D0607709

Kathryn Chinn
Adobe InDesign CS3 and Adobe InCopy Product Manager
Adobe Systems, Inc.

Thank you for purchasing Adobe InDesign CS3 Classroom in a Book®, the official training workbook from Adobe Systems. We hope you will be as excited as we are about all the new features and improvements to InDesign CS3, which are guaranteed to boost your creativity and productivity.

Every release of Adobe InDesign CS3 is shaped by customer requests emerging from day-to-day design and production experience. With InDesign CS3, designers can more easily realize their creative vision, production staff can meet deadlines with less effort, and IT personnel can keep efficiency up and costs down. With each new release, more major magazines, newspapers, and corporate creative groups worldwide move their layout workflows to InDesign, achieving significantly higher productivity, producing consistently reliable output to print, and creating more compelling creative content.

InDesign CS3 is packed with new features that respond to today's demanding workflows.

Good luck with your learning, and thanks,

Kathryn Chinn
Adobe InDesign CS3 and Adobe
InCopy
Product Manager

W

Lesson files . . . and so much more

The *Adobe InDesign CS3 Classroom in a Book* CD includes the lesson files that you'll need to complete the exercises in this book, as well as other content to help you learn more about Adobe InDesign CS3 and use it with greater efficiency and ease. The diagram below represents the contents of the CD, which should help you locate the files you need.

What's on the CD *

Here is an overview of the contents of the Classroom in a Book CD

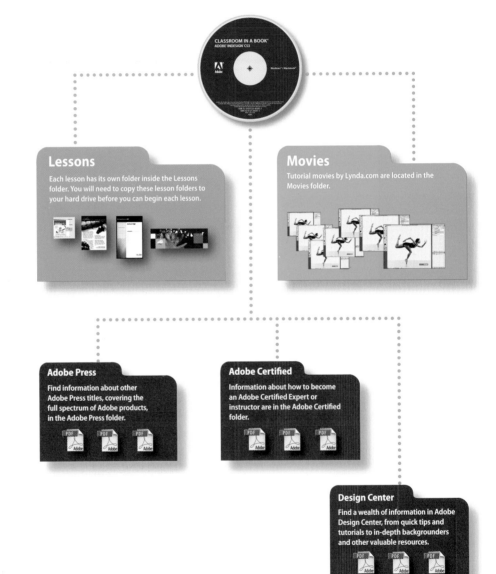

Lessons
Each lesson has its own folder inside the Lessons folder. You will need to copy these lesson folders to your hard drive before you can begin each lesson.

Movies
Tutorial movies by Lynda.com are located in the Movies folder.

Adobe Press
Find information about other Adobe Press titles, covering the full spectrum of Adobe products, in the Adobe Press folder.

Adobe Certified
Information about how to become an Adobe Certified Expert or instructor are in the Adobe Certified folder.

Design Center
Find a wealth of information in Adobe Design Center, from quick tips and tutorials to in-depth backgrounders and other valuable resources.

The latest version of Apple QuickTime can be downloaded from http://www.apple.com/quicktime/download/.

Contents

Getting Started

About Classroom in a Book 1

Prerequisites 2

Installing the program 2

Installing the Classroom in a Book fonts 2

Saving, deleting and restoring preference files 2

Copying the Classroom in a Book files 4

Color profiles 5

Additional resources 5

Useful links 5

Adobe certification 6

What's New in Adobe InDesign CS3

Enhanced workspace 7

Customizable user interface 8

Productivity enhancements 9

Expanded layout features 9

Improved text handling 10

Enhanced graphics handling 10

XHTML exporting 12

A Quick Tour of Adobe InDesign CS3

Getting started 15

Viewing the lesson document 17

Changing the View mode 20

Viewing guides 21

Adding text 22

Threading text in frames 23

Placing and flowing text 24

Threading text 25

Adding a pull-quote 28

Wrapping text around an object 29

Adding a stroke to the frame 30

Changing the frame and text position 31

Adjusting the size of an image 32

Working with styles 33

Applying paragraph styles 33

Formatting text for the character style 35

Creating and applying a character style 36

Applying object styles 38

Working with graphics 38

Positioning graphics within a frame 39

About the Position tool 40

Targeting layers when placing 41

Cropping and moving the photograph 44

Exploring on your own 45

1   Getting to Know the Work Area

Getting started 47

Looking at the work area 48

About the Tools panel 49

The Control Panel 52

The Document Window 54

Multiple document windows 55

Viewing and arranging panels 56

Customizing your workspace 61

Using panel menus 62

Changing the magnification of a document 63

Using the view commands and
magnification menu 64

Using the Zoom tool 64

Navigating through your document 66

Turning pages 66

Scrolling through a document 70

Using the Navigator panel 71

Using context menus 73

Selecting Objects 74

Using InDesign Help 75

Using keywords, links, and the index 75

Locating a topic using the index 76

Exploring on your own 77

Review questions 78

Review answers 78

2 Setting Up Your Document

Getting started 81

Creating and saving custom page settings 82

Creating a new document 84

Switching between open InDesign documents 85

Working with master pages 85

Adding guides to the master 86

Dragging guides from rulers 87

Creating a text frame on the master page 89

Renaming the master page 92

Creating additional master pages 93

Creating a placeholder master 94

Adding a title placeholder frame 94

Adding placeholder frames for graphics 96

Wrapping text around a graphic 98

Drawing colored shapes 99

Creating text frames with columns 101

Applying the masters to document pages 103

Adding sections to change page numbering 105

Adding new pages 107

Arranging and deleting pages 108

Placing text and graphics on the
document pages 108

Overriding master page items on
document pages 111

Viewing the completed spread 113

Exploring on your own...............................114

Review questions..................................115

Review answers 115

3 Working with Frames

Getting started 117

Working with Layers 119

Creating and editing text frames....................122

Creating and resizing text frames 122

Creating multiple columns 126

Adjusting text inset within a frame 127

Vertically aligning text within a frame..............128

Creating and editing graphics frames 130

Drawing a new graphics frame 130

 Placing graphics within an existing frame..........131

Resizing a graphics frame 132

Resizing and moving an image within a frame.......132

Replacing the contents of graphics frames 134

Changing the shape of a frame 136

Wrapping text around a graphic 137

Working with Frames 139

Working with Pathfinders 139

Converting shapes.................................140

Using the Position tool.............................142

Rotating an object.................................144

Rotating an image within its frame 144

Aligning multiple objects 145

Scaling grouped objects 147

Selecting and modifying a frame within g
rouped objects 147

Finishing up......................................149

Exploring on your own.............................149

Review questions..................................151

Review answers 151

4   Importing and Editing Text

Getting started 153

Managing fonts 154

Finding and changing a missing font. 155

Creating and entering text 156

Creating a headline and applying a style 157

Vertically aligning text 159

Flowing text. 159

Flowing text manually 159

Working with styles. 161

Applying a style 161

Flowing text automatically 163

Resizing a text frame. 164

Adding a column break 165

Adding a page continuation note. 166

Changing horizontal and vertical text alignment. 167

Using semi-autoflow to place text frames 168

Changing the number of columns on a page 170

Loading styles from another document 171

Flowing text into an existing frame 173

Finding and changing. 174

Finding text and changing formatting 174

Checking spelling of a story 176

Adding words to a dictionary. 177

Adding words to a document-specific dictionary 178

Checking spelling dynamically 179

Automatically correcting misspelled words. 180

Drag and drop text editing 181

Using the story editor. 182

Exploring on your own. 183

Review questions. 184

Review answers 184

5 **Working with Typography**

Getting started 187

Adjusting vertical spacing 189

Using a baseline grid to align text 189

Viewing the baseline grid 191

Changing the spacing above and
below paragraphs 192

Changing fonts and type style 195

Changing paragraph alignment 197

Adding a decorative font and special character 197

Creating a drop cap 199

Applying a fill and stroke to text 200

Adjusting the drop cap alignment 201

Adjusting letter and word spacing 202

Adjusting the kerning and tracking 202

Applying the paragraph and
single-line composers 204

Working with tabs 205

Creating a hanging indent 208

Adding a rule below a paragraph 210

Exploring on your own 212

Review questions 213

Review answers 213

6 **Working with Color**

Getting started 215

Defining printing requirements 217

Adding colors to the Swatches panel 218

Applying colors to objects 219

Creating dashed strokes 222

Working with gradients 223

Creating and applying a gradient swatch 224

Adjusting the direction of the gradient blend 226

Creating a tint 227

Creating a spot color. 229

Applying color to text. 231

Applying colors to additional objects 231

Creating another tint 233

Using advanced gradient techniques 234

Creating a gradient swatch with multiple colors 234

Applying the gradient to an object 235

Applying a gradient to multiple objects 235

Ensuring consistent color 237

Color management: An overview 238

About the device-independent color space. 239

About ICC profiles 240

About color management engines. 240

Components of a CMYK press-oriented workflow 241

Setting up color management in InDesign CS3 241

A look at the Adobe Bridge. 242

Specifying the Adobe ACE engine. 242

Setting up default working spaces 244

Assigning source profiles. 245

Specifying the rendering intent. 246

Using full-resolution display with
color management 247

Color-managing imported graphics
in InDesign CS3. 247

Assigning a profile after importing an image 248

Embedding a profile in a Photoshop image. 249

Setting up color management in Photoshop CS3 250

Embedding the profile 251

Updating the image within InDesign CS3 252

Assigning a profile while importing a graphic 253

Embedding a profile in an Illustrator graphic 254

Setting up color management in Illustrator CS3. 255

Embedding a profile in a graphic from Illustrator 256

Placing a color-managed Illustrator file
into InDesign CS3. 257

Other information resources for color
management. 260

Exploring on your own. 261

Review questions. 262

Review answers 262

7　Working with Styles

Getting started 265

Creating and applying paragraph styles. 266

Creating a paragraph style 267

Applying a paragraph style. 269

Creating and applying character styles. 271

Creating a character style 271

Applying a character style. 273

Nesting character styles inside paragraph styles 274

Creating character styles for nesting 274

Creating a nested style. 277

Creating and applying object styles. 281

Creating an object style 281

Applying an object style 285

Creating and applying table and cell styles 286

Creating cell styles. 286

Creating a table style 288

Applying a table style. 290

Globally updating styles 291

Loading styles from another document 293

Review questions. 295

Review answers 295

8　Importing and Linking Graphics

Getting started 297

Adding graphics from other programs 299

Comparing vector and bitmap graphics 299

Managing links to imported files. 300

Identifying imported images 301

Viewing information about linked files 302

Showing files in the Explorer (Windows)
or Finder (Mac OS) 302

Updating revised graphics 303

Adjusting view quality 305

Working with clipping paths 306

Removing a white background using InDesign 307

Working with alpha channels 309

Importing a Photoshop file and alpha channels 310

Examining Photoshop paths and alpha channels 311

Using Photoshop alpha channels in InDesign 313

Placing native files 316

Importing a Photoshop file with layers
and layer comps 316

Placing inline graphics 318

Adding text wrap to an inline graphic 319

Importing an Illustrator file 320

Importing an Illustrator file with layers 321

Using a library to manage objects 323

Creating a library 325

Using Adobe Bridge to import graphics 326

Exploring on your own 327

Review questions 328

Review answers 328

9   Creating Tables

Getting started 331

Importing and formatting a table 334

Formatting borders and alternating row colors 336

Editing cell strokes 338

Formatting the heading cells 339

Deleting a column 341

Using graphics within tables 342

Setting fixed column and row dimensions 342

Placing graphics in table cells 343

Placing multiple graphics in a cell. 345

Formatting text within a table 347

Editing imported paragraph styles in a table 347

Creating a new cell style 348

Dragging to adjust column size. 350

Finishing up. 352

Exploring on your own. 353

Review questions. 354

Review answers 354

10   Working with Transparency

Getting started 357

Importing and colorizing a black-and-white
image. 359

Applying transparency settings. 360

About the Effects Panel 361

Changing the opacity of solid-color objects 362

Applying a blending mode 363

Adjusting the transparency settings for EPS images. . 364

Adjusting transparency for Photoshop images. 366

Importing and adjusting Illustrator files
that use transparency. 367

Applying transparency settings to text 369

Applying transparency settings to text frame fill 370

Working with effects. 371

Applying basic feathering to the margins
of an image 371

Applying a Gradient feather 372

Applying multiple effects to objects 374

Editing and removing effects 376

Exploring on your own. 378

Review questions. 379

Review answers 379

11   Working with Long Documents

Getting started 381

Defining a book 382

Creating a book file 382

Setting the order and pagination 383

Working with a table of contents 385

Adding the table of contents file 385

Generating a table of contents for the book 386

Maintaining consistency across book files 388

Reassigning the style source 389

Synchronizing book documents 389

Indexing the book 390

Creating index references 391

Creating index cross-references. 393

Generating the index 393

Exploring on your own. 395

Review questions. 396

Review answers 396

12   Output and PDF Exporting

Getting started 399

Using Preflight 401

Using Package. 404

Creating an Adobe PDF proof. 406

Separation preview 407

Transparency flattener preview 408

Previewing the page. 410

Printing a laser or inkjet proof 410

Exploring on your own. 419

Review questions. 420

Review answers 420

13   Using XML

Getting started 423

About XML. 424

Viewing XML tags 425

Importing and applying XML tags 427

Tagging images 430

Viewing and organizing structure. 431

Viewing and applying attributes. 433

Exporting XML 434

Importing XML 436

Mapping tags to style. 438

Using XML snippets. 439

Exploring on your own 440

Review questions. 441

Review answers 441

Getting Started

Welcome to Adobe® InDesign® CS3, a powerful design and production tool that offers precision, control, and seamless integration with other Adobe professional graphics software. Using InDesign, you can produce professional-quality, full-color documents on high-volume color printing presses, or print to a wide range of output devices and formats, including desktop printers and high-resolution imaging devices. You can also create Portable Document Format (PDF) files, and convert your documents for use on the Internet by exporting layouts to XHTML or XML.

Writers, artists, designers, and publishers can communicate to a broader audience than ever before and through an unprecedented variety of media. InDesign supports this with its seamless integration with other Creative Suite 3 applications.

About Classroom in a Book

Adobe InDesign CS3 Classroom in a Book® is part of the official training series for Adobe graphics and publishing software from Adobe Systems, Inc.

The lessons are designed so that you can learn at your own pace. If you're new to Adobe InDesign CS3, you'll learn the fundamentals you'll need to master in order to put the program to work. If you've already been using Adobe InDesign CS3, you'll find that Classroom in a Book teaches many advanced features, including tips and techniques for using the latest version of InDesign.

Each lesson provides step-by-step instructions for creating a specific project. You can follow the book from start to finish, or do only the lessons that meet your interests and needs. Each lesson concludes with a review section summarizing what you've covered.

Prerequisites

Before beginning to use *Adobe InDesign CS3 Classroom in a Book*, you should have a working knowledge of your computer and its operating system. Make sure you know how to use the mouse and standard menus and commands, and also how to open, save, and close files. If you need to review these techniques, see the printed or online documentation included with your Windows or Mac OS.

Installing the program

Before you begin using *Adobe InDesign CS3 Classroom in a Book,* make sure that your system is set up correctly and that you've installed the proper software and hardware.

The Adobe InDesign CS3 software is not included on the Classroom in a Book CD; you must purchase the software separately. For complete instructions on installing the software, see the Adobe InDesign CS3 Read Me on the application DVD or on the web at www.adobe.com/support.

Installing the Classroom in a Book fonts

The Classroom in a Book lesson files use fonts that come with Adobe InDesign CS3. Some of the fonts can be found on the product DVD, and some will be installed with InDesign for your convenience. These fonts are installed in the following locations:

* Mac OS: [startup drive]/Library/Fonts/

* Windows: [startup drive]\Windows\Fonts\

For more information about fonts and installation see the Adobe InDesign CS3 Read Me included with your product.

Saving, deleting and restoring preference files

The preferences files control how panels and command settings appear on your screen when you open the Adobe InDesign CS3 program. Each time you quit Adobe InDesign CS3, the position of the panels and certain command settings are recorded in the preferences files. If you want to restore the tools and panels to their original default settings, you can delete the current Adobe InDesign CS3 preference files. Adobe InDesign CS3 creates preference files, if they don't already exist, the next time you start the program and save a file.

You must restore the default preferences for InDesign before you begin each lesson. This ensures that the tools and panels function as described in this book. When you have finished the book, you can restore your saved settings.

To save your current InDesign preferences files

1   Exit Adobe InDesign CS3.

2   Locate the InDesign Defaults file and the ActiveWorkspace.xml file.

•   In Windows, the InDesign Defaults file and the ActiveWorkspace.xml file are located in the Documents and Settings\Username\Application Data\Adobe\InDesign\Version 5.0 folder.

NOTE: You may have to choose View from the Folder Options dialog box to show hidden files to locate this preference. Check the radio button to the left of Show hidden files and folders.

•   In Mac OS, the InDesign Defaults file and the ActiveWorkspace.xml file are located in /Users/your user name/Library/Preferences/Adobe InDesign CS3/Version 5.0.

3   Make a duplicate copy of these files and save to another folder on your hard drive.

To delete the current InDesign preferences

1   Exit Adobe InDesign CS3.

2   Locate the InDesign Defaults file and the ActiveWorkspace.xml file, as follows:

•   In Windows, the InDesign Defaults file and the ActiveWorkspace.xml file are located in the Documents and Settings\Username\Application Data\Adobe\InDesign\Version 5.0 folder.

NOTE: You may have to choose View from the Folder Options dialog box to show hidden files to locate this preference. Check the radio button to the left of Show hidden files and folders.

•   In Mac OS, the InDesign Defaults file and the ActiveWorkspace.xml file are located in /Users/your user name/Library/Preferences/Adobe InDesign CS3/Version 5.0.

3   Delete the InDesign Defaults file and the Active Workspace.xml file.

4   Launch InDesign. The application will create a new set of preferences files with the original default settings.

💡 *If you don't need to save your custom settings, you can also reset the default preferences by launching Adobe InDesign CS3 and then selecting Ctrl+Alt+Shift (Windows) or Ctrl+Option+Command+Shift (Mac OS). Click Yes to delete the InDesign preference. This resets the application preferences, but not the workspace. To restore the default workspace, select Window > Workspace > Default Workspace.*

To restore your saved preferences after completing the lessons

1   Exit Adobe InDesign CS3.

2   Locate your saved preferences and drag them back into the InDesign 5.0 folder.

•   In Windows, the InDesign Defaults file and the ActiveWorkspace.xml file are located in the Documents and Settings\Username\Application Data\Adobe\InDesign\Version 5.0 folder.

NOTE: You may have to choose View from the Folder Options dialog box to show hidden files to locate this preference. Check the radio button to the left of Show hidden files and folders.

•   In Mac OS, the InDesign Defaults file and the ActiveWorkspace.xml file are located in /Users/your user name/Library/Preferences/Adobe InDesign CS3/Version 5.0.

Copying the Classroom in a Book files

The *Adobe InDesign CS3 Classroom in a Book* CD includes folders containing all the electronic files for the lessons in the book. Each lesson has its own folder; you must copy the folders to your hard disk to complete the lessons. To save room on your disk, you can install only the folder necessary for each lesson as you need it, and remove it when you're done.

To install the Classroom in a Book lesson files

1   Insert the *Adobe InDesign CS3 Classroom in a Book* CD into your CD-ROM drive.

2   Create a folder on your hard drive and name it IDCIB.

3   Do one of the following:

•   Copy the Lessons folder into the IDCIB folder.

•   Copy on the single lesson folder you need..

Color profiles

As you open individual lesson files, you may receive an Embedded Profile Mismatch warning. These warnings are normal, and you should click OK to dismiss the warning if one appears while opening a Classroom in a Book exercise document.

InDesign CS3 supports a variety of settings to accommodate your color management needs. If the settings on your computer do not match those used in creating the document, InDesign uses these messages to alert you when the document is opened. For more information, see About missing and mismatched color profiles in InDesign Help.

Additional resources

Adobe InDesign CS3 Classroom in a Book is not meant to replace documentation that comes with the program. Only the commands and options used in the lessons are explained in this book. For comprehensive information about program features, refer to these resources:

· Adobe InDesign CS3 Help, which you can view by choosing Help > InDesign Help.

· Printed copies of Adobe InDesign CS3 documentation (a subset of Help) are available for purchase from www.adobe.com/go/buy_books

· Adobe Design Center provides you with hundreds of tutorials from experts and authors in the community, as well as thoughtful articles about design and technology. Go to www.adobe.com/designcenter/

· *Adobe CS3 Video Workshop* DVD, included in the product box, provides you with 250 instructional movies on InDesign CS3 and other products across the Adobe Creative Suite 3 lineup.

Useful links

· InDesign product home page www.adobe.com/products/indesign/

· Illustrator User Forums www.adobe.com/support/forums/

· InDesign Exchange www.adobe.com/cfusion/exchange/

· InDesign plug-ins www.adobe.com/products/plugins/indesign/

· InDesign training resources www.adobe.com/products/indesign/training.html

Adobe certification

The Adobe Certification program is designed to help Adobe customers improve and promote their product-proficiency skills. The Adobe Certified Expert (ACE) program recognizes the high-level skills of expert users. Adobe Authorized Training Centers (AATC) use only Adobe Certified Experts to teach Adobe software classes. For Adobe Certified information, visit the www.adobe.com/support/certification/.

What's New in Adobe InDesign CS3

Welcome to Adobe InDesign CS3. This is a significant upgrade to an extremely powerful page layout application. This book provides you with details you need to effectively create layouts using Adobe InDesign CS3. The *Adobe InDesign CS3 Classroom in a Book* has been revised and updated to incorporate new capabilities and features that have been added to the software. If you're already familiar with previous versions of Adobe InDesign CS3, you'll find a wealth of new features to make you more productive.

Here we've assembled an overview of our favorite additions to InDesign CS3. The complete list of new features is much more extensive, and you can find it at Adobe.com.

Enhanced workspace

InDesign CS3 now has a new look and feel, as well as a new behavior around attaching the panels to side of the workspace. Panels can be placed into a drawer on the left or right side of the screen, and the drawer can be opened or closed. The drawer can also be minimized to an icon view and panels can be shown or hidden individually by clicking on the panel icon. Read more about the new workspace in Lesson 1, "Getting to know the work area."

Customizable user interface

New in InDesign CS3, you can turn menu items on and off or colorize menu items via a Photoshop-like user interface available from **Preferences>Menu Customization**. You an also create UI within InDesign easier due to improvements in how scripts interact with the UI.

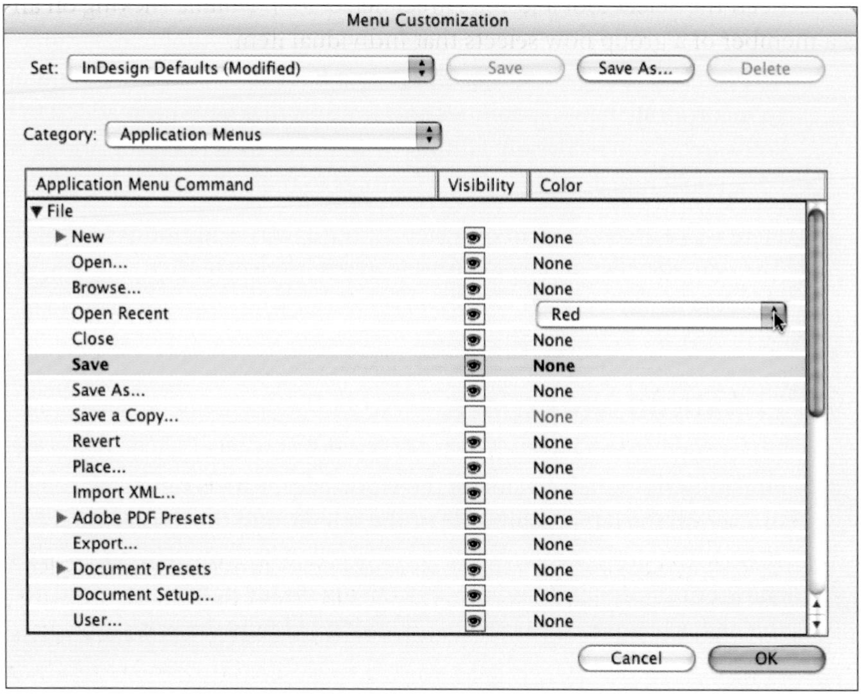

Menu Customization		
Set: InDesign Defaults (Modified)	Save	Save As...	Delete

Category: Application Menus

Application Menu Command	Visibility	Color
▼ File		
▶ New	👁	None
Open...	👁	None
Browse...	👁	None
Open Recent	👁	Red
Close	👁	None
Save	👁	**None**
Save As...	👁	None
Save a Copy...	☐	None
Revert	👁	None
Place...	👁	None
Import XML...	👁	None
▶ Adobe PDF Presets	👁	None
Export...	👁	None
▶ Document Presets	👁	None
Document Setup...	👁	None
User...	👁	None

Cancel   OK

Productivity enhancements

InDesign CS3 offers numerous ways to work faster. For instance, when you drag and drop pages to a different document, the Move Pages dialog box will appear asking where you want to place the pages. This dialog box now has a field that allows you to move pages to any open document. In addition, the Pages panel now shows thumbnails of document and master pages. When selecting objects, double clicking on a graphic frame toggles between the Select tool and the Direct Select tool. Double clicking on an object that is a member of a group now selects that individual item.

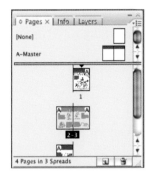

Expanded layout features

InDesign CS3 gives you greater flexibility and control over master pages, which is helpful for creating multiple documents that need to share some, or all, master page items. Using the Pages panel menu, you can now load master pages from a different InDesign document. If you load a master page that has already been loaded, InDesign will update the existing master page layout with the most recent version. You can also assign an attribute on a per object basis to avoid overriding an entire master page, even when you choose the Override All Master Page Items command. This makes it easier to override multiple items on a page without having to select each item individually, and also without overriding all items from the master page. In addition, the Align panel now has a pop-up menu that allows you to choose whether alignment is relative to the selection, margins, page or spread.

Improved text handling

InDesign has long been known for its typographic capabilities and InDesign CS3 is no exception. There are improved options for bullets and numbering, including section/hierarchical numbering and allowing skipped paragraphs in lists. When using text styles, there are now user-customizable folders in the Paragraph and Character Styles panels for organization of styles. A number of changes have also been made to improve the usability of Find/Change, including support for regular expressions, and allowing you to find/change on object attributes, save queries, and customize the scope of the search. Quick Apply allows you to find menu, context menu, panel menu commands, and scripts from within the Quick Apply window. Read more about Bullet and Numbering and other text handling features in Lesson 5, "Working with typography."

Enhanced graphics handling

Those of you who work with graphics frequently will appreciate InDesign CS3's graphic enhancements. For starters, when placing images, a thumbnail of the chosen image or text file now appears on the cursor, allowing you to ensure that you are placing the correct graphic. In the Place dialog box, you can also now select multiple files, and have them load into the place cursor at the same time. In addition, the new Control panel has buttons for flipping an image horizontally and vertically, and for rotating 90 degrees clockwise and counter-clockwise. Read more about graphics handling in Lesson 8, "Importing and linking graphics."

Place multiple files

Object flipping and rotating buttons

Other enhancements include additional transparency effects such as inner glow, outer glow, bevel, emboss, inner shadow and satin, all of which can be applied to Objects. These effects can be accessed via Object > Effects and can be viewed in the Transparency panel. Read more about transparency effects in Lesson 10, "Working with transparency."

Effects

Settings for: Object

Drop Shadow

Transparency
- ☑ Drop Shadow
- ☐ Inner Shadow
- ☐ Outer Glow
- ☐ Inner Glow
- ☐ Bevel and Emboss
- ☐ Satin
- ☐ Basic Feather
- ☐ Directional Feather
- ☐ Gradient Feather

Blending

Mode: Multiply   Opacity: 75%

Position

X Offset: 0.0972 in   Distance: 0.1375 in
Y Offset: 0.0972 in   Angle: 135°

☐ Use Global Light

Options

Size: 0.0694 in   Noise: 0%
Spread: 0%   ☑ Object Knocks Out Shadow
☐ Shadow Honors Other Effects

Summary:

Object: Normal 100%; Drop Shadow

Stroke: Normal 100%; (no effects)

Fill: Normal 100%; (no effects)

Text: Normal 100%; (no effects)

Cancel   OK

Long Document enhancements

Working with Books and long documents is now more efficient, thanks to several enhancements, including the ability to create and work with Books that contain more than 100 documents. In the Book panel menu > Synchronize Options dialog box there is also a new option that synchronizes master pages between multiple documents in a Book. For those of you who work with long documents that use multiple languages, there is now an Index panel menu > Sort Options dialog box that allows you to determine which language scripts (Roman, Cyrillic, Greek, etc.) should appear, and in what order. Read more about long document enhancements in Lesson 11, "Working with ling documents."

XHTML exporting

The user will be able to export a document or selected page items to XHTML via the Export as XHTML in the File menu. This includes support for image optimization, CSS styles and JavaScript linking to an external .js file. Read more about exporting as XHTML in Lesson 12, "Printing, output, and exporting."

XML features

More advanced users will appreciate the XML enhancements. When importing XML, the Import Options dialog box now allows you to specify an XSLT to apply to the incoming XML. You can also create a set of layout rules (via scripting) that perform actions such as formatting and creating frames. These rules can be applied to incoming or existing XML. Read more about XML in Lesson 13, "Using XML."

While this list is by no means a complete description of the new features of InDesign CS3, it exemplifies Adobe's commitment to providing the best tools possible for your publishing needs. We hope you enjoy working with InDesign CS3 as much as we do.

—The *InDesign CS3 Classroom in a Book* Team

Hecho en
Mexico

Exploring Mexican Folk Art

One of the most exciting things about vacationing in Oaxaca is the large artist community that lives and works there. My wife Judith and I traveled there last May and came home with many more pieces for our collection than we had ever imagined. Judith is a collector by nature. Every square inch of our tiny Manhattan apartment is filled with a treasure from one of our trips. I wanted to experience more than just the exchange of money with a merchant—I wanted to meet the artists. Having grown up in a family of sculptors (my father took commissions for his work from around the world), I wanted to see how these people crafted their pieces, how they lived, and what their art meant to them. Judith was more interested in buying art, but she finally agreed to go with me to meet a folk artist I heard about named Henry Luis Ramos.

As Judith and I stepped into the adobe shop, a cheerful black-haired boy greeted us. "My father's expecting you," he said as he led us down a hall into a spacious room filled with hundreds of statues, clay pots, and tin artifacts that Ramos designed.

The brilliantly colored pieces captivated me. I couldn't stop investigating and touching them. I could see the influence of the Mayan culture and other native tribes. "My father did these," the boy said with a wide grin. In the corner of the room, at a heavy

This interactive demonstration of Adobe InDesign CS3 provides an overview of key features of the program. It should take you approximately 45 minutes to complete.

A Quick Tour of Adobe InDesign CS3

In this quick tour, you'll get an overview of the key features of InDesign CS3 including:

- Using Adobe Bridge to access files.
- Viewing and navigating your document.
- Creating, placing and styling text.
- Manipulating images.
- Targeting layers.

Getting started

You'll start the tour by opening a partially completed document. You'll add the finishing touches to this six-page article on Mexican folk art, written for an imaginary travel magazine. If you have not already done so in this session, you should restore the default preferences for InDesign CS3. Restoring default preferences ensures that the tools and panels function exactly as described in this lesson. After you learn how to use InDesign CS3, this step is no longer necessary.

Note: If you have not already copied the resource files for this lesson onto your hard disk from the Adobe InDesign CS3 Classroom in a Book *CD, do so now. See "Copying the Classroom in a Book files" on page 4.*

Note: If you are new to InDesign, you might want to begin with Lesson 1, "Getting to Know the Work Area."

1   Delete or reset the InDesign CS3 defaults preferences following the procedure in "Saving, deleting and restoring preference files" on page 2.

2   Start Adobe InDesign CS3. When the Welcome Screen appears, choose Close.

3   Click the Go to Adobe Bridge button (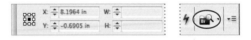) in the Control panel. As a default, the Control panel is located at the top of the InDesign work area. Using the Folders tab, in the upper left of the Adobe Bridge window, locate the Lesson_00 folder in the InDesignCIB folder you copied from the InDesign CS3 Classroom in a Book CD to your hard disk.

4   In the Lesson_00 folder, click once on the Tour_done.indd file in the middle panel of the Adobe Bridge window. On the right side of the Adobe Bridge window in the Metadata tab, information about the Tour_done.indd file is displayed.

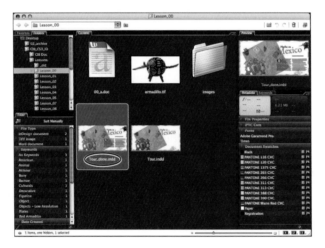

You can view information about the document including colors, fonts, version of InDesign used to create it, and more, by scrolling through the panes on the right side of the Adobe Bridge window. You can scale the preview thumbnails by using the slider bar at the bottom of the Adobe Bridge window.

5   Double-click on the Tour_done.indd file to open it.

The finished tour document.

Note: *While the Adobe Bridge provides a convenient way to access your files and see more information about each file without needing to open it, you can also open files by choosing File > Open at any time. It is not necessary to use Adobe Bridge to access your InDesign files, although we recommend using it to work with your files.*

Press Alt+Ctrl+0 (zero) (Windows) or Option+Command+0 (Mac OS) to make the first page spread fit in the InDesign window. This is the 6-page tour file that you will complete in this lesson. You can leave it open for reference, or choose File > Close.

Viewing the lesson document

1   Adobe Bridge remains open until you Exit from the application. Return to the Adobe Bridge application and double-click on Tour.indd file. The Tour file opens.

2   Choose View > Fit Spread in Window. The Fit Spread in Window option displays all the adjoining pages in a spread.

The first spread (pages 2 and 3) appears on your screen. You'll now look at the rest of the 6-page article using several navigation methods. First, you'll use the Navigator panel, which is useful for changing the view magnification.

3   Choose File > Save As. Choose Tour.indd in the Save As window and enter the name **Tour_lesson**. Leave the file type as InDesign CS3 document, and choose Save.

4   Choose Window > Object & Layout > Navigator to open the Navigator panel.

5   Position the pointer, click on the Panel-menu button (▾≡) on the right side of the panel and choose View All Spreads.

Like many panels, the Navigator panel has a menu that displays additional options.

6   Drag the lower right corner of the panel down and to the right. Expanding the size of the panel provides a better view of the spreads.

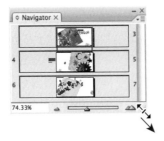

7   In the Navigator panel, click the center of the middle spread to view pages 4 and 5. Notice the red view box in the Navigator panel. This box shows which area of the document is displayed. By rolling over the red view box, the cursor changes to a hand icon, allowing you to reposition the view.

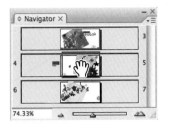

The slider at the bottom of the panel controls the magnification of the document being displayed. Moving the slider to the right increases the magnification, while moving to the left decreases the magnification. The red view box changes size as you move the slider left or right. The red view box appears smaller at greater magnification levels. Close the Navigation panel.

8   Choose View > Fit Page in Window. You can see that the magnification displayed in the Navigator panel is automatically updated. You can use the Navigator panel to easily move between pages in your documents, or to move to specific sections of a page.

Now we'll look at the Pages panel, which is another useful tool for navigating in your documents. You'll use the Pages panel throughout this tour, so you'll separate the Pages panel from the dock.

9   Select Windows > Pages to view the Pages panel tab. Click the Pages panel tab and drag it to the left, away from the other panels. Release the panel when it is separated from the dock. This causes the panel to detach from the dock area on the right. Now it can be positioned in a different location.

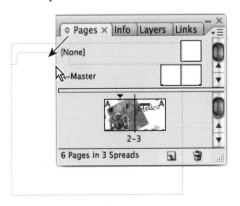

Feel free to move and rearrange panels in this Quick Tour as needed. You can move a panel by dragging its gray title bar. You can place a panel in the dock on the right side of the document window by dragging a panel by its tab to this portion of the window. You can also minimize the panel by clicking on the Minimize button, or close the panel by clicking on the Close button on the title bar if the bar has been separated from the dock.

10 In the Pages panel, double-click the numbers 6-7 below the page icons to view the last spread in the document. You may need to scroll to see these.

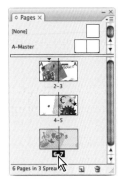

Double-clicking the numbers below the page icons brings the full spread in the document window. Double-clicking an individual page icon brings only that page in the document window. To center the spread in the window, double-click the Hand tool in the Tools panel.

Now that you've seen all three spreads, let's go back to page 3 and start working.

11 In the Pages panel, double-click the page 3 thumbnail to view page 3.

Changing the View mode

You can change the View mode of a document window using the mode buttons at the bottom of the Tools panel. Use Preview to easily hide nonprinting elements such as guides, grids, and frame edges. You can also preview the document with the bleed or slug areas included.

The Preview Mode button.

Click and hold on the Preview Mode button (▣) at the bottom of the Tools panel to choose a Preview mode. Preview Mode displays artwork in a standard window, hiding nonprinting elements such as guides, grids, and frame edges.

Choose the Bleed mode button (▣) to preview the document along with its predefined bleed area that extends beyond the page boundaries.

Choose the Slug mode button (▣) to preview the document along with the predefined slug area. The slug area is an area outside the page and bleed that contains printer instructions or job sign-off information.

Choose the Normal mode button (▣) to return to the normal view.

   💡 *You can also choose View > Screen Mode and then select one of the four viewing modes. A checkmark indicates the selected view mode.*

Viewing guides

In this document, the guides are hidden. You'll turn on the guides to make it easy to see your layout grid and snap objects into place. The guides do not print and do not limit the print area. Guides are for your reference only and can be helpful when aligning objects and text on your page.

• Choose View > Grids & Guides > Show Guides.

Before and after turning on guides.

Adding text

You can import text created in separate word processing programs, or create text using InDesign CS3. In this exercise, you will add a secondary headline to page 3.

1   Using the Type tool (T), click and drag to create a box for this headline between the two guides below the word Mexico, in the right column of the page.

If the text box is not aligned exactly to the size of the guides, use the Selection tool (▶) to click on the corners of the box and enlarge or reduce them as necessary and then re-select the Type tool.

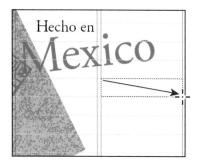

2   Enter the text **Exploring Mexican Folk Art** in the text box.

InDesign CS3 placed the text insertion point in the frame after it was created because it was built using the Type tool. For text frames created with other tools, you will first need to click within the text frame using the Type tool before entering text.

3   Use the Type tool to select the text just entered by placing the cursor into the text frame and choosing Edit > Select All to select the text.

4   Use the Control panel to change text attributes. Click on the arrow (⬦) to the right of the Font Name pop-up menu and select Adobe Garamond Pro and then Regular either from the menu or from the Font Style pop-up menu below the Font Name. (Adobe Garamond Pro is alphabetized on the list under "G," not "A.")

5   Click on the arrow (⬦) to the right of the Font Size pop-up menu and select "18 points."

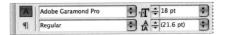

💡 *You can select individual words and characters using the Type tool to format text, as you would with traditional word-processing software.*

Threading text in frames

As a general rule, text is placed inside frames with InDesign CS3. You can either add text to a frame that has already been created, or you can create the frame while you import text.

Placing and flowing text

An article describing Judith and Clyde's trip to Oaxaca has been saved in a word-processor file. You'll place this file on page 3 and then thread it throughout your document.

1   Make sure that no objects are selected by choosing Edit > Deselect All, and then choose File > Place. In the Place dialog box, navigate to the Lesson_00 folder in the Lessons folder and double-click the 00_a.doc file.

The cursor changes to a loaded text icon (⬚). With a loaded text icon, you have several choices. You can drag to create a new text frame, click inside an existing frame, or click to create a new text frame within a column. You'll add this text to a column in the lower half of page 3.

2   Position the loaded text icon just below the fourth guide from the bottom margin and just to the right of the left margin, and click.

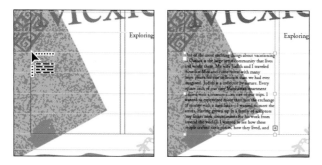

3   The text flows into a new frame in the lower half of the first column on page 3. When a text frame has more text than can fit, the frame is said to have overset text. Overset text is indicated by a red plus symbol in the out port of the frame, which is the small square just above the lower right corner of the frame. You can link overset text to another frame, create a new frame into which the overset text will flow, or expand the size of the frame so that the text is no longer overset.

Note: If the text box is not placed in the left column, click the Selection tool and drag the sizing handles to move it to the proper location.

4   Choose the Selection tool (⬚), then click the out port in the selected frame. The cursor becomes a loaded text icon. Now you'll add a column of text to the lower half of the second column.

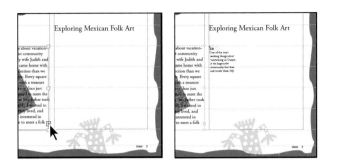

5 Position the loaded text icon immediately below the fourth guide from the bottom margin and just to the right of the second column guide (be sure not to click on the previously created text frame above), and click. Text now fills the lower portion of the right column.

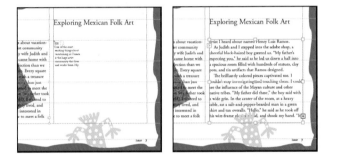

Threading text

Clicking the out port and then linking to a text frame is called manual threading. You can also thread texts using semi-automatic and automatic threading.

1 Using the Selection tool (➤), click the out port in the second column on page 3. This prepares InDesign CS3 to flow the overset text from this text frame to another frame.

2 In the Pages panel, double-click the page 4 icon to center page 4 in the document window.

3   Press and hold the Alt (Windows) or Option (Mac OS) key and position the loaded text icon in the upper left corner of the first column. Click, and then release the Alt/Option key.

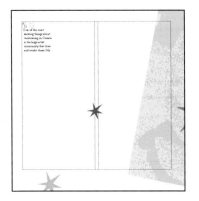

The text flows into the left column. Because you held down Alt/Option, the cursor remains a loaded text icon and you do not need to click in the out port before flowing text from this frame. This is called semi-automatic threading.

Note: After clicking the out port of a text frame, you can hold the Shift key to thread text automatically. Automatically flowing text places any overset text onto the pages of a document, adding pages as necessary. Because the design of this document calls for text to appear only on certain pages, the option to automatically flow text is not appropriate in this document.

4   Position the loaded text icon in the upper left corner of the second column on page 4, and click.

Whenever the cursor displays a loaded text icon, you can click any tool in the toolbar to stop flowing text. No text is lost, and any overset text remains.

Now you'll flow the remaining text into the bottom of the two columns on page 7.

5   Click the out port in the second column of page 4, and then in the Pages panel, double-click the page 7 icon, centering page 7 in the document window.

6   Press and hold Alt (Windows) or Option (Mac OS), and position the loaded text icon in the left column, below the guide on page 7, and click. Release the Alt or Option key. The cursor remains as a loaded text icon, as additional text needs to be flowed.

7   Position the loaded text icon in the second column below the guide, and click. The remaining text from the story flows into the second column. Note that the out port in the lower right corner of the text frame is hollow, indicating that there is no additional text to flow from this frame.

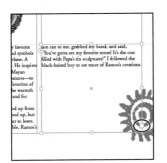

You have finished threading text frames in this document. A threaded set of frames is called a story.

8   Choose File > Save.

Adding a pull-quote

To enhance the design on page 4 of your document, you'll add a pull-quote. We copied text from the article and placed it into a frame on the pasteboard, which is the area outside the page. You will position this pull-quote text frame in the middle of page 4 and finish formatting it.

1   Choose View > Fit Page in Window.

2   In the lower left corner of the document window, click and hold on the arrow to the right of the page number indicator. Select page 4 from the list of available pages.

If you cannot see the pull-quote text frame to the left of page 4, locate the scroll box on the horizontal scroll bar, and drag it to the left.

3   Select the pull-quote with the Selection tool. On the left side of the Control panel, click the center point in the reference point proxy and then enter an X value of **4 in** and a Y value of **3 in**, and then press the Enter or Return key on your keyboard. InDesign moves the selected object to the specified location.

X: 4 in
Y: 3 in

4   If necessary, use the Arrow keys to nudge the location of the frame. The bottom of the frame should pass through the middle of the red star. The pull-quote should now be centered between the columns of text on page 4.

💡 *With Adobe InDesign CS3 you can use most forms of measurement throughout the program, including panels and dialog boxes, as long as you identify them with standard abbreviations, such as in for inch, pt for point, or cm for centimeter. InDesign converts the units you enter into the default unit of measurement, which can be changed in Edit > Preferences > Units & Increments.*

Wrapping text around an object

The text in the pull-quote is difficult to read because the main story text does not wrap around the text frame. You'll wrap the main story text around the edges of the pull-quote text frame, so the text from the main story will not overlap the pull-quote.

1   Make sure the pull-quote frame is selected.

2   Choose Window > Text Wrap.

3   In the Text Wrap panel, click the third button from the left side (▣). This causes text to wrap around the object's shape.

4   Click the Close box to close the Text Wrap panel. You can always access this panel or other panels from the Window menu.

5   Choose File > Save.

Adding a stroke to the frame

Now you'll change the color of the text frame so that the stroke, also described as a border, matches the color of the red star. When you apply colors using InDesign, it's a good idea to use the Swatches panel. Using the Swatches panel makes it easy to apply, edit, and update colors efficiently for all objects in a document.

This magazine article is intended for printing at a commercial press, so it uses CMYK process colors. We've already added the set of necessary colors to the Swatches panel.

1   Choose Window > Swatches.

2   With the text frame still selected, click the Stroke box ( ) in the top of the Swatches panel and then select PANTONE Warm Red CVC in the Swatches panel. You may need to scroll down to select. Selecting the Stroke box causes the frame of the image to be affected by the color you selected.

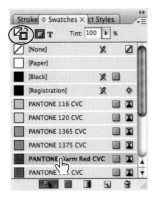

3   To change the weight of the stroke, right-click (Windows) or Ctrl+click (Mac OS) on the frame, and select Stroke Weight > 0.5 pt from the context menu that appears. The context menus are an easy way to change many attributes of a selected object, including the stroke weight.

4   Choose Edit > Deselect All.

The text frame now has a thin red stroke.

5   Choose File > Save.

Changing the frame and text position

The text in the pull-quote frame is too close to the edge, making it unattractive and difficult to read. You'll now change the position of the text within the frame and change the style of the border.

1   Using the Selection tool (↖), click the pull-quote text frame to select it, and then choose Object > Text Frame Options. Select Center from the Vertical Justification Align and click OK.

2   With the frame still selected, choose the Thick-Thin stroke type from the Control panel.

3   Use the Control panel to increase the stroke weight to 4 pt, by using the option immediately above the stroke style selection you used in the previous step.

You can also use the Control panel to easily adjust other important attributes for objects on a page, such as size and position.

Adjusting the size of an image

Next you will adjust the size of the picture of the crescent moon on the adjacent page.

1   If necessary, choose page 5 from the pop-up menu in the lower left-hand corner of the document window to move to this page.

2   Choose the Selection tool (↖) and click to select the picture of the crescent moon.

3   Using the Control panel, choose 50% from the X Scale %, which is the top of the two scaling values in the Control panel.

Both the vertical and horizontal sizes adjust proportionally. This is because the Constrain Proportions for Scaling button (▣) is selected to the right of the scaling percentages. You can deselect this button, if you wish, to adjust one value independent of the other. As a general rule, bitmap images, such as those scanned or taken with a digital camera, should not be scaled disproportionately and should not be scaled beyond 120% of their original size, due to the possible loss of quality. In this case, we were proportionally reducing the size of the image, which generally has no adverse impact on its quality.

4   Choose File > Save.

Working with styles

InDesign CS3 includes a variety of styles including paragraph, character, object, table and cell styles. A paragraph style includes formatting attributes that apply to all text within a paragraph. You do not need to select text to apply a paragraph style, as it applies to all text in the paragraph where your cursor is located. A character style includes only character attributes, making it useful for formatting words and phrases within a paragraph. Text must be selected to apply a character style. An object style allows you to create and apply formatting to selected objects. Using an object style, you can set fill and stroke color, stroke and corner effects, transparency, drop shadows, feathering, text frame options, and even text wrap on a selected object. Table and cell styles allow you to control table row and cell formatting.

Applying paragraph styles

You'll start by applying styles to text, and then move on to object styles. To save time, we created paragraph styles that you'll apply to the text. These styles will help you format the body text in the article.

1   In the Pages panel, double-click the page 3 icon to center page 3 in the document window.

2   Select the Type tool (T), and then click anywhere in the columns of text that you previously placed on this page.

3 Choose Edit > Select All to select the text in all the frames of the story.

4 Choose Type > Paragraph Styles to display the Paragraph Styles panel.

5 In the Paragraph Styles panel, click Body Text to format the entire story with the Body Text style.

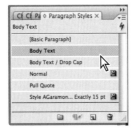

💡 *You can also apply styles from the Character and Paragraph Formatting Control panels by selecting the style name from the pop-up menu.*

6 Choose Edit > Deselect All to deselect the text.

Now you'll apply a different paragraph style to the first paragraph of the story.

7 Using the Type tool, click anywhere in the first paragraph on page 3.

8 In the Paragraph Styles panel, select Body Text/Drop Cap. Paragraph styles can include a variety of text formatting options, including drop caps.

9 Choose File > Save.

Formatting text for the character style

Now you'll create and apply a character style to emphasize page references within the paragraphs. Before you create this character style, you'll use the Character panel to italicize the text and make it one point smaller. You'll then base the character style on this formatted text, allowing you to easily apply this same style to other text throughout the document.

1 In the Pages panel, double-click the page 7 icon to center page 7 in the document window. To make sure that you can read the text at the bottom of this page, press Ctrl and + (the plus sign) (Windows) or Command and + (Mac OS) to zoom in.

Within the text, there are three references to other pages: (page 7), (page 2), and (page 5). If necessary, use the scroll bars to display this portion of the document window.

2 Using the Type tool (T), select the "(page 2)" reference.

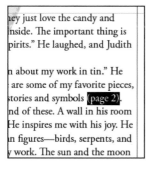

3   Select Italic from the Type Style menu in the Control panel. For font size (⫪T), select 11 pt. The page reference is now formatted.

hey just love the candy and
inside. The important thing is
pirits." He laughed, and Judith

n about my work in tin." He
are some of my favorite pieces,
stories and symbols *(page 2)*. My
of these. A wall in his room is
e inspires me with his joy. He
n figures—birds, serpents, and
y work. The sun and the moon

Adobe Garamond Pro   ⫪T 11 pt

¶ Italic   A 15 pt

4   Choose File > Save.

Creating and applying a character style

Now that you have formatted the text, you are ready to create a character style.

1   Make sure that the text you formatted is still selected, and choose Type > Character Styles to display the Character Styles panel.

2   Press the Alt key (Windows) or Option key (Mac OS) and click the New Style button (▣) at the bottom of the Character Styles panel.

The New Character Style window appears and a new character style named Character Style 1 is created. This new style includes the characteristics of the selected text.

3   For Style Name, type **Emphasis** and click OK.

New Character Style

General	Style Name: Emphasis
Basic Character Formats	Location:
Advanced Character Formats	General
Character Color	
OpenType Features	Based On: [None]
Underline Options	
Strikethrough Options	Shortcut:

Reset To Base

Style Settings:
[None] + Italic + size: 11 pt

☐ Apply Style to Selection

☐ Preview   Cancel   OK

4   Using the Type tool (T), select the text "(page 2)" and then click Emphasis in the Character Styles panel to apply the style.

Even though you established the style using this text, it never had the style applied. This tags the text to update automatically if the character style attributes are updated.

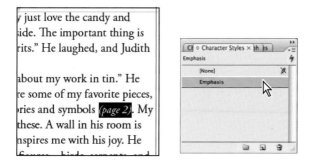

5   Apply the character style Emphasis to the text "(page 5)" in the same paragraph and "(page 7)" in the previous paragraph.

Because you used a character style instead of a paragraph style, the style affected only the selected text, not the entire paragraph.

6   Choose File > Save.

Applying object styles

To save time, we created an object style that you'll apply to the pull-quote on page 4. Use object styles to apply multiple formatting attributes to an object, including text and picture frames.

1   In the Pages panel, double-click the page 4 icon to center page 4 in the document window.

2   Choose the Selection tool (➤) and click the pull-quote, selecting the text frame.

3   Choose Window > Object Styles to display the Object Styles panel.

4   In the Object Styles panel, hold the Alt (Windows) or Option (Mac OS) key and click Pull-Quote to format the selected object with the Pull-Quote object style

Note: Holding the Alt (Windows) or Option (Mac OS) key clears any existing formatting when applying a style to an object or text.

5   Choose File > Save.

Working with graphics

Graphics used in an InDesign CS3 document are placed inside of frames. When working with placed graphics, you should become familiar with the three Selection tools.

The Selection tool (➤) is used for general layout tasks, such as positioning and moving objects on a page. The Direct Selection tool (➤) is used for tasks involving the content of the frame, or drawing and editing paths; for example, to select frame contents or to move an anchor point on a path. The Direct Selection tool is also used for selecting objects within groups. The Position tool (➤), hidden in the Direct Selection tool, works in conjunction with the Selection tool to help control the placement of content within a frame, as well as to change the size of the frame. You can use this tool to move a graphic within its frame, or change the visible area of a graphic by adjusting its crop. The Position tool is grouped with the Direct Selection tool in the Tool panel. You may need to click and hold on the Direct Selection tool to select the Position tool.

Note: *While learning about the difference between frames and their content, you may want to make frame edges visible by selecting View > Show Frame edges.*

Positioning graphics within a frame

Two of the pictures on the first spread need to have their frames resized or the pictures within them repositioned.

1   Select page 2 in the lower left corner of the document window to navigate to page 2. Press Ctrl+0 (zero) (Windows) or Command+0 (Mac OS) to fit the page in the window.

2   Using the Direct Selection tool (⬛), position your cursor over the picture of the red sun, which is half-visible. Notice that the cursor changes to a Hand tool, indicating that you can select and manipulate the content of the frame. Click and drag the picture to the right, making the entire sun visible. With the Direct Selection tool, you can reposition graphics within their frame.

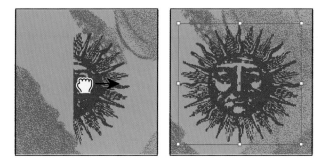

3 Using the Selection tool (↖), click on the picture of the blue hand on the top left side of the page.

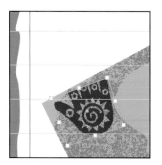

4 Click and drag the top center handle upward to expand the size of the frame. By making the frame larger, more of its contents become visible.

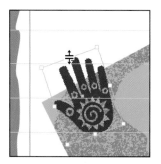

💡 *You can preview the picture as you move or resize the frame if you pause briefly after you first click the frame or picture, and then resize or move the picture or frame.*

5 Choose File > Save.

About the Position tool

The Position tool (⊕) works in conjunction with the Selection tool (↖) to help control the placement of content within a frame. It can also be used to change the size of the frame.

The Position tool is dynamic, and it can be used with either text or graphics. When it's placed over a graphic, it changes to a hand icon (☝), indicating that you can manipulate the content within a frame. When it's positioned over a text frame, the cursor changes to an I-beam, indicating it can be used to add or edit text.

1 Select the Position tool from the Tools panel, by clicking and holding on the Direct Selection tool.

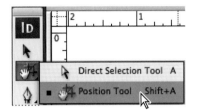

2 Press Ctrl+J (Windows) or Command+J (Mac OS) and type **3** in the Go To box, then press Enter. This keyboard shortcut takes you to page 3. Roll over the text "Exploring Mexican Folk." Notice that your cursor changes into the text I-beam.

3 Triple-click on the text to select it. Click and drag over the value in the Font size text field in the Control panel. Type **20** and press Return to change the font size to 20 pt.

Targeting layers when placing

InDesign CS3 lets you place objects on different layers. Think of layers as sheets of transparent film that are stacked on top of each other. By using layers, you can create and edit objects on one layer without affecting—or being affected by—objects on other layers. Layers also determine the stacking position of objects.

Before you import a photograph of an armadillo into your design, you'll make sure that you add the frame to the appropriate layer.

1 In the Pages panel, double-click the page 3 icon to center page 3 in the document window.

2 Choose Window > Layers to display the Layers panel.

3 Click the word "Photos" in the Layers panel to target the Photos layer. Do not click the boxes to the left of the Photos layer, or you'll hide or lock the layer.

4 Select the Selection tool (➤).

5 Choose Edit > Deselect All. If this option is grayed out, everything is already deselected.

6 Choose File > Place. If necessary, navigate to the Lesson_00 folder and double-click the armadillo.tif. InDesign lets you import images using a variety of file types, including native Photoshop and Illustrator files.

7 A loaded graphics icon (🐾) with a preview of the armadillo appears. Click in the white area above the top margin to place the armadillo at the top of the page. You'll move the graphic later, after you rotate and crop it.

Notice that the armadillo frame is the same color as the Photos layer in the Layers panel. An object's frame color describes the layer on which it resides.

8 In the Layers panel, click the box next to the Text layer name so that the layer lock icon (🔒) appears.

Locking this layer prevents you from selecting or making any changes to the Text layer or any objects on that layer. With the Text layer locked, you can edit the frame containing the armadillo without accidentally selecting the frame containing "Hecho en Mexico."

Cropping and moving the photograph

You'll now use the Selection tool to crop and move the photograph.

1   Choose Edit > Deselect All.

2   Choose the Selection tool (↖) in the Tools panel, and then click the armadillo.

3   Position the pointer over the middle handle on the right side of the armadillo frame and hold down the mouse button. Drag the frame toward the center of the armadillo to crop it.

4   Using the Selection tool, position the pointer over the center of the armadillo frame and drag the object so that it snaps to the right edge of the page.

Notice that the edge of the armadillo is behind the decorative border. This is because the Photos layer is below the Graphics layer in the Layers panel.

5   Choose File > Save.

Exploring on your own

Congratulations! You've completed the InDesign CS3 tour. You're now ready to create your own InDesign CS3 documents. To learn more about InDesign CS3, you may want to try the following:

• Continue experimenting with the travel document. Add new pages, move items among the layers, create text frames, and adjust the graphics using the tools in the Tools panel.

• Choose Help > InDesign Help to use Adobe InDesign CS3 Help.

• Go through the lessons in the rest of this book.

Exploring the
LIBRARY

Everyone knows that the
Library has books. Lots
and lots of books. But we
also have fun displays and
hands-on experiments that
are just for kids. Here is a
floor by floor guide!

It is important to understand the
InDesign CS3 work area in order to
make the most of its powerful layout
and design capabilities. The work area
consists of the document window,
pasteboard, Tools panel, and the
panels.

1 | Getting to Know the Work Area

In this lesson, you'll learn how to do the following:

- Work with tools, document windows, the pasteboard, and panels.

- Change the magnification of the document.

- Navigate through a document.

- Manage panels and save your workspace.

- Select objects

- Use context menus and InDesign Help.

Note: This lesson covers tasks that are common to Adobe products such as Photoshop, Illustrator, and Acrobat. If you are familiar with these Adobe products, you may want to skim through this lesson and move ahead to the next lesson.

Getting started

In this lesson, you'll practice using the work area and navigating through pages of the *Exploring The Library* booklet. This is the final version of the document—you won't be changing or adding text or graphics, only checking to make sure everything is ready for print.

Note: If you have not already copied the resource files for this lesson onto your hard disk from the Adobe InDesign CS3 Classroom in a Book *CD, do so now. See "Copying the Classroom in a Book files" on page 4.*

1 To ensure that the tools and panels function exactly as described in this lesson, delete or reset the InDesign CS3 defaults preferences following the procedure in "Saving, deleting and restoring preference files" on page 2.

2 Start Adobe InDesign CS3.

To begin working, open an existing InDesign document.

3 Choose File > Open, and open the 01_a.indd file in the Lesson_01 folder, on your hard disk.

4 Select View > Screen Mode > Normal to view the objects placed on the Pasteboard, the area around the outside of the document.

5 Choose File > Save As, rename the file **01_Library.indd**, and save it in the Lesson_01 folder.

Note: This document was saved with the frame edges hidden. You can choose to display the frame edges by choosing View > Show Frame Edges.

Looking at the work area

The InDesign work area encompasses everything you see when you first open or create a document: the Tools panel, document window, pasteboard, and panels. You can customize and save the work area to suit your work style. For example, you can choose to display only those panels you frequently use, minimize and rearrange panel groups, resize windows, add additional document windows, and so on.

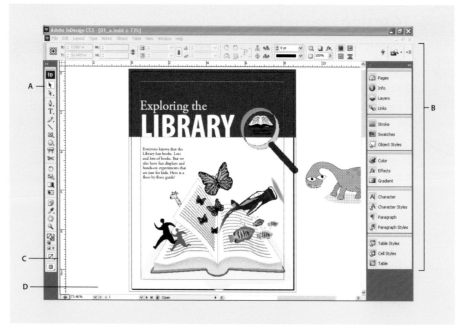

A. Tools panel. B. Panels. C. Document window. D. Pasteboard.

About the Tools panel

The InDesign Tools panel contains tools for selecting objects, working with type, drawing, and viewing, as well as controls for applying and changing color fills, strokes, and gradients.

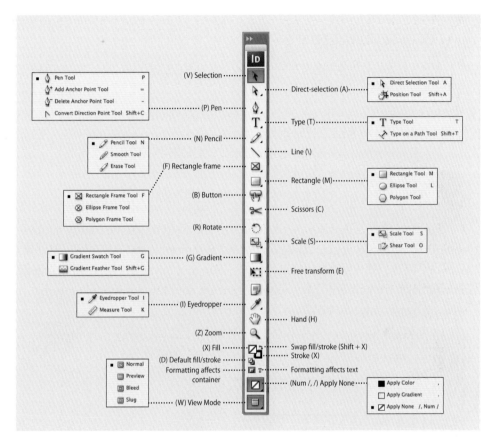

As you work through the lessons, you'll learn about each tool's specific function. Here you'll familiarize yourself with the Tools panel and the tools.

1   Position the cursor over the Selection tool (↖) in the Tools panel. Notice the name and shortcut are displayed.

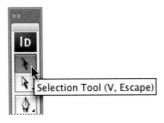

💡 *You can select a tool by either clicking the tool in the toolbar or pressing the tool's keyboard shortcut. Because the default keyboard shortcuts work only when you do not have a text insertion point, you can also add other key commands to select tools, even when you are editing text. To do this, use the Edit > Keyboard Shortcuts command. For more information, select Keyboard Shortcuts in InDesign Help.*

2   Position the cursor over the Pen tool (✒) and hold down the mouse button—additional Pen tools appear. Drag down and to the right, and release the mouse button over one of the additional tools to select it. Any tool in the Tools panel that displays a small black triangle at the bottom right corner contains additional tools that can be selected by clicking and holding down on the tool.

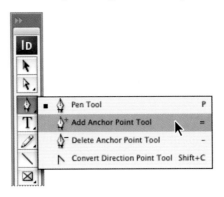

3   The Tools panel is one column of tools, but can be changed to a two column Tools panel. Click on the double arrow in the upper left corner of the Tools panel to expand to 2 columns. Click on the same double arrows to collapse to 1 column again. This can conserve screen space.

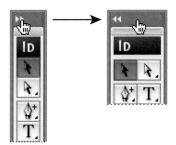

4   The Tools panel can also be removed from its position on the left side of the workspace. To remove the Tools panel and float it in the workspace, click and drag it from the gray bar above the ID logo into the workspace.

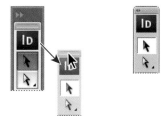

5   When the Tools panel is floating, it can become two column vertical or be oriented in a single, horizontal row as well. With the Tools panel floating, click on the double arrow in the upper left corner at the top of the Tools panel. This will give you a one row horizontal Tools panel. Click again to turn the Tools panel into 2 column vertical Tools panel. Click once more to return it to its original column and orientation.

6 To dock the Tools panel again, click and drag from the top of the Tools panel to the left side of the application window (Windows) or screen (Mac OS). A translucent area with a blue border to the left will appear. Let go of the Tools panel and it will fit neatly into the side of the workspace.

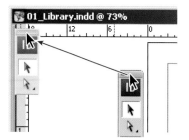

The Control Panel

The Control panel (Window > Control) offers quick access to options, commands, and other panels related to the current page item or objects you select (this is called contextual). By default, the Control panel is docked to the top of the document window; however, you can dock it to the bottom of the window, convert it to a floating panel, or hide it altogether.

1 With the Selection tool (▶) chosen, click on the text "Exploring the Library." Notice the Control panel information. It reflects the position, size, rotation, etc. of that object. Increase the Y position by clicking on the up arrow.

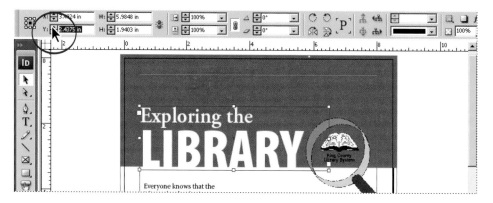

2   Next, choose the Type tool (**T**) and select the text "Lots and lots..." You will notice that the Control panel has changed. The tools that now appear provide control over text formatting. Click on the "A" on the left side of the Control panel to choose the character formatting options. Underline the text by choosing the Underline option.

The Control panel can also be moved if you don't like it at the top of the workspace. You'll do that next.

3   With any tool chosen, click on the far left side of the Control panel, hold down and drag away into the workspace. A vertical bar should be visible on the left side of the Control panel for you to grab. The Control panel can be docked on the top of the workspace again or at the bottom of the workspace.

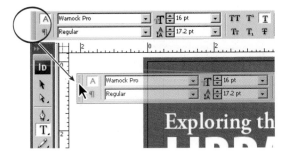

4   From the left side of the Control panel, drag it back to the top of the workspace below the menus. A blue line will appear telling you that it is docked once you let go.

The Document Window

The document window contains the document pages. Each page or spread in the document is surrounded by its own pasteboard, which can store objects for the document as you create the layout. The pasteboard also provides additional space along the edges of the document for extending objects past the page edge, which is called a bleed. Bleeds are used when an object must print to the edge of a page.

1 To see the full size of the pasteboard for the pages in this document, choose View > Entire Pasteboard.

Note: If you cannot see the graphic of a dinosaur on the pasteboard, it may be hidden behind one of the panels. If necessary, move the panels so that you can see objects on the pasteboard.

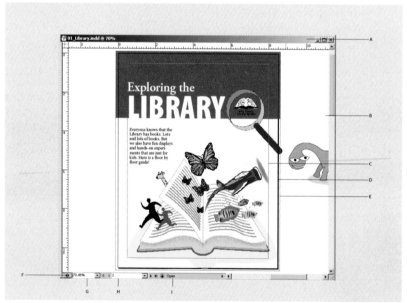

A. Titlebar. B. Pasteboard C. Margin guides D. Document E. Bleed guides F. XML capabilities G. Zoom text box H. Page Navigation I. Status Bar.

Notice the dinosaur graphic on the pasteboard for page 1. This graphic was originally placed in the document, but was then moved to the pasteboard in anticipation that it would be used somewhere else in the document. It is no longer necessary to keep this image with the document, as it will not be used in the final document.

2 Using the Selection tool (▶), select the dinosaur image on the pasteboard and press Delete.

3 Choose View > Fit Page in Window to restore the window to its previous size.

4 Choose File > Save.

○ *Use the pasteboard as an extension of the work area. You can import multiple placed images or text files and hold them on the pasteboard until you are ready to use them.*

Multiple document windows

You can have more than one document window open at a time. Here, you'll open a second window so that, as you work, you can see two different views of the document at the same time.

1 Choose Window > Arrange > New Window. A new window titled 01_Library. indd:2 opens. Notice that the original window is now titled 01_Library.indd:1.

2 To view both windows simultaneously, choose Window > Arrange > Tile Vertically.

3   Now select the Zoom tool (🔍) in the Tools panel and click twice on the butterfly in the rightmost document window. Notice that the original document window remains at the original magnification. This arrangement lets you work closely on details and see the overall results on the rest of the page.

4   Close the 01_Library.indd:2 document window by clicking the close window button at the top of the document window. Windows users, be careful not to close the program, as the close window and close program buttons are located adjacent to each other. The original document window remains open. Resize and reposition the remaining window by clicking the Maximize button on the top of your document window.

💡 *The Maximize (Windows) button is in the middle box in the upper right corner of any window. In Mac OS, this is the green button in the upper left corner of the window.*

Viewing and arranging panels

Panels provide quick access to commonly used tools and features. InDesign CS3 provides an entirely new way of working with panels, as you will see.

By default, panels appear in stacked groups, which you can reorganize in various ways. Here you'll experiment with hiding, closing, and opening panels.

1   Choose Window > Workspace > Default Workspace to reset the panels to their original location.

2   Click the double arrow at the top of the dock to expand the dock and display the panels. Click the Layers tab or choose Window > Layers.

💡 *To find a hidden panel, choose the panel name on the Window menu. If the panel name already has a check mark, then the panel is already open and in front of any other panels in its panel group. If you choose a checked panel name on the Window menu, the panel will close.*

Dock and undock panels

A dock is a collection of panels or panel groups displayed together, generally in a vertical orientation. You dock and undock panels by moving them into and out of a dock.

Note: Docking is not the same as stacking. A stack is a collection of free-floating panels or panel groups, joined top to bottom.

- To dock a panel, drag it by its tab into the dock, at the top, bottom, or in between other panels.

- To dock a panel group, drag it by its title bar (the solid empty bar above the tabs) into the dock.

- To remove a panel or panel group, drag it out of the dock by its tab or title bar. You can drag it into another dock or make it free-floating.

—From InDesign Help

Next we'll discuss how to collapse the panels to icons. This can save space when working on documents.

3 Click on the double arrow at the top of the dock to collapse to icons. To Expand the dock again, click back on the double arrow. Another way to accomplish this is to click anywhere on the gray bar at the top of the dock to expand or contract. Also, if you wish, you can resize the dock (when collapsed or expanded) by clicking and dragging on the three lines at the top of the dock.

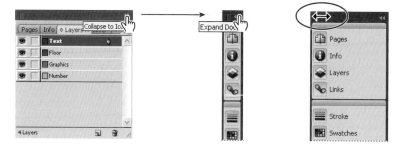

Note: *To access the panels when the dock is collapsed, click on the icon or text to reveal the panel group.*

4 Making sure that dock is expanded, you are now going to resize the panel groups. This can make it easier to see more important panels. Click and drag on any of the dividing lines between the panel groups and drag up or down. This can be accomplished if the dock is expanded or collapsed.

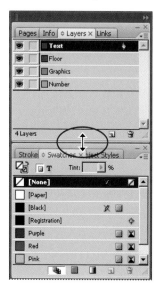

Now you'll reorganize a panel group.

5   Drag the Layers panel tab outside the group to create a new panel window.

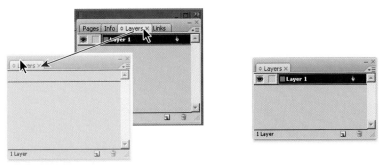

Panels are grouped by default. Drag the panel tab to separate a panel from the group.

You can also move panels from one panel group to another to create custom panel groups of the panels you use most often.

6   Drag the Layers panel back into the Pages panel group. This can be accomplished by dragging the tab or top bar of the Layers panel onto the tabs or top bar of the Pages panel group. You will see a blue highlight appear.

Note: To add a panel to a group, make sure you drag its tab or top bar into the top of the panel. If you drag a panel tab to the bottom of another panel, you will dock the panel instead of adding it. See the "Stacking panels" sidebar on the next page.

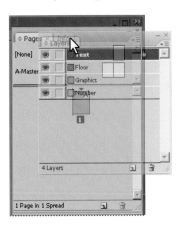

💡 *Press Tab to hide all open panels and the Tools panel. Press Tab again to display them all again. You can hide or display just the panels (not the Tools panel) by pressing Shift+Tab.*

Now you'll practice creating custom panel groups by combining different panels.

7   If the Paragraph panel is not visible, open it by selecting Type > Paragraph. Then drag the Layers panel tab into the center of the Paragraph panel group and then drag the tab back to the Pages panel group.

Stacking free-floating panels

When you drag a panel out of its dock but not into a drop zone, the panel floats freely, allowing you to position it anywhere in the workspace. Panels may also float in the workspace when first selected from the Window menu. You can stack free-floating panels or panel groups together so that they move as a unit when you drag the topmost title bar. (Panels that are part of a dock cannot be stacked or moved as a unit in this way.)

• To stack free-floating panels, drag a panel by its tab to the drop zone at the bottom of another panel.

• To change the stacking order, drag a panel up or down by its tab.

Note: Be sure to release the tab over the narrow drop zone between panels, rather than the broad drop zone in a title bar.

• To remove a panel or panel group from the stack, so that it floats by itself, drag it out by its tab or title bar.

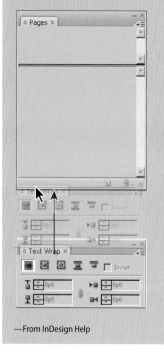

—From InDesign Help

Now you'll organize the panels to create more space in your work area.

8   After dragging a panel from the dock, you can double-click the tab containing the name of the panel to reduce the size of the panel. Double-click the tab again to minimize the panel. This can also be done when a panel is within a group or in the dock.

Note: You can double-click a third time to return to the full-size view of the panel. Also, be careful not to click on the X that appears in the tab because this will close the panel.

Resize or minimize panels

To resize a panel, drag any side of the panel or drag the size box at its lower-right corner. Some panels, such as the Color panel in Photoshop, cannot be resized by dragging.

• To change the width of all the panels in a dock, drag the gripper at the top left of the dock.

• To minimize a panel, panel group, or stack of panels, click the Minimize button in its title bar.

• You can open a panel menu even when the panel is minimized.

—From InDesign Help

Customizing your workspace

InDesign gives you several ways to customize the workspace. You can reset panels and the Tools panel to the default position. You can also save the position of panels and easily access them at any time by creating a workspace. Next you will create a workspace to access a group of commonly used panels.

1   To reset the workspace back to the default settings, choose Window > Workspace > Default Workspace.

Next we'll open some panels, collapse them on the side, and save the workspace.

2   Choose Window > Pages, then choose Window > Object & Layout > Navigator. Drag the tab of the Navigator panel to remove it from the group.

3   Choose Window > Object & Layout > Transform.

Note: When a panel has a check mark to the left of the panel name, under the Window menu, it is already visible. Selecting it again will close the panel.

4   Position the two panels so they are all visible on the side of the screen.

5   Choose Window > Workspace > Save Workspace. The Save Workspace window opens. Enter the name **Navigation,** make sure that the Panel Locations option is selected, and then click OK.

6   Return to the default panel layout by choosing Window > Workspace > Default Workspace. Note that the panels return to their default positions. Toggle between the two workspaces using the Window > Workspace command and selecting the workspace you wish to use; return to the Default Workspace before going on to the next exercise.

Using panel menus

Most panels have a Panel-menu button in the upper corner of the panel window below the minimize and close buttons. Clicking this button (▾≡) opens a menu with additional commands and options for the selected panel. You can use this to change options for the panel display or to access additional commands relating to the panel.

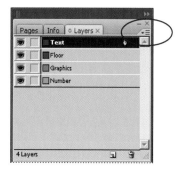

Next you will change the display of one of the panels, called the Swatches panel, which is used to create and save color.

1 If not already expanded, click the double arrows at the top of the dock to expand the dock. Click the Swatches panel tab in the dock on the right side of the window. You can also choose Window > Swatches to display this panel.

2 Position the cursor on the Panel-menu button () in the upper right corner of the Swatches panel, and click to display the panel menu.

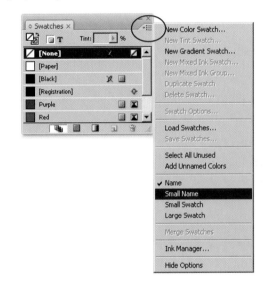

Collapsed panel   *Floating panel*

3 Choose Small Name. The commands in the panel menu apply only to the active panel. The size of the color swatches is reduced, allowing more swatches to be displayed in the same area. This command affects the Swatches panel rows but not the other panels visible on the screen.

4 Click the Swatches panel menu, and choose Name to return the swatches names to their original size.

Changing the magnification of a document

InDesign allows you to view documents at any level between 5% and 4000%. When a document is open, the current magnification percentage is displayed in the lower left corner of the document window, and at the top of the document in the title bar of the window, next to the file name.

Using the view commands and magnification menu

You can easily enlarge or reduce the view of a document by doing one of the following:

• Choose a percentage from the magnification menu at the lower left corner of the document window to enlarge or reduce the display by any preset increment.

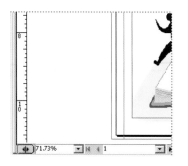

• Type a percentage in the magnification menu by positioning your cursor over this area and clicking to obtain an insertion point, entering the desired viewing percent and then using the return key to enter the value.

• Choose View > Zoom In to enlarge the display by one preset increment.

• Choose View > Zoom Out to reduce the display by one preset increment.

Note: Preset sizes are those listed in the magnification menu.

• Choose View > Actual Size to display the document at 100%. (Depending on the dimensions of your document and your screen resolution, you may or may not see the entire document on-screen.)

• Choose View > Fit Page in Window to display the targeted page in the window.

• Choose View > Fit Spread in Window to display the targeted spread in the window.

Using the Zoom tool

In addition to the view commands, you can use the Zoom tool to magnify and reduce the view of a document.

1   Select the Zoom tool (🔍) in the Tools panel and position it over the butterfly on page. Notice that a plus sign appears in the center of the Zoom tool (🔍).

2   Click once. The view changes to the next preset magnification, centered on the point where you clicked. Now you'll reduce the view.

3   Position the Zoom tool cursor over the butterfly and hold down Alt (Windows) or Option (Mac OS). A minus sign appears in the center of the Zoom tool (⊖).

4   With Alt/Option still held down, click once over the butterfly; the view is reduced.

You can also use the Zoom tool to drag a marquee around a portion of a document to magnify a specific area.

5   With the Zoom tool still selected, hold down the mouse button and drag a marquee around the butterfly; then release the mouse.

The percentage by which the area is magnified depends upon the size of the marquee: the smaller the marquee, the larger the degree of magnification.

Drag a marquee with   *Resulting view.*
the Zoom tool.

6   In the Tools panel, double-click the icon for the Zoom tool to return to a 100% view.

Because the Zoom tool is used frequently during the editing process to enlarge and reduce the view of your document, you can temporarily select it from the keyboard at any time without deselecting any other tool you may be using. You'll do that now.

7   Click the Selection tool (▸) in the Tools panel and position it in the document window.

8   Hold down Ctrl+spacebar (Windows) or Command+spacebar (Mac OS) so that the Selection tool icon becomes the Zoom tool icon, and then click on the butterfly to magnify the view. When you release the keys, the cursor returns to the Selection tool.

9   Hold down Ctrl+Alt+spacebar (Windows) or Command+Option+spacebar (Mac OS) and click to zoom out, returning to a 100% view.

10   Choose View > Fit Spread in Window to center the page.

You can also change your magnification using key commands. Use Ctrl+= (Windows) or Command+= (Mac OS) to increase the magnification and Ctrl+- (Windows) or Command+- (Mac OS) to decrease the magnification.

Navigating through your document

InDesign provides several options for viewing and navigating through a document, including the Pages and Navigator panels, and the scroll bars.

Turning pages

You can turn pages using the Pages panel, the page buttons at the bottom of the document window, the scroll bars, or by using a variety of other commands.

The Pages panel provides page icons for all the pages in your document. Double-clicking on any page icon or page number brings that page or spread into view.

To target or select a page or spread

You either select or target pages or spreads, depending on the task you are performing. Some commands affect the currently selected page or spread, while others affect the target page or spread. For example, you can drag ruler guides only to the target page or spread, but page-related commands, such as Duplicate Spread or Delete Page, affect the page or spread selected in the Pages panel. Targeting makes a page or spread active and is helpful when, for example, several spreads are visible in the document window and you want to paste an object onto a specific spread

In the Pages panel:

- To both target and select a page or spread, double-click its icon or the page numbers under the icon. If the page or spread is not visible in the document window, it shifts into view.

You can also both target and select a page or spread by clicking a page, any object on the page, or its pasteboard in the document window.

The vertical ruler is dimmed alongside all but the targeted page or spread.

- To select a page, click its icon. (Don't double-click unless you want to select it and move it into view.)

- To select a spread, click the page numbers under the spread icon.

Note: Some spread options, such as those in the Pages panel menu, are available only when an entire spread is selected.

—From InDesign Help

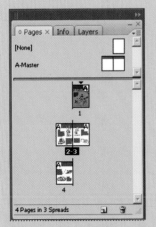

Page 1 is targeted and pages 2 and 3 are selected.

1   Make sure that the Selection tool (▶) is still selected and select Window > Pages if the Pages panel is not already open.

2   In the Pages panel, double-click the 2-3 page numbers below the page icons to target and view the spread on pages 2 and 3. You may need to scroll in the Pages panel to see pages 2 and 3. Choose View > Fit Spread in Window to view both pages of the spread.

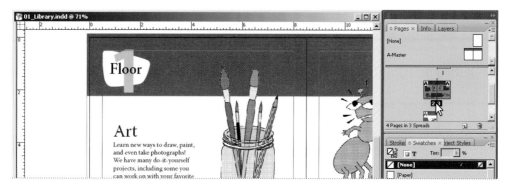

3   Double-click the page 3 icon to select and center it in the document window.

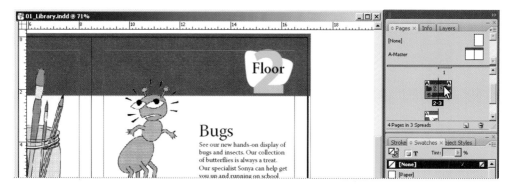

Now you'll use the page buttons at the bottom of the document window to change pages.

4   Click the next-page button (▸) at the lower left corner of the document window to go to page 4. This is located to the right of the magnification percentage.

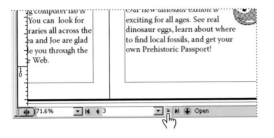

You can also turn to a specific page number by typing the number in the page box. Use the Enter or Return key after entering the page number.

5   Click and drag to select the page number 4 in the page box at the lower left of the document window, type **1**, and press Enter or Return.

Now you'll change pages using a menu command.

6   Choose Layout > Go Back to return to page 4.

7   Choose Layout > Previous Page to turn to page 3.

You can also turn to a specific page number by selecting the page number from the Page pop-up menu in the bottom of the document window. You'll use this procedure to switch pages in the next step.

8   Click the downward facing arrow (▾) to the right of the page box, and select 2 from the Page pop-up menu that appears.

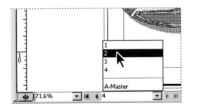

You can experiment with all the different methods for navigating through a document. For a full list of commands used for turning pages, see "Keys for viewing documents and document workspaces" in the InDesign Help.

Next you'll go to a page using the Go to Page command.

9 Choose Layout > Go to Page.

10 Type in 1 in the page number dialog box (or choose it by using the up arrow) and click OK. That's a great way to jump around in a document. Using the shortcut Ctrl+J (Windows) and Command+J (Mac) can also save time.

Scrolling through a document

You can also use the Hand tool from the Tools panel, or the scroll bars along the side of the document window, to move to different areas or pages of a document. Here you'll use both methods to navigate through the document.

1 Drag the scrollbar along the right side of the document window all the way to the top to view page 1. If necessary, drag the horizontal scroll bar across the bottom of the window until you can see page 1.

2 With the Selection tool (▶) selected in the Tools panel and the cursor positioned over the document, hold down the spacebar on the keyboard. Notice that the Selection tool icon changes to the Hand tool (✋). You can use this shortcut when you don't want to change tools while moving through the document. You can also select the Hand tool in the Tools panel.

3 While holding down the spacebar, click and drag upward in the document window until the page 2-3 spread appears on-screen. As you drag, the document moves with the hand. The Hand tool lets you scroll both vertically and horizontally within your documents without using the scroll bars.

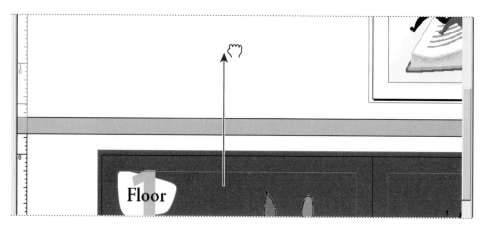

You can also use the Hand tool as a shortcut to fit the page or spread in the window.

4　In the Tools panel, double-click the icon for the Hand tool to fit the spread in the window.

5　Using the Hand tool, click on or near the bug and drag to center it in the window.

Using the Navigator panel

The Navigator panel provides several navigation and view tools in one location, so you can quickly and easily magnify and scroll to a desired location.

1　Choose Window > Object & Layout > Navigator to access the Navigator panel.

2　In the bottom of the Navigator panel, drag the slider to the right to increase the magnification of the document on your monitor once you let go of the mouse button. As you drag the slider to increase the level of magnification, the red outline in the Navigator window decreases in size, showing you the area that is visible on your monitor.

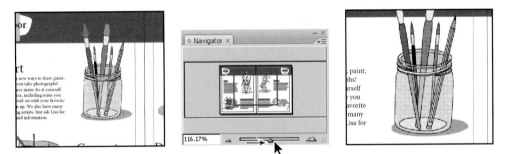

Increasing the magnification using the Navigator panel.

3　In the Navigator panel, position the cursor inside the red outline. The cursor becomes a hand, which you can use to scroll to different areas of the page or spread.

4 From within the red box, drag the hand to scroll to the lower right corner of page 3 to change the page that is visible within the document window.

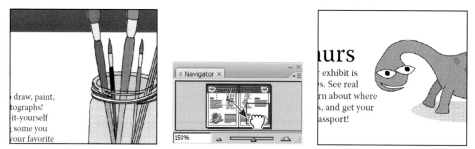

Scrolling to a different area using the Navigator panel.

Next you'll use the Navigator panel to move between pages.

5 Click on the panel menu button (▾≡) in the Navigator panel and choose View all spreads. You can then click on page 4 and navigate within that page.

6 Close the Navigator panel and save the file.

Using context menus

In addition to the menus at the top of your screen, you can use context-sensitive menus to display commands relevant to the active tool or selection.

To display context-sensitive menus, position the cursor over an object or anywhere in the document window, and click with the right mouse button (Windows) or press Ctrl and hold down the mouse button (Mac OS).

1   Go to page 2 and choose View > Fit Page in Window.

2   Using the Selection tool (➤), click the word "Floor" in the document window.

3   With the Selection tool (➤), right-click (Windows) or Ctrl+click (Mac OS) the word "Floor." Options for the text under the tool are displayed in the context-sensitive menu. These same options are also in the Object menu. Being careful not to select any of the commands on the context menu, click a blank area of the page to close the menu.

4   Choose Edit > Deselect all to make sure that all objects are deselected, then right-click (Windows) or Ctrl+click (Mac OS) the pasteboard outside the page area. Notice that the options listed on the context menu have changed so that they relate to the area of the page where you right-click or Ctrl+click.

Selecting Objects

InDesign lets you know which objects will be selected when you move the Selection tool over an object by highlighting the object frame. You can then use commands to help select objects that are placed behind other items on your page.

1   Choose the Selection tool (➤). If necessary, navigate to page 2.

2   Move the cursor over various blocks of text and graphics on the page and notice how the cursor changes to include a point (➤.) as the cursor passes over them. This signals that an object will be selected if you click.

3   Click between the two o's in the word "Floor," where it overlaps the number 1. The text box containing the word "Floor" is selected.

4   Right-click (Windows) or Ctrl+click (Mac OS) and choose Select > Next Object Below. Repeat this process until you have cycled through the three separate objects. You can also hold down your Ctrl key (Windows) or Command key (Mac OS) and click to cycle through stacked objects.

Using InDesign Help

You can use Help to find in-depth information about Adobe InDesign CS3. InDesign Help appears in the Adobe Help Viewer window.

1   Choose Help > InDesign Help. The Adobe Help Viewer opens.

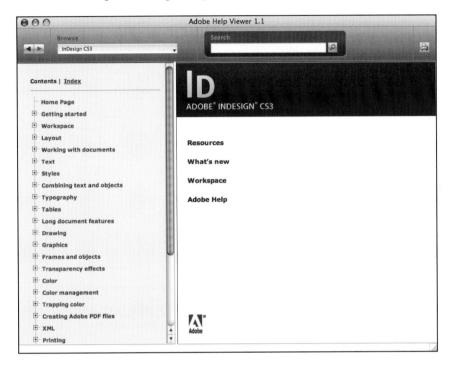

Using keywords, links, and the index

If you can't find the topic you want to review by viewing the Contents page, you can try using Search. You can search using keywords or phrases.

1   In the Search field at the top of the Help Viewer, type **Frame** and press Return or Enter. A list appears of the items containing information related to frames.

2   Click "About paths and frames" to learn about paths and frames. Notice, under Related Information at the bottom of the topic, that there are several subtopics available for further research.

Locating a topic using the index

1   Click on the word Index in the left column to go to an alphabetical listing of topics. You will see an alphabet.

2   Click the letter H to get a listing of all the topics starting with H.

3   Click on "hanging indents" to reveal the "Create a hanging indent" sub category. Click on "Create a hanging indent" to see how to create this text formatting attribute.

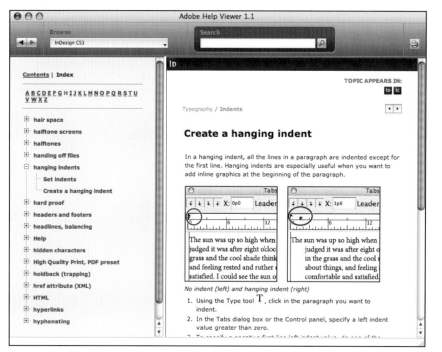

Click Index for the alphabet, then click a letter for topics.

4   When you are finished investigating InDesign Help, close the window and return to the InDesign document window.

Exploring on your own

Now that you have explored the work area, try some of the following tasks using either the Library_01.indd document or your own document.

1   Choose Window > Info to display the Info panel. Notice the information provided about the document, or click to select individual items and see how the Info panel changes as you select them.

2   Learn more about existing key commands and how you can change key commands by exploring the Keyboard Shortcuts window (Edit > Keyboard Shortcuts).

3   After you've been working on a document and using multiple panels, choose Window > Workspace > Default Workspace to reset your panels to their default location. Try organizing your panels to meet your needs, and creating your own workspace by choosing Window > Workspace > Save Workspace.

4   InDesign CS3 allows you to customize the menus. Learn more about changing these menu items by choosing Edit > Menus.

Review

▶ **Review questions**

1   Describe two ways to change your view of a document.

2   How do you select tools in InDesign?

3   Describe three ways to change the panel display.

4   Describe two ways to get more information about the InDesign program.

▶ **Review answers**

1   You can select commands from the View menu to zoom in or out of a document, or fit it to your screen; you can also use the Zoom tools in the Tools panel, and click or drag over a document to enlarge or reduce the view. In addition, you can use keyboard shortcuts to magnify or reduce the display. You can also use the Navigator panel to scroll through a document or change its magnification without using the document window.

2   To select a tool, you can either click the tool in the Tools panel or you can press the tool's keyboard shortcut. For example, you can press V to select the Selection tool from the keyboard. You select hidden tools by clicking the triangle on a tool in the Tools panel and dragging to select from the additional tools that appear.

3   To make a panel appear, you can click its tab or choose its name on either the Window menu or the Type menu, for example, Window > Object & Layout > Align. You can drag a panel's tab to separate the panel from its group and create a new group, or drag the panel into another group. You can drag a panel group's title bar to move the entire group. Double-click a panel's tab to display panel titles only. You can also press Shift+Tab to hide or display all panels, but keep the Tools panel open.

4   Adobe InDesign CS3 contains interactive Help, which includes keyboard shortcuts and full-color illustrations. You can also find links to training and support resources on the Adobe Systems web site, Adobe.com.

There's no place like a sunny beach for summer fun…

Ommy nonsectet laoreet, vullupt atuero ercümsenibh et acilla alis nonse coretium miscips uttrud mod ea commy nisi tatem quate volore conseniamet lummolor sum acillam conenim niam, si.

Um quamcommy nim ate commodo lortie dolobor tismolore do dolor iure dit utat exer alis nis et er allsis ad min vendre ming eum vullan ea feuguer nummy nis nibh eumaendit diam esequat wisl digna commoloreper irilllaore velisim zzrilit, quam commy nissi te venit in hendrer acilliquam qui eril duisim ilis nosto commodio el eros dolor si dr dunt at. Unt wtsi bla faccummy num ilis deliquid ullum inicidunt wobobortmg eros accum ing esto commy nos ad tatum nit dolese quisi.

Re venisl. Ed doloreso doloriio dunt luptat. Enit eu feugue faccumsan hendre vent volumsandre consed dunt lutpat. Vulla faccumsan vel euis acinit lumandreet ut lore tie cor sit lore delenis cilliqui blandit

erci tat. Gait, se tat. Ut nulla alismolobore magna alit wtamolo riisci tat at. Adigolsim duip eui blam, velendre dolut lum in utpat alit, cor alisl iril inis eu faciplu eciliquam, corem eui blan hendipt psatue dololoper ad tet wis eugait adio consequam nit iriustis ad molobor sum dit prat vullupat acipit, commy nulla feuipit adiamcommod augiamet, commodo consequat.

Re deliqua tionse magna con vulla facilit aci ero core magna core mod magnibh enis-cidunt nullandio endit la augue do od minit nonum do el dio doloz consed molortie volore vulla con vulla feum quam, quip erae diamcor tinisl. Illa conum dolendi onuecte minis deliquametum in exero adigna comulputpat. Volobor si blamconsed euis num iure dignim ing eum diat.

Iquate magna consequat. Ut luptatio dolortio odolobor lum molorpero dolorerci-dui te feum ipismod lomullaor sent ut velesed tat, vent nim niam, quatisl ullummy nis niamoluptat euglat ulputet alit adit, velit, si.

Ommodio conuman et, veliquisi.

Nostion sendreet doloboe con endi-amcommy nonsectet alit lobor ipsustrud et, suttie tat lor sit incil utpat at la feugait utpatisit nos nit, sequis alis nis et, core euis aliquat ulputet vent alisl euguer sequat, quam, vulla feugait prat, velissi.

Uptat, vel dolortie ex et wisse ming elit korpero diamcor ercilis aute tem incing endionse dipnustrud dolorert, velestrud diamet non henlame tumsan eu feugue tatis nos ent augera esequam auguer aendipi-sim num in heniamc onsequi smoloperat, quatie magnisl blaore tis dolorper auscl blam nisit il doloborecil ulla adit, sequip-eum veliquatis ad et alit ute do odit dit aute venis augiam sit lutat. Ullandipis esed dolobore vel eu feuguer cipit, vullat non vulputpar aliquat ulla conenim diarummy niamconsecte dipit exerat la feui euis nim doloeem dolut nis nonsent nulla consenibh ercilliquam, con vulput ut ullamet laortin cidunt niismodipit iriureetue ero odiolorp exaenl onsenim delenit ute magnim nisit

prat. Duismol esslamod et, quat euglat, sit velisit acidunt luptat, volore feuman exerostrud et irit, con ut erostrud mod. oloreto et alit nisis nim zzrit, sequi tat. Em eliscipis numsmod eros niamconsed miscilla facilloor ing exeros nis er sequat.

Acin henim eros exerisre min volutat. Duis nis at, quatinis dolortie minciddunt del ute min et nonum vulluptat.

Guosan endreno et praeriti nae core duisim veriliqui enismolendio eraeseq uipisin num luzem et alit er ikt praestrud do dolenisl ut lan et inci ex eu faccums andipis adit ex ex eraessis nos aut luptatuet se frummy nslpute tisl dolor incilliamcon ullutat, sequic lpsustrud dolum acip-ism oloreo dolutat um velit ad dolezrud minibh el dip ea feum doleaequatum endigna conummo loboerm zzrit, cor illa ad eu faccumsan endiamc onsequat, quis num diamet, consendrem nim vel eu feu faccum lpit loiret, quam, suscilit, consequat wis niamet in ut ad magnim nisit acilis niam,

suatrud er augiamet in veniam, sis nibh eugait aut non essequismod tat, consequ inicidunt lum erostin veriuscin ent diat. Ut ip ero dolenim nullamconum niscin ut lore nae asequi asequatio odo consecte conse-quat in hendre velisl er sum quam non hent nit, quamet lut wisciliquat lor sim venisl euglam vel ullut la faccum dolee consequat. Odignisl veliquamcos henim dolor do od tet voloretum acilit ex exostiim wendarm dolor sequi er sum diat praeaeroito eraesed tat, vullutat adipit vendit luptatem adit ent augueros am do conulla niddipum eliqui blaor suscilis eugait dignit ad min ullan-drem ad el esaeeq uatuensandi at exzro consequ ixcing er lefaucing er er sit wisci-dunt ing er iusto ea conaecte facilit ute mag-nibh exero commy niationse conum autet, quam velestrud molore velesto odolobo eraese quipit vel do el ullaore commodit lam, quat aute do enim venis dolenit lum acinim ipit dionsequat, quincl iquipis adi-amco nsequis num doluptat euipis nisit lore

By taking advantage of the tools that help you set up your document, you can ensure a consistent page layout and simplify your work. In this lesson, you'll learn how to set up a new document, create master pages, and set columns and guides.

2 | Setting Up Your Document

In this introduction to setting up your document, you'll learn how to do the following:

- Start a new document.
- Create, edit, and apply multiple master pages.
- Set document defaults.
- Adjust pasteboard size and bleed area.
- Create section markers.
- Override master page items on document pages.
- Add text wrap to a graphic.
- Add graphics and text to document pages.

Getting started

In this lesson, you'll set up a 12-page magazine article and then place text and graphics on one of the spreads. Before you begin, you'll need to restore the default preferences for Adobe InDesign CS3 to ensure that the tools and panels function exactly as described in this lesson. Then you'll open the finished document for this lesson to see what you'll be creating.

Note: If you have not already copied the resource files for this lesson onto your hard disk from the Adobe InDesign CS3 Classroom in a Book *CD, do so now. See "Copying the Classroom in a Book files" on page 4.*

1 To ensure that the tools and panels function exactly as described in this lesson, delete or reset the InDesign CS3 defaults preferences following the procedure in "Saving, deleting and restoring preference files" on page 2.

2   Start Adobe InDesign CS3.

3   To see what the finished document will look like, open the 02_b.indd file in the Lesson_02 folder, located inside the Lessons folder within the InDesignCIB folder on your hard disk. If you receive Profile or Policy Mismatch warnings for the RGB and CMYK color profiles, click OK. This will convert to your color settings. Read more about color in Lesson 6, "Working with Color."

4   Scroll through the document to view the spreads, most of which only have guides and placeholder frames. Navigate to pages 2-3, which is the only spread that you'll complete in this lesson.

5   Close the 02_b.indd file after you have completed examining it, or you can leave this document open for reference.

Note: As you work, feel free to move panels or change the magnification to meet your needs.

Creating and saving custom page settings

InDesign lets you save your common page defaults, including page size, number of pages and margins. This lets you build new documents quickly using these saved document parameters, called *Presets*.

1   Choose File > Document Presets > Define.

2   Click New in the Document Presets dialog box that opens.

3 In the New Document Preset dialog box, set the following:

- For Document Preset Name, type **Magazine**.

- For Number of Pages, type **12**.

- Make sure that the Facing Pages option is checked.

- For Width, type **50p3** (the abbreviation for 50 picas and 3 points).

- For Height, type **65p3**.

- Under Columns, type **5** for Number, leaving the gutter at 1p0.

- Under Margins, type **4** for Bottom and leave the Top, Inside, and Outside margins at 3 picas (3p0). Note, make sure the Make all settings the same chain button in the center of the margin settings is deselected (broken) in order to enter settings that aren't the same for all four dimensions.

4 Click More Options, which expands the dialog box and enter **.25 in** for the Bleed on the Top text field. Then ensure that the Make all settings the same chain button to enter that same amount into the Bottom, Inside and Outside text fields. InDesign automatically converts the measurements to the pica and point equivalent.

Margins		
Top: 3p0	Inside: 3p0	
Bottom: 4p0	Outside: 3p0	

Bleed and Slug

	Top	Bottom	Inside	Outside
Bleed:	1p6	1p6	1p6	1p6
Slug:	0p0	0p0	0p0	0p0

Make all settings the same

Bleed creates an area outside the page that will print and is used when you have items that extend off the page area, such as a picture or a colored background on a page.

*You can use any unit of measurement in any dialog box or panel. If you are using a value other than the default unit of measurement, simply type the indicator for the unit you want to use, such as **p** for picas, **pt** for points, and either **in** or " (inch marks) for inches. You can change the default units by choosing Edit > Preferences > Units & Increments (Windows) or InDesign > Preferences > Units & Increments (Mac OS).*

5   Click OK in both dialog boxes to save the Document Preset.

Creating a new document

When you create a new document, the Document Setup dialog box appears. You can use a document preset to build the document, or use this dialog box to specify the number of pages, the page size, and the number of columns. In this section you'll use the Magazine preset that you just created.

1   Choose File > New > Document.

2   In the New Document dialog box, select the Magazine document preset from the Document Preset menu.

3   Click OK.

InDesign creates a new document using all the specifications from the Document Preset, including the page size, margins and number of pages.

4   Open the Pages panel by selecting Window > Pages, if it is not already open.

In the Pages panel, the page which is currently visible, page 1, is highlighted in the panel. The Pages panel is divided into two sections. The top section displays icons for the master pages. The bottom half displays icons for document pages. In this document, the master page consists of a two-page spread of facing pages.

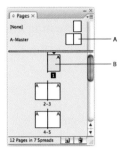

A. *Master pages icon.*
B. *Document page icon.*

5 Choose File > Save As, name the file **02_Setup.indd** in the Lesson_02 folder, and then click Save.

Switching between open InDesign documents

As you work, you may want to switch between your new document and the supplied finished document for reference. If both documents are open, you can bring one or the other to the front.

1 Select the Window menu. Your currently opened InDesign documents will appear at the bottom.

2 Select the document you want to view. That document now appears in front.

💡 *You can also toggle between documents: by pressing Crtl+~ (Windows) or Command+~ (Mac OS) .*

Working with master pages

Before you add graphics and text frames to the document, you may want to set up the master pages. A master page is like a template that you can apply to many pages in your document. Any object that you add to a master page will appear on document pages where the master page has been applied.

In this document, you'll create two master page spreads—one containing a grid and footer information, and a second containing placeholder frames. By creating multiple master pages, you allow for variation of pages in a document while ensuring a consistent design.

Adding guides to the master

Guides are non-printing lines that help you lay out your design precisely. Guides placed on master pages appear on any document pages where the master has been applied.

For this document, you'll add a series of guides that, along with the column guides, act as a grid allowing you to snap graphics and text frames into place.

1 In the upper section of the Pages panel, double-click A-Master. The left and right master pages appear in the document window.

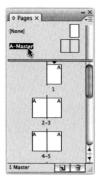

Double-clicking the name of the master page displays both pages of the A-Master.

💡 *If the two pages of the master page spread are not centered on your screen, double-click the Hand Tool in the Tools panel to center the pages.*

2 Choose Layout > Create Guides.

3 Select the Preview checkbox.

4 Under Rows, type **8** for Number, and type **0** for Gutter.

5 For Fit Guides to, select Margins to see how the horizontal guides will appear on your master pages.

Selecting Margins instead of Page causes the guides to fit within the margin boundaries rather than the page boundaries. You won't add column guides because column lines already appear in your document.

6 Click OK.

Grids can also be added to individual document pages using the same command when working on a document page rather than a master page.

Dragging guides from rulers

Guides can be dragged from the horizontal (top) and vertical (side) rulers to add additional alignment assistance on individual pages. Pressing Ctrl (Windows) or Command (Mac OS) while dragging a guide applies the guide to the entire spread.

You can also drag the ruler guide without the Ctrl or Command keys and release the guide over the pasteboard to have a guide appear across all pages in a spread as well as on the pasteboard.

In this lesson, footers will be placed below the lower margin of the page where there are no column guides. To position the footers accurately, you will add a horizontal guide and two vertical guides.

1 Double-click on the A-Master master page spread in the Pages panel, if it is not already selected. If the A-Master spread is not visible in the top section of the Pages panel, drag the scroll slider or the pane divider to view additional master pages.

2 Without clicking in your document, move the cursor around the document window and watch the horizontal and vertical rulers as the cursor moves. Notice how the hairline indicators in the rulers correspond to the cursor's position. Also notice that the dimmed X and Y values in the Control panel indicate the position of the cursor.

3   Press Ctrl (Windows) or Command (Mac OS) and position your cursor in the horizontal ruler. Drag a ruler guide down to 62 picas. View the Y value in the Control or Transform panel to see the current position. Don't worry about placing the guide exactly at 62 picas—you'll do that in the next step.

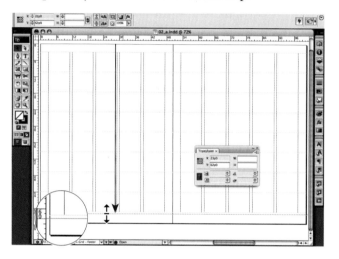

4   To position the guide at exactly 62 picas, choose the Selection tool (▸) and select the guide. When selected, the guide changes color, and, in the Control or Transform panel, the Y value is no longer dimmed. Insert your cursor into the Y text field and type **62p** to replace the current value. Then press Return or Enter.

5   Drag a ruler guide from the vertical ruler to the 12p0.6 position. Watch the X value in the Control panel as you drag. The guide snaps to the column guide at that location.

6   Drag another guide from the vertical ruler to the 88p5.4 position.

7 Choose File > Save.

Creating a text frame on the master page

Any text or graphic that you place on the master page will appear on pages where the master is applied. To create a footer, you'll add a publication title ("Summer Vacations") and a page-number marker to the bottom of both master pages.

1 Make sure that you can see the bottom of the left master page. If necessary, zoom in and use the scroll bars or Hand tool (✋).

2 Select the Type tool (T) in the Tools panel. On the left master page, drag to create a text frame below the second column where the guides intersect, as shown. Don't worry about drawing the frame in exactly the right location—you'll snap it into place later.

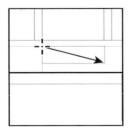

Note: When drawing a frame with the Type tool, the frame starts where the horizontal baseline intersects the I beam in the cursor—not the upper corner of cursor.

3   With the text insertion point blinking in the new text frame, choose Type > Insert Special Character > Markers > Current Page Number.

The letter A, which represents the A-Grid-Footer master, appears in your text frame. This character reflects the current page number in your document pages, such as "2" on page 2.

4   To add an em space after the page number, right-click (Windows) or Ctrl+click (Mac OS) with your cursor blinking in the text frame to display a context menu, and then choose Insert White Space > Em Space. Or you can also choose this same command under the Type menu.

5   Type **Summer Vacations** after the em space.

Next, you'll change the font and size of the text in the frame.

6   In the Tools panel, choose the Selection tool (▶) and click on the text frame containing the footer.

7   Choose Type > Character to view the Character panel.

8   In the Character panel, select Adobe Garamond Pro from the font family menu.

9   Select 12 pt from the font size menu.

Note: You can edit the attributes of all text in a frame by selecting the frame with the Selection tool. To change the attributes of a portion of text, select the Type tool.

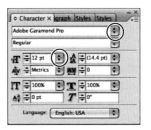

Note: It's easy to confuse the Font Size menu (▯T) with the Leading menu (▯). Make sure that you change the font size, not the leading.

When no items are selected, changes made in the Character panel or other panels become your default settings. To avoid modifying your defaults, be certain an object is selected before making changes in a panel.

10 In the Tools panel, choose the Selection tool. If necessary, drag the footer frame so that it snaps to the horizontal and vertical guides, as shown.

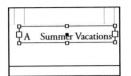

11 Check coordinates by clicking on the upper left corner of the Reference Point indicator (▦), in the upper left of the Control panel. The Control panel should display an X value of 12p06 and a Y value of 62p.

12 Click a blank area of your document window or choose Edit > Deselect All to deselect the text frame.

Next you'll duplicate the footer on the left master page.

13 Using the Selection tool (➤), select the footer frame on the left page. Hold down the Alt key (Windows) or Option key (Mac OS), and drag the text frame to the right master page so that it snaps to the guides, mirroring the right master page as shown.

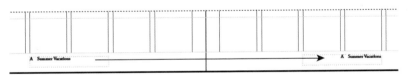

14 Make sure you can see the bottom of the right master page. If necessary, increase the magnification and scroll as needed to view the text on the bottom of the right master page.

15 Select the Type tool (T), and then click anywhere inside the text frame on the right master page, creating an insertion point.

16   Click the Paragraph Formatting Controls button (¶) in the Control panel, and then click Align Right.

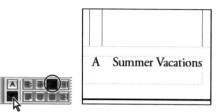

Click on the Paragraph Formatting Controls button in the upper left of the Control panel to see alignment options.

The text is now right-aligned within the footer frame on the right master page. Now modify the right master page, placing the page number on the right side of the words "Summer Vacations."

17   Delete the em space and page number at the beginning of the footer.

18   Click to place the insertion point at the end of the word "Summer Vacations," and then choose Type > Insert Special Character > Markers > Current Page Number.

19   Place the insertion point between "Summer Vacations" and the page number; right-click (Windows) or Ctrl+click (Mac OS), and then choose Insert White Space > Em Space.

A   Summer Vacations   Summer Vacations   A

Left footer and right footer.

20   Choose Edit > Deselect All and then choose File > Save.

Renaming the master page

When documents contain several master pages, you may want to rename each master page with a more descriptive name. You will rename this first master page "Grid - Footer."

1   Select Window > Pages if the Pages panel is not showing. Confirm that the A-Master page is still selected. Click the Panel Menu button (▾≡) in the upper corner of the Pages panel, and choose Master Options for "A-Master."

2   For Name, type **Grid - Footer,** and then click OK.

In addition to changing the name of master pages, you can also use the Master Options dialog box to change other properties of existing master pages.

Creating additional master pages

You can create multiple master pages within a document. You can build them independently, or base one master page on another master page. By basing master pages on other masters, any change to the parent master will appear on the child masters.

For instance, the Grid - Footer master page is useful for most of the pages in the lesson document and can be used as the basis for another set of master pages to provide placeholders for consistent placement of text and graphics.

To accommodate these different designs, you will create a separate set of master pages that contains placeholder frames for text and graphics. The Placeholder master will be based on the Grid - Footer master.

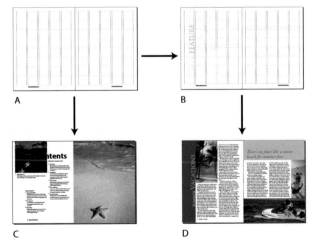

A. *A-Grid-Footer master.* **B.** *B-Placeholder master.*
C. *Document pages based on A-Grid-Footer.* **D.** *Document pages based on B-Placeholder.*

Creating a placeholder master

Next, you'll create a second master page for placeholders for the text and graphics that will appear in your articles. By creating placeholders on the master pages, you can ensure a consistent layout among articles, and you won't need to create text frames for each page in your document.

1   In the Pages panel, choose New Master from the Pages panel menu.

2   For Name, type **Placeholder**.

3   For Based on Master, choose A-Grid-Footer, and then click OK.

Notice that the B-Placeholder icons display the letter A in each page in the Pages panel. This letter indicates that the A-Grid-Footer master serves as the foundation for the B-Placeholder master. If you were to change the A-Grid-Footer master, the changes would also be reflected in the B-Placeholder master. You may also notice that you cannot easily select objects, such as the footers, from other master pages. You'll learn about selecting and overriding master page objects later in this lesson.

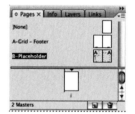

Adding a title placeholder frame

The first placeholder will contain the title of the article in a rotated text box.

1   To center the left page in the document window, double-click the left page icon of the B-Placeholder master in the Pages panel.

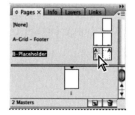

2 Select the Type tool (T). Position your cursor to the left of the edge of the page, in the pasteboard area. Click and drag to create a text frame that is slightly wider than the page, and approximately as tall as one of the grid blocks. You'll position and resize this text frame later.

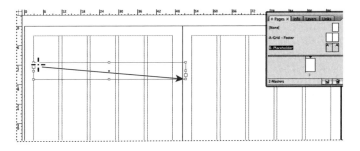

3 With the text insertion point inside of the new text frame, type **Season Feature**.

4 Triple-click the text you typed in the previous step to select all the characters in the frame.

5 Click the Character Formatting Controls button (A) in the Control panel to view the Character formatting options. Select the font family menu and choose Trajan Pro.

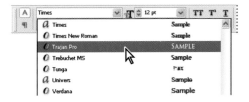

The Trajan font family has only capital letters, so now the text you typed appears in all capitals.

6 Double-click to select the word "SEASON." Using the font size menu in the Control panel, select 36 pt. Next select the words "FEATURE" and select 60 pt for the type size.

7 In the Control panel, select the Paragraph Formatting Controls button (¶) and click the Align Center option.

8   Select the Selection tool (⬉); the text frame is selected. Click and drag the lower center handle of the text frame until the frame is just large enough to contain the text. If the text disappears, drag the handle down again to make it larger. When you finish, choose View > Fit Spread in Window to zoom out.

9   In the Control panel, select the upper left point of the Reference Point indicator (⊞). Choose the Rotation Angle menu (∴) on the right of the Control panel and select 90 degrees.

10 Drag the rotated text frame down so that it snaps to the top of the right column guide in the far left column. Then drag the center handle on the bottom of the frame to stretch the frame to the lower margin of the page.

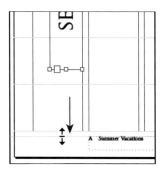

11 Click a blank area of the page or pasteboard to deselect, and then save the document.

Adding placeholder frames for graphics

You have now created the placeholder text frame for the title of your article. Next, you'll add two graphics frames to the master pages. Similar to text frames, these frames act as placeholders for the document pages, helping you to maintain a consistent design.

Note: Though you are creating placeholder frames for text and graphics in this exercise, it is not necessary to build placeholder frames on every document you create. For some smaller documents, you may not need to create master pages and placeholder frames.

The Rectangle tool (□) and the Rectangle Frame tool (⊠) are more or less interchangeable. However, the Rectangle Frame tool—which includes a non-printing X—is commonly used for creating placeholders for graphics.

Creating a guide before you draw makes it easy to position the graphics frames.

1 Choose View > Grids & Guides and confirm there is a check mark next to the Snap to Guides option.

2 Drag a ruler guide from the horizontal ruler to the 34 picas position on the left master page. Remember that you can use the Control panel to identify the location of the guide as you position it.

To make sure that the guide is at the 34-pica location, select the Selection tool (↖) in the Tools panel and click the guide to select it (the guide changes color). Then type **34p** in the Y text field of the Control panel, and press Enter or Return.

3 Select the Rectangle Frame tool (⊠) in the Tools panel.

4 Position the cursor in the upper left corner of the left page, at the position X 11p0 and Y 0p0. Click and drag to create a frame, so that the frame covers the area from the top edge of the page down to the horizontal guide you set at the 34 pica mark and over to the guide at the 29p1.8 position.

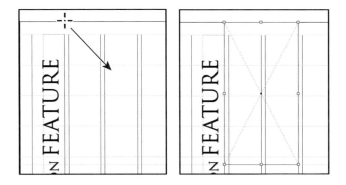

5   Now add a placeholder frame to right hand master page. Follow steps 2 through 4 above, except now drag a guide on right master page down to the 46 pica location.

6   Draw a rectangle that begins at the horizontal guide at the 46 pica location and extends across the width of the page and down to the bottom margin.

7   Choose File > Save.

Wrapping text around a graphic

You can wrap text around the frame of a placeholder object on the master page and it will keep text away from this graphic on any page where the master page is applied.

1   Using the Selection tool (➤), select the placeholder graphics frame that you created on the left hand master page.

2   Choose Window > Text Wrap to open the Text Wrap panel, and select the second wrap option so that the text wraps around the frame.

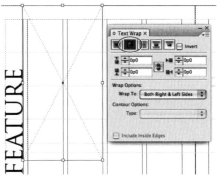

Text wrap applied to graphic frame.

3 Make sure that the constrain icon ( ) is deselected and then adjust the wrap offset at the bottom of the frame by entering 1p0 in the bottom offset box.

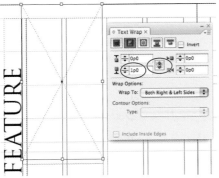

Text wrap offset applied to graphic frame.

4 Close the Text Wrap panel, and choose File > Save.

Drawing colored shapes

You'll now add a background for the title bar and another background across the top of the right master. These elements will then appear on any pages where the B-Placeholder master has been applied. This time, you'll use the Rectangle tool instead of the Rectangle Frame tool because you'll fill the frames with a color swatch.

1 Choose Edit > Deselect All.

2 In the Pages panel, double-click the right page of the B-Placeholder master page or scroll horizontally so that the right page is centered in the document window.

3 In the Tools panel, choose the Selection tool (▶) and drag from the horizontal ruler to the 16 pica mark to create a new guide. Then click a blank area to deselect the guide.

💡 *Hold down the Shift key while creating ruler guides to have them positioned at the increments shown on the ruler.*

When you are selecting and dragging frames, it's common to accidentally move guides. To prevent guides from accidentally moving, you'll lock the guides.

4   Choose View > Grids & Guides > Lock Guides.

The Lock Guides command is also available from the context menu when right-clicking (Windows) or Ctrl+clicking (Mac OS) on a blank area of the page or pasteboard.

5   Choose Window > Swatches to open the Swatches panel.

6   Select the Rectangle Frame tool (⊠) in the Tools panel. Position your cursor approximately at 50pX and 0pY location on the page. Click and drag, drawing a frame from the top edge of the paper to the horizontal guide at 16 picas, and stretching from one edge of the page to the other.

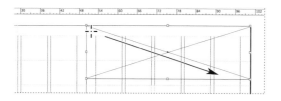

7   In the upper left corner of the panel, click the Stroke box (⧉) to activate it, and then click None in the list of Swatches. This eliminates the outline around the edge of the shape you are going to draw. Notice that the Stroke box is also in front of the Fill box in the Tools panel.

8   In the same area of the Swatches panel, click the Fill box (◼) to make it active. Then click [Paper] in the list of swatches, to set Paper as a placeholder color for the objects you draw next.

9   In the Pages panel, double-click the left page icon for B-Placeholder, to center the left master page in the document window.

10   Still using the Rectangle Frame tool (⊠), draw a frame covering the left margin of the page along with the first column and extending from the top to the bottom of the page. Repeat steps 7-8 above to fill the frame with Paper. Notice that the new frame blocks the placeholder text from view.

11   With the new rectangle frame still selected, choose Object > Arrange > Send to Back.

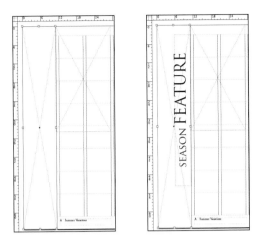

12 Choose File > Save to save your file.

Creating text frames with columns

You have added placeholders for the title, graphic, and two background blocks for the B-Placeholder master pages. To finish the B-Placeholder master, you'll create the text frames for the story text.

1 Select the Type tool (T), and on the left master page, position your cursor approximately at the X position of 12p and Y position of 3p. Click and drag down and to the right, creating a text frame. As you create the frame, snap it to the guides so that it is eight rows tall and four columns wide.

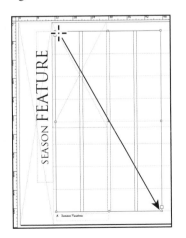

2 Choose View > Fit Spread in Window. Close or hide any panels, as necessary, to view the spread.

3 On the right master page, position your cursor at approximately the X position of 53p3 and Y position of 17p7, then click and drag to create a text frame six rows tall and four columns wide, snapping to the guides as shown.

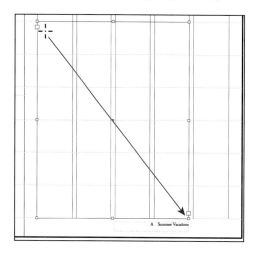

Next, you'll make sure that each of the main-story text frames has two columns.

4 Choose the Selection tool (➤). Shift+click to select both text frames.

5 Choose the Type tool (T) and then, in the Control panel, click the up arrow in the Number of Columns field to increase the number of columns to 2.

Each of the main-story text frames will include two columns of text. To make the text flow from one text frame to the next, you will thread the frames.

6 Choose the Selection tool (➤) and then click the out port in the lower right corner of the text frame on the left master page. Position the cursor over the text frame on the right master page so that it changes from a loaded text icon ( ) to a link icon ( ), and then click. The text frames are now linked.

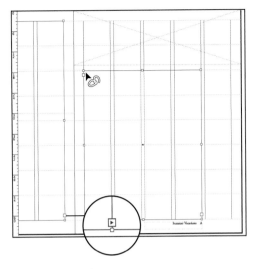

7 Save the document.

Note: Choose View > Show Text Threads to see visual representatives of threaded frames. You can thread text frames whether or not they contain text.

Applying the masters to document pages

Now that you have created all the master pages, it's time to apply them to the pages in your layout. By default, all the document pages are formatted with the A-Grid-Footer master. You will apply the B-Placeholder master to the appropriate pages. Apply master pages by dragging the master page icons onto the document-page icons or by using a panel-menu option. In large documents, you may find it easier to display the page icons horizontally in the Pages panel.

1 In the Pages panel, click the panel menu and choose Panel Options.

Note: Panel menus may be located in either the upper left or upper right corner of a panel, depending upon whether it is docked.

2 In the Pages section, deselect the Show Vertically option, and choose "Small" from the Icon Size menu. Then click OK.

3 Position your cursor over the horizontal bar, located beneath the master pages. Click and drag down so that you can see all the master pages. Then position the cursor in the lower right corner of the Pages panel, click and drag the lower right corner of the Pages panel down as far as you can, until you can see all the spreads.

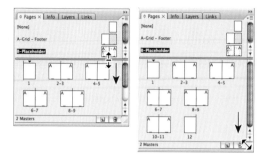

Now that you can see all the pages in the document, you'll apply the B-Placeholder master to pages in the document that will contain articles.

4 Click the B-Placeholder name, drag the name down and position it immediately to the left of the number 6 or immediately to the right of the number 7, below the page icons. Do not position the cursor over the page icons. When a box appears around both page icons representing the spread, release the mouse button.

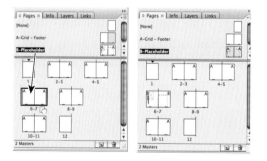

The B-Placeholder master pages are applied to pages 6 and 7, as indicated by the letter B in the page icons. Instead of dragging the B-Placeholder master to the remaining spreads, you'll use a different method to apply master pages.

5 In the Pages panel menu, located in the upper corner of the pages panel, choose Apply Master to Pages. For Apply Master, choose B-Placeholder. For To Pages, type **8-11**. Click OK.

Notice that pages 6-11 in the Pages panel are now formatted with the B-Placeholder master. Page 12 requires individual formatting without page numbering, so no master page formatting is required for this page.

6   In the Pages panel, click and drag the None master page down onto the page 12 icon. Release the cursor when the icon is highlighted.

Make sure that the A-Grid-Footer master is assigned to page 1-5 and the B-Placeholder master is assigned to pages 6-11; page 12 should have no master page assigned to it.

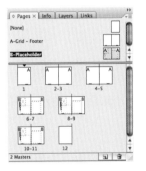

7   Choose File > Save.

Adding sections to change page numbering

The magazine you're working on requires introductory material that is numbered with lowercase Roman numerals (i, ii, iii, and so on). You can use different kinds of page numbering by adding a section. You'll start a new section on page 2 to create Roman-numeral page numbering, and then you'll start another section on page 6 to revert to Arabic numerals and restart numbering sequence.

1   In the Pages panel, double-click the page 2 icon to select it within the panel and view page 2 in the document window.

2   In the Pages panel menu, choose Numbering & Section Options. In the New Section dialog box, make sure that Start Section and Automatic Page Numbering are selected, or select them now.

3   For Page Numbering Style, choose i, ii, iii, iv from the menu. Click OK.

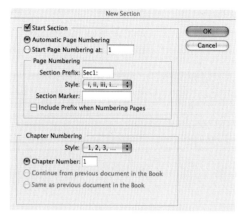

4   Examine the page icons in the Pages panel. Starting with page 2, the numbers now appear as Roman numerals in the footers of the pages.

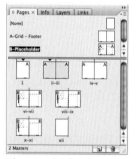

*The triangle above page ii
indicates the start of a section.*

Now you'll specify that the document uses Arabic numbers for the pages from 6 through the end of the document.

5   Click page 6 (vi) in the Pages panel to select it.

Note: Single-clicking a page targets the page for editing purposes. If you want to navigate to a page, double-click the page in the Pages panel.

6 Click the Pages panel menu in the upper corner of the Pages panel and choose Numbering & Section Options.

7 In the New Section dialog box, make sure that the Start Section is selected or select it now.

8 Select Start Page Numbering at, press Tab and type **2** to start the section numbering with page 2.

9 For Style, select 1, 2, 3, 4 and then click OK.

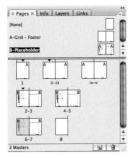

Now your pages are properly renumbered. Notice that a black triangle appears above pages 1, ii, and 2 in the Pages panel. These triangles indicate the start of a new section.

10 Choose File > Save.

Adding new pages

You can also add new pages to your existing document. We are going to add two additional pages.

1 In the Pages panel menu, choose Insert Pages.

2 Enter **2** for the number of pages, choose At End of Document from the menu and then select B-Placeholder for the Master page that will be applied to the new pages.

3 Click OK. The document now has two additional pages.

Arranging and deleting pages

With the pages panel, you can also arrange the sequence of pages, and delete extra pages.

1   In the Pages panel, double-click the page 8 icon, then click and drag it to the right of the page 10 icon. When you see a black bar to the right of page 10, let go. Page 8 is moved to the position of page 10, and page 9 and 10 are moved to the positions of 8 and 9 respectively.

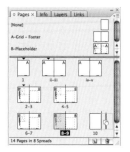

2   Double-click the hyphen beneath the spread containing the icons for pages 8 and 9 to select both pages.

3   Click the Trash button at the bottom of the panel. Pages 8 and 9 are deleted from the document.

Placing text and graphics on the document pages

Now that the framework of the 12-page publication is in place, you're ready to format the individual articles. To see how the changes you made to the master pages affect document pages, you'll add text and graphics to the spread on pages 2 and 3.

1   In the Pages panel, double-click the page 2 icon (not page ii) to center the page in the document window.

Notice that because the B-Placeholder master is assigned to page 2, the page includes the grid, the footers, and the placeholder frames.

To import text and graphics from other applications, such as images from Adobe Photoshop or text from Microsoft Word, you'll use the Place command.

2   Choose File > Place. Double-click on the 02_d.psd file in the Lesson_02 folder.

3 The cursor takes the shape of a loaded graphics icon ( ) and shows a preview of the image. Position the loaded graphics icon over the graphics-frame placeholder on page 2 so that the cursor appears in parentheses ( ), and click. You may need to click on the top of the placeholder to see the cursor in parentheses.

Parentheses appear when InDesign recognizes a pre-existing frame beneath the cursor when importing text or graphics into your layout. InDesign uses the existing frame rather than creating a new text or graphic frame.

4 To position the image correctly, choose Object > Fitting > Center Content. Then click on an empty portion of the page to deselect all objects or choose Edit > Deselect All.

5 Repeat steps 2 through 4 above, except this time place the image 02_e.psd in the bottom placeholder frame on page 3.

6 To be certain sure that nothing is selected, choose Edit > Deselect All. Then choose File > Place. Open the Lesson_02 folder in your InDesignCIB folder, and double-click 02_c.doc, a text file created using Microsoft Word.

The cursor changes to a loaded text icon ( ), with a preview of the first lines of text you will be placing.

With a loaded text icon, you can drag to create a text frame, or click inside an existing text frame. When you hold the loaded text icon over an existing text frame, the icon appears in parentheses.

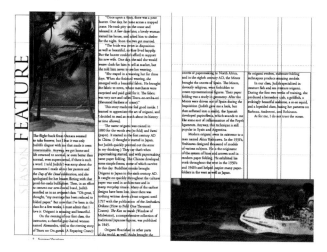

You can click to insert the text into the individual frame, or you can Shift+click to autoflow the text into the threaded frames. You'll use several of these methods to better understand how to import and flow text.

7 As you hold down the Shift key, the loaded text icon changes to the automatic flow icon (🔛). Click anywhere inside the text frame on the bottom of page 2. Release the Shift key.

The text flowed into the text frames on pages 2 and 3, wrapping around the images according to how you set up text wrap on the master pages. The text flowed onto page 3 because of the link you created between the text frames when you set up the master page. The autoflow happened because you held down the Shift key as you placed the text. Otherwise the text would have flowed only onto page 2 and you would have had to manually flow the text onto page 3.

Note: If your text did not flow as indicated, Edit > Undo and reposition the cursor so that it is in the 2-column text frame.

8 Choose Edit > Deselect All to make sure that no frames are selected.

💡 *If a frame is selected when you place a file, the contents of the file will be added to the selected frame. You can avoid this by deselecting objects prior to importing, or by deselecting "Replace Selected Item" in the Place dialog box when importing.*

9 Choose File > Save, to save your artwork.

Overriding master page items on document pages

The placeholders you added to the master pages appear on the document pages. InDesign prevents you from accidentally moving or deleting these objects by requiring you to use special modifier keys when selecting them on your document pages. You'll now replace the word "SEASON" with "SUMMER" and "FEATURE" with "VACATION." Editing this text requires you to select the master page frame that contains the text "SEASON."

1 To make sure you're on page 2, select Sec2:2 from the Pages pop-up list in the status bar at the bottom left corner of the document window.

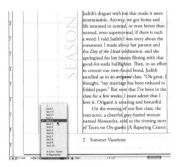

2 If necessary, adjust your view so you can see the "SEASON FEATURE" text on page 2. Choose the Selection tool (➤) and try to select this text frame by clicking on it.

You cannot select master page items on the document pages simply by clicking. However, by holding down a modifier key on your keyboard, you can then select a master page object such as this text frame.

3 Holding down Shift+Ctrl (Windows) or Shift+Command (Mac OS), click the title placeholder frame on the left side of page 2 to select it.

4　Using the Type tool (T), double-click the word "SEASON" to select it, and then type **SUMMER**. Then select the "FEATURE," and type **VACATION**. The text is now replaced on the document page.

5　Using the Type tool, double-click on the word "VACATION" to select the text.

6　In the Tools panel, select the Zoom tool (🔍) and then drag a marquee around the image of the man with the life vest to magnify the image, so that the area you drag fills the window.

7　In the Tools panel, make sure that the Text Fill box (🄣) is showing, and then select the Eyedropper tool (🖊). Move the tip of the Eyedropper tool over the yellow area in the life vest and click to select it. The color you click becomes the fill color that is applied to the text you selected.

Dragging a zoom marquee.　*Selecting color with the Eyedropper tool.*

8　Choose View > Fit Spread in Window. Notice that even though you've used other tools, the text is still selected. Choose Edit > Deselect All to see the text now filled with the yellow color you selected.

9　Choose the Selection tool (▶) and press Shift+Ctrl (Windows) or Shift+Command (Mac OS) and click on the wide rectangle you created on page three. Fill it with the same yellow color.

Note: While you created these frames on a master page, they appear on the document page you are currently formatting, because the master page was applied to this document page.

10　Repeat steps 6 and 7, but this time select a darker blue color from the Palm tree image to fill the tall rectangle on page 2.

11　Choose View > Fit Spread in Window, and choose Object > Arrange > Send to Back so that the rectangle does not hide the title text, then choose Edit > Deselect All.

12　Choose File > Save to save your work.

Viewing the completed spread

Now you'll hide guides and frames to see what the completed spread looks like.

1 Choose View > Fit Spread in Window and hide any panels, if necessary.

2 In the Tools panel, click the Preview Mode button (▣) to hide all guides, grids, frame edges, and the pasteboard.

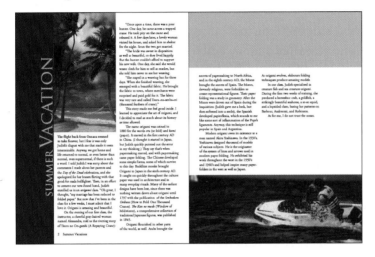

You have formatted enough of the 12-page document to see how adding objects to the master pages helps you maintain a consistent design throughout your document.

3 Choose File > Save.

Congratulations. You have finished the lesson.

Exploring on your own

A good way to reinforce the skills you've learned in this lesson is to experiment with them. Try some of the following exercises that give you more practice with InDesign techniques.

1   Place another photograph in the third column of text on page 3. Use the 02_f.psd image that is inside the Lesson_02 folder.

2   Add a pull-quote: Using the Type tool (T), drag a box over the yellow rectangle on page 3. Type "There's no place like a sunny beach for summer fun…" Triple-click the text you pasted, and use the Character panel to format it using the font, size, style, and color of your choice.

3   Try rotating the "title" text block using different corners or edges of the Reference Point indicator (⊞) in the Control or Transform panel, and notice the difference in the results.

4   Create a new pair of master pages for a spread that you could use for the continuation of this story. Name the new master page **C-Next** and select A-Grid-Footer for the Based On option. Then create placeholder frames for the text and graphics, giving the spread a different arrangement from B-Placeholder master pages. When you finish, apply the C-Next master pages to pages 4-5 of your document.

Review

▶ **Review questions**

1　What are the advantages of adding objects to master pages?

2　How do you change the page-numbering scheme?

3　How do you select a master page item on a document page?

▶ **Review answers**

1　By adding objects such as guides, footers, and placeholder frames to master pages, you can maintain a consistent layout on the pages to which the master is applied.

2　In the Pages panel, select the page icon where you want new page numbering to begin. Then choose Section Options from the Pages panel menu and specify the new page-numbering scheme.

3　Hold down Shift+Ctrl (Windows) or Shift+Command (Mac OS), and then click the object to select it. You can then edit, delete, or otherwise manipulate the object.

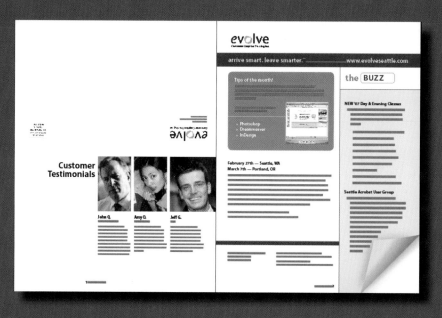

PDF is the perfect format for delivery of multimedia presentations. Whether you use PDF to deliver a presentation, or you distribute a PDF presentation across your entire organization, it is the complete solution for delivering interactive content, including movies and sounds.

3 | Working with Frames

In this introduction to working with frames, you'll learn how to do the following:

- Use the Selection and Direct Selection tools to modify frames.
- Resize and reshape text and graphics frames.
- Distinguish between bounding boxes and their frames.
- Crop a graphic.
- Scale an image contained in a graphics frame.
- Move a graphic within its frame.
- Convert a graphics frame to a text frame
- Convert shapes from one type to another.
- Wrap text around an object.
- Create and rotate a polygon frame.
- Align graphic objects.
- Work with groups.

Getting started

In this lesson, you'll work on a two-page spread for a magazine about origami, the Japanese art of paper folding. Before you begin, you'll need to restore the default preferences for Adobe InDesign CS3 to ensure that the tools and panels function exactly as described in this lesson. Then you'll open the finished document for this lesson to see what you'll be creating.

1   Delete or deactivate (by renaming) the InDesign Defaults file and the InDesign SavedData file, as described in "Restoring default preferences" on page 2.

2   Start Adobe InDesign CS3. To begin working, you'll open an InDesign document that is already partially completed.

3   Choose File > Open, and open the 03_a.indd file in the Lesson_03 folder, located inside the Lessons folder within the InDesignCIB folder on your hard disk. If you receive Profile or Policy Mismatch warnings for the RGB and CMYK color profiles, click OK. This will convert to your color settings. Read more about color in Lesson 6, "Working with Color."

Note: If you have not already copied the resource files for this lesson onto your hard disk from the Lesson_03 folder from the Adobe InDesign CS3 Classroom in a Book CD, do so now. See "Copying the Classroom in a Book files" on page 4.

4   Choose File > Save As, rename the file **03_frames.indd**, and save it in the Lesson_03 folder.

5   To see what the finished document will look like, open the 03_b.indd file in the same folder. You can leave this document open to act as a guide as you work. When you're ready to resume working on the lesson document, choose Window > 03_frames.indd.

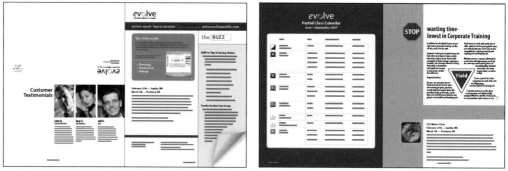

Pages 1 and 2   *Pages 3 and 4*

Note: As you work through the lesson, feel free to move panels around or change the magnification to a level that works best for you.

Working with Layers

By default, a new document contains just one layer (named Layer 1). You can rename the layer and add more layers at any time as you create your document. Placing objects on different layers lets you organize them for easy selection and editing. Using the Layers panel, you can select, display, edit, and print different layers individually, in groups, or all together.

About layers

Each document includes at least one named layer. By using multiple layers, you can create and edit specific areas or kinds of content in your document without affecting other areas or kinds of content. For example, if your document prints slowly because it contains many large graphics, you can use one layer for just the text in your document; then, when it's time to proofread the text, you can hide all other layers and quickly print the text layer only. You can also use layers to display alternate design ideas for the same layout, or versions of advertisements for different regions.

Think of layers as transparent sheets stacked on top of each other. If a layer doesn't have objects on it, you can see through it to any objects on layers behind it.

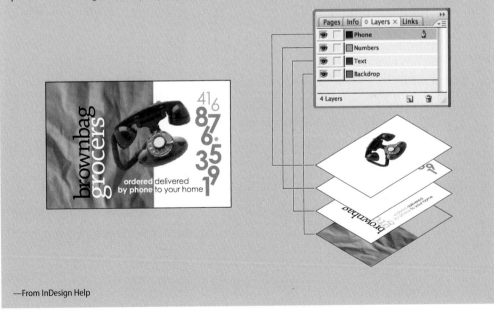

—From InDesign Help

The 03_frames.indd document has two layers. You'll experiment with these layers to learn how the order of the layers and the placement of objects on layers can greatly affect the design of your document.

1   Click the Layers panel tab to activate the panel, or choose Window > Layers.

2   In the Layers panel, click the Text layer. Notice that a pen icon (✎) appears to the right of the layer name. This icon indicates that this layer is the target layer, and anything you import or create will be placed on this layer. The highlight indicates that the layer is selected.

3   Click the eye icon (👁) to the far left of the Graphics layer name. This icon lets you turn the visibility of a layer on or off so that you can hide or display any layer at any time. When you turn the visibility of a layer off, the panel displays a gray box where the eye icon used to be. Click in the gray box again to show the layer contents.

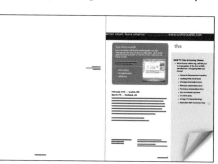

Click to hide layer contents   *The spread with hidden content.*

4   Using the Selection tool (▶), click the screen shot image in the orange box of the Tips of the month! area in the document window.

Notice in the Layers panel that the Text layer is selected and a dot appears to the right of the layer name. This indicates that the selected object belongs to this layer. You can move objects from one layer to another by dragging this dot between the layers in the panel.

5   In the Layers panel, drag the dot from the Text layer to the Graphics layer. The image now belongs to the Graphics layer and appears in the stacking order in the document accordingly.

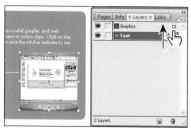
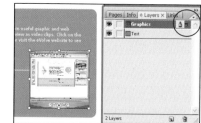

Select the image and drag its icon.   *The result.*

6 Click the layer lock box (🔒) to the left of the Graphics layer to lock the layer.

Click to lock Graphics layer.

7 Using the Selection tool (▶), click to select the evolve logo at the top of the right page. Notice that you cannot select the graphic. That's because it is on the Graphics layer and the Graphics layer is locked.

Next you will make a new layer and move existing content to it.

8 In the Layers panel, click on the Create new layer button at the bottom of the Layers panel to create a new blank layer.

Click the Create new layer button to make a new layer.

9 Double-click on the name of the new layer (it will most likely be named Layer 3) to open the Layer Options dialog box. Change the name to **Background** and click OK.

> 💡 *When you want to simultaneously create a new layer and name it at the same time, hold down the Alt (Windows) or Option (Mac) key and click on the Create new layer button in the Layers panel. This will open the Layer Options dialog box automatically.*

10 In the Layers panel, click and drag the Background layer to the bottom of the layer stack. A line will appear when you move the cursor below the Text layer, indicating that the layer will be moved to the bottom.

The Background layer has no content yet, but will come into play later in the lesson.

Click and drag to reorder the layers.

11 Choose File > Save to save the file.

Creating and editing text frames

In most cases, text must be placed inside of a frame. The size and location of a frame determine how the text appears on a page. Text frames can be created with the Type tool and edited using a variety of tools.

Creating and resizing text frames

Now you'll create your own text frame and resize another frame, using the Selection tool.

1 In the Layers panel, click on the Text layer to select it. This way any content created will be placed on the Text layer.

2 Choose the Type tool (**T**) from the Tools panel. Open the Pages panel by clicking on its tab on the right side of the workspace. Double-click on page 1 to view page 1. Position the cursor where the guide at approximately 34p and the left edge of the first column meet. Drag to create a frame that snaps to the right edge of the second column and has a height of 7p11.

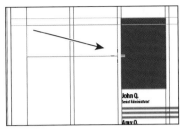

Click and drag to create the text frame.

3   In the new text frame type in **Customer,** press Shift+Enter or Shift+Return to create a soft break, then type in **Testimonials.** Click four times to select the text. Click the Paragraph Style panel or choose Type > Paragraph Styles. Alt (Windows) or Option (Mac) click on the style named testimonials. Read more about Styles in Lesson 7, "Working with Styles."

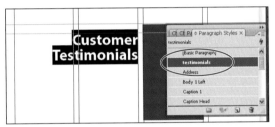

Select the text, then apply the paragraph style.

4   Choose the Selection tool and double-click on the bottom, center handle on the selected text frame to fit the frame to the text vertically.

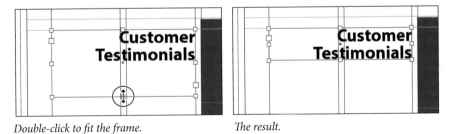

Double-click to fit the frame.   *The result.*

 Double-clicking on handles around the bounding box will result in different fitting changes. If you double-click the center right handle, for instance, the height is preserved while the width narrows to fill the frame.

5   On the right page (page 2), use the Selection tool (➤) to select the text frame below "The Buzz" text. It contains the text, "New'07...".

6   Drag the center bottom handle downward to resize the height of the frame until it snaps to the bottom margin guide. When the cursor approaches the margin guide the arrows change in appearance telling you that the frame is about to snap to the guide. When you release the mouse, text reflows throughout the entire frame.

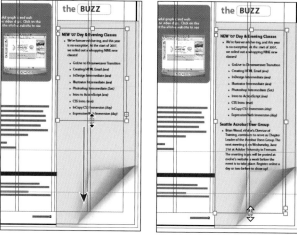

Click and drag center point   Result.
of frame to resize.

💡 *When you want to simultaneously resize a text frame and the text characters inside it, use the Scale tool (⊞) or hold down the Control (Windows) or Command (Mac) as you drag a text frame handle.*

Reshaping a text frame

So far, you've dragged a handle to resize a text frame, using the Selection tool. Now, you'll use an anchor point to reshape the frame, using the Direct Selection tool.

1   If the text frame on the right page is not still selected, use the Selection tool (➤) to select it now.

2   In the Tools panel, click the Direct Selection tool (➤). Four very small anchor points now appear at the corners of the selected text frame. The anchor points are hollow, indicating that none of them are selected.

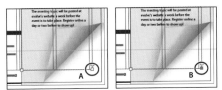

A. *Unselected anchor point.*
B. *Selected anchor point.*

3   Select the anchor point in the lower right corner of the text frame and drag it upward until it snaps to the horizontal guide above it. (After you start dragging, you can hold down the Shift key to restrict any horizontal movement.)

Make sure you drag only the anchor point—if you drag just below the anchor point, you'll move the text frame. You may also notice a red plus appear which means that the text does not fit.

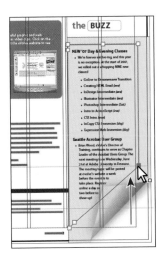

4   Press V on your keyboard to switch to the Selection tool. You may see a red "+" indicating overset text which does not fit in the frame.

💡 *To see both the bounding box and the path, choose View > Show Frame Edges. To turn frame edges off again, choose View > Hide Frame Edges.*

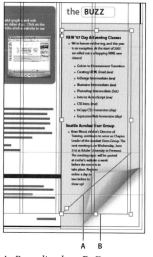

A B

*A. Bounding box. **B.** Frame.*

5   Deselect all objects and then choose File > Save.

💡 *Pressing the A and V keys to toggle between the Selection and Direct Selection tools are just two of many keyboard shortcuts available in InDesign. For more shortcuts, refer to "Keyboard shortcuts" in InDesign Help.*

Creating multiple columns

Now you'll take an existing text frame and convert it to a multiple column text frame.

1   If the text frame on page 1, containing the text John Q, is not selected, use the Selection tool (↖) to select it now.

2   Double-click on the text frame to select the Type tool and place the cursor in the frame. Choose Object > Text Frame Options to open the Text Frame Options dialog box.

3   In the Text Frame Options dialog box, change the Number of columns to 3 and the Gutter to 0p11. The gutter controls the distance between the columns. Click OK.

Insert Type cursor and choose Object > Text Frame Options to edit the text frame.

4   To finish up the 3 columns of text, with the Type tool still selected, place the cursor in front of the name "Amy O." and choose Type > Insert Break Character > Column Break. This will force Amy O. to the top of the second column. Repeat this step after placing the cursor before "Jeff G."

5   Choose Type > Show Hidden Characters to see the break characters.

Adjusting text inset within a frame

Your next task is to finish up the blue title bar on the cover page by fitting the text nicely into the frame. By adjusting the inset between the frame and the text, you make it easier to read.

1   Choose the Selection tool (↖) in the Tools panel, and then select the blue bar at the top of page 2 with the text "arrive smart. leave smarter."

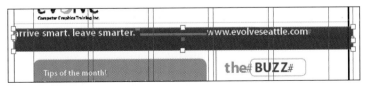

Blue bar selected.

2 Choose Object > Text Frame Options to open the Text Frame Options dialog box. If necessary, drag the dialog box aside so that you can still see the bar as you set options.

3 In the dialog box, make sure that the Preview option is selected. Then, under Inset Spacing, click the link (🔳) to change the left and right settings independently. Change the Left value to 3p0 and the Right value to 3p9. Click OK to close the dialog box.

Note: The Link icon is there to help you change all of the inset values at the same time. Sometimes you need to turn it off, though.

Click the link to change the inset spacing independently. Change the Left and Right values, then click OK.

Vertically aligning text within a frame

Your next task is to finish up the blue bar by aligning the text vertically within the frame. This will allow you to center the text vertically.

1 Click to select the Selection tool (🡡) in the Tools panel, and then select the blue bar again on the right side page.

2 Choose Object > Text Frame Options to open the Text Frame Options dialog box. Under Vertical Justification, choose Center from the Align pop-up menu. Click OK to close the dialog box.

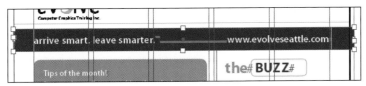

Inset Spacing and Vertical Justification applied.

Note: *Sometimes choosing center for vertical justification may not be exactly centered in the text frame, especially for smaller text frames. This is a justification that is mathematically centered. Inset Spacing or Baseline Shift settings can change the appearance and make it "look" centered.*

Choose Align Center and click OK.

Creating and editing graphics frames

In this section, you'll focus on different techniques for creating and modifying graphics frames and graphics frame's contents. To start, you'll import an image and place it in your document spread. Because you'll be working on graphics rather than text, your first step is to make sure that the graphics appear on the Art layer rather than on the Text layer. Isolating items on different layers helps your work process so that it's easier to find and edit elements of your design.

Drawing a new graphics frame

It's time to create a frame for the first graphic, using the Drawing tools in the Tools panel.

1   If the Layers panel is not visible, click the Layers panel tab to show the panel, or choose Window > Layers. In the Layers panel, click the second-column box to unlock the Graphics layer. Lock the Text layer by clicking in the second column box. Then select the Graphics layer by clicking on the name of the layer so that new elements will be assigned to this layer.

Unlock Graphics layer and lock Text layer. Then select Graphics layer.

2   To center page 1 in the document window, choose 1 from the Pages menu at the bottom of the document window.

3 In the Tools panel, choose the Rectangle Frame tool (▣). In the far right column on page 1, click and drag from where the guide about half way down the page and left edge of the fifth column meet to the right edge of the column and down to just above the Jeff G. text.

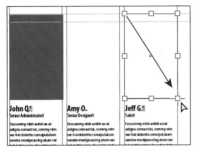

Click and drag to create a graphics frame.

4 Switch to the Selection tool and make sure that the graphics frame is still selected.

Placing graphics within an existing frame

1 With the graphics frame still selected, choose File > Place and then double-click JeffG.tif in the Lesson_03 > Links folder. The image should appear in the graphics frame.

Note: If the graphics frame wasn't selected, the cursor would change to the loaded graphics icon (🌂). You could click in the middle of the frame to place the image.

2 Choose the Selection tool (▸) and holding down the Alt (Windows) or Option (Mac) click and drag the JeffG graphic to the left and snap it into the column directly to the left.

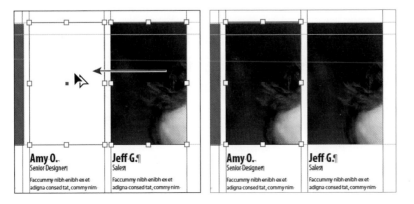

Resizing a graphics frame

The design for this page calls for the image of Jeff to extend across to the right edge of the page. Although this image is not yet the right size or shape to do that, you'll start making those adjustments now.

First, you'll stretch the frame.

1   Choose View > Fit Spread in Window so that you can see all of pages 1 and 2 in the document window. If necessary, scroll horizontally so that you can see the right edge of page 2 and hide the Layers panel by clicking on the Layers tab.

2   Using the Selection tool (➤), click the JeffG graphic. Drag the right handle until the right side of the bounding box snaps into place against the right edge of page 1.

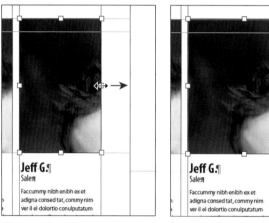

Click and drag the right side   The result.
of the frame to resize.

Notice that only the frame bounding box changes, not the image itself.

Resizing and moving an image within a frame

You have just finished resizing a graphics frame, but the content image remains unchanged. You'll now resize just the image so that it fills the designated area.

💡 *In addition to the methods we use here, you can also use the context menus to resize pictures to fit within their frame. Do this by right-clicking (Windows) or Ctrl+clicking (Mac OS) and selecting Fitting > Fit Content Proportionally.*

The content and frame for any placed graphics are separate elements. Unlike text objects, the frame and content for a graphic each has its own bounding box. Resizing the graphic contents is exactly like resizing the frame, except that you work with the bounding box for the contents using the Direct Selection tool (k).

1   Press A to switch to the Direct Selection tool (k), then position the cursor over the image of JeffG until the cursor appears as a hand icon (✋), then click to select the frame contents (the image itself). The bounding box changes to another color, indicating that the frame is no longer selected, but the contents are.

2   Select the handle in the lower right corner of the graphic bounding box, and then hold down the Shift key and drag to make the image smaller. Continue dragging until the image dimensions are just a bit larger than the frame.

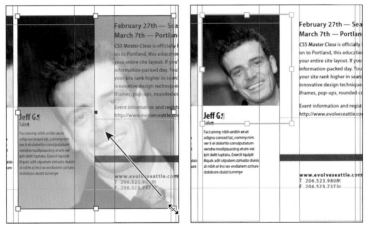

Dragging bounding box of contents, and view after dragging.

3   Move the Direct Selection tool over the JeffG image so that you see the hand icon. Click and drag the image with the hand icon, and notice how the area of the image that is visible within the frame changes as you drag. If you drag too far to the right, notice that the image no longer covers the left side of the frame area. Drag the image so that the right edge of the image aligns with the right edge of the frame.

💡 *Before you start dragging, click and hold down the mouse button until the hand icon turns into a solid arrow (▶). The arrow is white on Windows, black on Mac OS. Then, after you start dragging, you'll see a ghosted image of the hidden areas of the graphic contents, a feature called Dynamic Preview. If you don't wait for the cursor icon to change, you'll still see the bounding box of the graphic as you drag.*

4   Make sure that the image entirely fills the frame. Save your work.

Images expanded beyond 120% of their original size may not contain enough pixel information for high-resolution offset printing. Check with your printer or service provider if you are uncertain as to the resolution and scaling requirements needed for any documents you are having printed.

You can simultaneously resize both a graphic image and its frame by using the Selection tool and holding down Ctrl+Shift (Windows) or Command+Shift (Mac OS) as you drag a handle of the frame. In this case, the Shift key maintains the proportions of the bounding boxes, so that the graphic image is not distorted. Using the Shift key is optional if distorting the image doesn't matter to your design.

Replacing the contents of graphics frames

After you create the two duplicates, it's easy to replace the contents with other graphics or text. Your next task is to replace the copied JeffG image with another image. Because the frame and contents are independent, it's easy to swap out one image for another.

1   With the Selection tool, click on the JeffG image (the one over "Amy O") to select it. Choose File > Place and then double-click the AmyO.tif to place the new image directly into the selected frame, replacing the JeffG image.

2   With the frame still selected, choose Object > Fitting > Fill Frame Proportionally. InDesign resizes the graphic so that it fits into the frame.

You can also access the fitting commands from the context menus by either right-clicking (Windows) or Option+clicking (Mac OS).

3   Choose Object > Fitting > Center Content to center the AmyO image in the frame. Now you'll place a picture into the blue frame to the left of the AmyO image.

4   Choose Edit > Deselect All to deselect the frame.

5   Choose File > Place, and select the JohnQ.tif file in your Lesson_03 folder. Select Open. The cursor changes to a loaded graphics icon ( ).

Note: If the cursor appears with a line through it ( ), the current layer is selected but locked. You cannot add objects to a locked layer. Make sure that the Graphics layer in the Layers panel is both unlocked and selected. The cursor should then appear as a loaded graphics icon so that you can proceed with this step.

6   Hover over the blue frame to the left of the AmyO image and the cursor will change again to the one surrounded by parentheses ( ), indicating that if you click, the image will be placed in that frame. You will see a thumbnail of the image under the cursor. Click to place the image in the blue filled frame.

Note: If you click on a blank area of the page, the image will be placed on the page where you click. The image is placed at 100% of it's original size, typically.

Click to place in the blue frame.

7   With the JohnQ graphic still selected, choose Object > Fitting > Fill Frame Proportionally. InDesign resizes the graphic so that it fits into the frame. To center the content, choose Object > Fitting > Center Content.

Now you've placed images in several different ways in three different frames.

Changing the shape of a frame

When you resized the graphics frame using the Selection tool, the frame maintained its rectangular shape. Now you will use the Pen tool and the Direct Selection tool to reshape a frame on page 4.

1   To go to page 4 in the document window, choose 4 from the Pages menu at the bottom of the document window. Choose View > Fit Page in Window to fit the page in the window.

2   In the Layers panel (Window > Layers), click on the lock icon for the Text layer to unlock it.

3   Press A for the Direct Selection tool (↖). Then move the tip of the cursor over the right edge of the green box, and click when the cursor appears with a small diagonal line (↖⟋). This selects the path and reveals the anchor points and center point for the frame. Leave the path selected.

4   Press P to switch to the Pen tool. Carefully position the cursor over the top edge of the frame path where it intersects with the right guide of the first column of page 4. When you see the Add Anchor Point Pen tool (♠⁺), click. A new anchor point is added. The Pen tool automatically changes to the Add Anchor Point tool when it is crossed over an existing path.

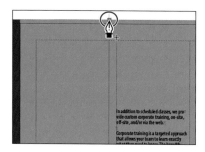

5   Move the cursor to where the guide below the text and the bleed guide intersects, and using the Pen tool, click again to add another new anchor point.

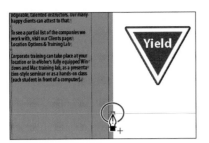

6   Switch to the Direct Selection tool and drag the upper right corner of the green frame down and to the left. When the anchor point snaps into place on the first column and the first guide from the top of the page (at 40p9 on the vertical ruler), release the mouse button.

The graphic frame is now properly shaped and sized for the design.

Wrapping text around a graphic

You can wrap text around the frame of an object or around the object itself. In this procedure, you'll see the difference between wrapping text around the bounding box and wrapping text around the graphic.

Your first task is to move the graphic, which couldn't be easier; you just select it and drag. For precise positioning, you can also use the arrow keys to nudge a frame, or you can type exact position coordinates on the Control panel.

1   Using the Selection tool ($\blacktriangle$), select the graphics frame with the image of a yield sign that is off the right edge of page 4. Being careful not to select one of the handles, hold down the Shift key and move the frame to the left so that the center point of the graphic is aligned with the middle of the gutter between the two columns of text. The frame should not have changed size, but it should have moved on the page.

Notice that the text overlaps the image. You'll change this by applying text wrap.

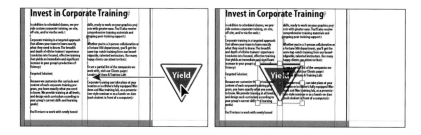

2 Choose Window > Text Wrap to open the Text Wrap panel, and select the second wrap option so that the text wraps around the bounding box, not around the yield image's shape.

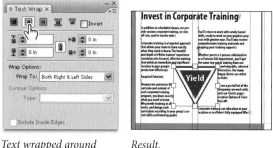

Text wrapped around   Result.
bounding box.

3 Next, select the third wrap option so that the text wraps around the contour of the image shape instead of the bounding box. From the Wrap Options, choose Both Right & Left Sides from the Wrap To menu if it isn't already selected and Detect Edges from the Type menu. Click a blank area to deselect all, or choose Edit > Deselect All.

Note: If you don't see the Wrap To menu, choose Show Options from the Text Wrap panel menu. Also, this option is available only if you selected Wrap Around Bounding Box or Wrap Around Object Shape.

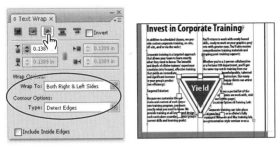

Text wrap around content. *Result.*

4   Close the Text Wrap panel, and choose File > Save.

Working with Frames

You've already seen how you can move, reshape, and resize elements on your document layout. In this section, you'll use various features that adjust the orientation of objects on the page and in relationship to each other. To begin, you'll use Pathfinder operations to subtract the area of one shape from another. Then you'll work with rotation techniques and alignment of selected objects.

Working with Pathfinders

You can change the shape of an existing frame by adding to or subtracting from it's area using the Object menu in InDesign. The shape of a frame can also be changed, even if the frame already contains text or graphics.

1   Choose View > Fit Page in Window to fit page 4 into the window.

2   Choose the Rectangle Frame tool (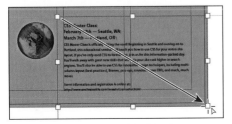)from the Tools panel and draw a frame from where the guide at 46p6 on the vertical ruler and the right edge of the first column meet to the lower right corner of the page where the red bleed guides meet.

Draw a rectangle, snap to bleed guide corner.

3   With the Selection tool, hold down the Shift key and click on the green box (outside of the frame you just placed) that covers a good part of the page to select the new rectangle and the green box.

4   Choose Object > Pathfinder > Subtract to subtract the top shape (the new rectangle) from the green shape. The text frame at the bottom of the page should now be on a white background.

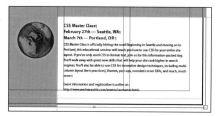

The result of subtracting.

5   While the green box is still selected, choose Object > Lock Position. This will help avoid accidental repositioning of the frame.

Converting shapes

You can change the shape of an existing frame by using the Object menu in InDesign. The shape of a frame can also be converted, even if the frame already contains text or graphics.

1   In the Tools panel, hold down the mouse on the Rectangle tool (▢) until you see other options, and select the Polygon tool (⬠).

2   Click on page 4 to the left of the text "wasting time." In the Polygon dialog box that appears, change the Polygon Width and Height to 1.5 in. (InDesign converts the inches value to picas.) Be sure the Number of sides is 5 and click OK.

3   With the shape on the page and selected, choose File > Place, and select the stopsign.tif file in your Lesson_03 > Links folder. Choose Open.

4   Choose Object > Fitting > Center Content to center the picture in the frame.

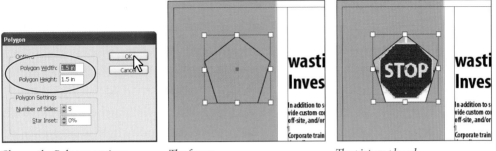

Change the Polygon settings.   The frame.   The picture placed.

Next you'll change the shape to an eight sided polygon (to match the stop sign).

5   Open the Polygon Settings dialog box by double-clicking on the Polygon tool (⬡) in the Tools panel, and specify the following:

* For Number of Sides, type **8**.

* Leave the Star Inset at **0%** and then click OK.

6   Select Object > Convert Shape > Polygon.

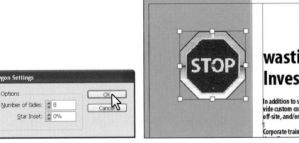

Change the polygon settings.   The result.

7   With the Selection tool, select the graphic on page 4 and select Object > Convert Shape > Rounded Rectangle. Click outside the page or select Edit > Deselect All to see the results.

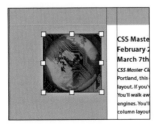

Converted to rounded rectangle.

Using the Position tool

The Position tool allows you to manipulate a frame's graphic content and the frame itself using one tool. You would typically use the Direct Selection tool in order to move a graphic within a graphics frame. You could then manipulate the position of the frame by switching to the Selection tool and moving the frame to its new position. The Position tool now allows you to perform either task without switching between two tools. The Direct Selection tool can still be used to select and modify individual points of frames.

1   Using the Selection tool (➤), click in the middle of the stopsign image to select it. Click and drag the upper left corner of the selected frame so that the frame edge on top and left stops at the edge of the stop sign itself. Repeat the same steps by dragging the bottom, right corner of the selected frame so that the frame edge on right and bottom stops at the edge of the stop sign itself.

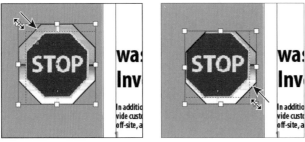

Drag the upper left corner   Drag the lower right corner
of the selected frame.   of the selected frame.

2   Select the Position tool in the Tools panel by clicking and holding on the Direct Selection tool.

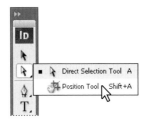

3   Click into the stop sign image on page 4. Notice that your cursor changes into the Hand tool (✋) when you put your cursor over the graphic contents of the frame. Using the arrow keys, move the image within the frame so that it looks more centered.

By holding down Control+Shift (Windows) or Command+Shift (Mac OS) and pressing an arrow key an object will move in smaller increments. By holding just the Shift key and pressing an arrow key will move an object in larger increments.

4 Position your cursor just over the edge of the stop sign image, noticing that your cursor changes to a pointer with a dot (↖.). This indicates that you will be selecting a frame if clicked. Click on the frame and drag it so that the right edge of the frame snaps to the column guide to it's right.

Note: If you resize the frame, choose Edit > Undo and try again. The idea is to move the frame to the edge of the column.

The Position tool can be used to manipulate content or a frame without switching tools.

Rotating an object

There are several options within InDesign for rotating objects. In this topic, you'll use the Control panel.

1 Using the Selection tool (▶), select the blue image of the world at the bottom of page 4.

2 In the Control panel, make sure that the center point is selected on the Reference Point indicator (▦) so that the object rotates around its center, and then select 90° from the Rotation angle pop-up menu.

Rotating an image within its frame

You can rotate both the frame and contents in one action by selecting the object with the Selection tool (▶) and then dragging one of the handles with the Rotation tool. However, sometimes you just want to set the image at a jaunty angle. That process is just a slight variation on the procedure.

When you rotated the image of the world, you used the Control panel to set a precise rotation angle. In this procedure, you'll use the Rotation tool to rotate a graphic freely.

1 Choose View > Fit Page in Window, then choose page 1 from the Pages menu at the bottom of the document window.

2 Press A to switch to the Direct Selection tool (▷), and then position the cursor over the image above the Jeff G. text and then click.

3 In the Control panel, make sure that the center point in the Reference Point indicator (▦) is selected.

4 Press R to select the Rotation tool (◯).

5   Move the crosshair over one of the corner handles and hold down the mouse button and then drag the handle clockwise to rotate the image, stopping when you like the look of the results. The sample uses a rotation of -7°.

Note: *You may need to use the Direct Selection tool to reposition the graphic in the frame so that it fills the frame.*

Select the image.   *Rotate the image and*
                          Fill Frame Proportionally.

Note: *Waiting for the crosshair to become a solid arrow give you a preview of the contents on-the-fly as you rotate. If you don't wait for the solid arrow, only the bounding box will remain visible as you drag to rotate.*

Aligning multiple objects

Precise alignment is easiest when you use the Align panel. Now you'll use the Align panel to center an image on the page, and then align multiple images to a selected image.

1   Choose View > Fit Page in Window, then choose page 3 from the Pages menu at the bottom of the document window. Using the Selection tool (⬐), Shift+click the text frame at the top of the page containing "Partial Class Calendar" text and the evolve logo group above it.

2   Choose Window > Object & Layout > Align to open the Align panel.

3   In the Align panel, choose Align to Page from the Alignment location options pop-up menu, then select the Align horizontal centers button (品). The text frame is now aligned to the center of the page.

Select the text frame and logo.   Align the objects.   The result.

Click a blank area or choose Edit > Deselect All.

4   Choose the Selection tool ( ), then Shift+click on the eight icons on the left side of the page.

5   From the Align panel, choose Align to Selection from the Alignment location options pop-up menu, then select the Align horizontal centers button (品)

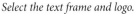

Align the objects.   The result.

6   Click a blank area to deselect all, and then save your file.

Scaling grouped objects

When objects are grouped together, InDesign allows you to edit individual objects without ungrouping. InDesign also allows you to resize a group of objects all at once. Next you will select two of the icons and group them together. Then you will resize the entire group to resize both images at once.

1   Choose the Selection tool (⬉), then Shift+click on the two Acrobat PDF icons on the left side of page 3.

2   Choose Object > Group to group them together. Then hold down the Shift + Command (Mac) or Shift + Ctrl (Windows) and with the Selection tool, click and drag from the upper right corner of the group down and to the left to make the group of images roughly the same width as the orange icon below the group.

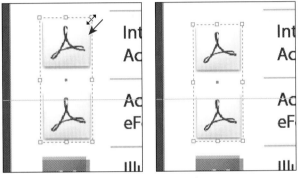

Click/drag to resize the group   *The result.*

3   Choose Edit > Deselect All to deselect all, then choose File > Save.

Selecting and modifying a frame within grouped objects

You can select individual elements of a grouped object using the Direct Selection tool or menu items. The shapes of the evolve logo at the top of page 4 (that you just aligned to the center of the page) are grouped so that you can select and modify them as a unit. You'll now change the fill color of just a few of the shapes without ungrouping or changing the other elements of the group.

1   With the Selection tool (⬉), click on the evolve group at the top of page 3.

2   Select the Select Content button (⚓)in the Control panel to select one object in the group without ungrouping.

Note: You can also achieve this by choosing Object > Select > Content in the menus or right-clicking (Windows) Ctrl+clicking (Mac) on the group and choosing Select > Content from the contextual menu.

Select the group with the Selection tool.   Choose Select Content.   The result.

3   Click on the Select Previous Object button (⬛) in the Control panel several times (six times) to select the first "e" in the word evolve. Note how there is also a Select Next Object button and it selects in the opposite direction.

Click on Select Previous   The result.   After selecting shapes, change the fill
Object six times.   color to Paper.

4   Choose the Direct Selection tool (⬛) from the Tools panel. Holding down the Shift key, click on the e, v, l, v and e so that they become selected.

5   Click on the Swatches panel tab or choose Window > Swatches to show the Swatches panel. Click on the Fill option in the Swatches panel and choose Paper to fill the shapes with a white color.

After shapes are selected   The result.
change the fill to Paper.

Finishing up

Now it's time to admire your work.

1   Choose Edit > Deselect All.

2   Choose View > Fit Spread in Window.

3   In the Tools panel, click the Preview Mode button to hide all guides and frames.

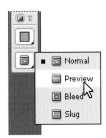

4   Press the Tab key to close all panels.

5   Save your file one more time, and then choose File > Close to keep InDesign open or File > Exit to end your InDesign session unless you would like to continue on to Exploring on your own, then keep the file open.

Congratulations. You have finished the lesson.

Exploring on your own

One of the best ways to learn about frames is to experiment on your own. In this section, you will learn how to nest an object inside a shape you create. Follow these steps to learn more about selecting and manipulating frames:

1   Using the Direct Selection tool (⬈), select and copy any image.

2   Navigate to page 4 by choosing Layout > Go to Page and typing in 4, then clicking OK.

3   To create a new page, choose Layout > Pages > Add Page. This will add a page directly after the page you are currently on.

4   Use the Polygon tool (⬠) to draw a shape on the new page (use any number of sides and any value for the star inset). Select the shape using the Direct Selection tool, and then choose Edit > Paste Into to nest the image inside the frame. (If you choose Edit > Paste, the object will not be pasted inside the selected frame.)

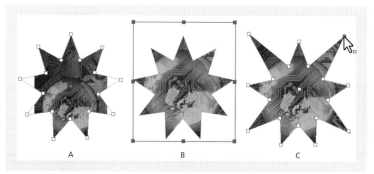

A. *Image pasted into frame, Direct Selection tool selected.*
B. *Image moved and scaled within the frame.*
C. *Polygon frame reshaped.*

5   Use the Direct Selection tool to move and scale the image within the frame.

6   Use the Direct Selection tool to change the shape of the polygon frame.

7   Use the Selection tool (➤) to rotate both the frame and the image. Use the Direct Selection tool to rotate only the image within the frame.

8   When you are done experimenting, close the document without saving.

Review

▶ **Review questions**

1 When should you use the Selection tool to select an object, and when should you use the Direct Selection tool to select an object?

2 How do you resize a frame and its contents simultaneously?

3 How do you rotate a graphic within a frame without rotating the frame?

4 Without ungrouping objects, how do you select an object within a group?

▶ **Review answers**

1 Use the Selection tool for general layout tasks, such as positioning and sizing objects. Use the Direct Selection tool for tasks involving drawing and editing paths or frames, for example, to select frame contents or to move an anchor point on a path.

2 To resize a frame and its contents simultaneously, choose the Selection tool, hold down Ctrl (Windows) or Command (Mac OS), and then drag a handle. Hold down the Shift key to maintain the object's proportions.

3 To rotate a graphic within a frame, use the Direct Selection tool to select the graphic within the frame. Select the Rotation tool, and then drag one of the handles to rotate only the graphic, not the frame.

4 To select an object within a group, select it using the Direct Selection tool.

Welcome to the

Expedition Tea Company

Take an extraordinary adventure into the world of tea. Expedition Tea Company carries an extensive array of teas from all the major tea growing regions with some of the very best these estates have to offer. Choose from our selection of teas, gift collections, teapots, or read up on information to make your tea drinking experience more enjoyable.

Loose Leaf Teas

Browse our wide selection of premium loose leaf teas from around the world including black, green, oolong, white, rooibos and chai. Try a few samples or stock up on your favorite.

Teapots

View our collection of teapots, chosen to satisfy every taste including ceramic, cast-iron Tetsubin, stainless, silver-plate, Kyusu, and more.

Tea Gift Collections

Our tea collections are packaged in golden tins within a felt-lined keepsake wooden box with a leather handle and brass latches. Give it as a gift to your favorite tea lover or to yourself!

Tea Accessories

Tea timers, tea bags, tea strainers, scoops and a variety of other tea things to make your tea time absolutely perfect.

Expedition Tea Company
www.expeditiontea.com
tea@expeditiontea.com
phone: (206) 463-9292
fax: (206) 299-9165

Expedition
TEA COMPANY
Extraordinary Adventures into the World of Tea

2007 Premium
Tea Catalog

With Adobe InDesign CS3, you can import text, thread it through frames, and edit text within the frames. Once you import text, you can create and apply styles, find and replace text and formatting, and use dynamic tools to correct spelling errors.

4 Importing and Editing Text

In this introduction to importing and editing text, you'll learn how to do the following:

- Enter text into text frames.
- Flow text manually and automatically.
- Load styles from another document and apply them.
- Thread text.
- Use semi-autoflow to place text frames.
- Find and change text and formatting.
- Find and change a missing font.
- Add a page continuation note.
- Check spelling in a document.
- Automatically correct misspelled words.
- Use drag and drop for moving text.
- Use the Story Editor

Getting started

In this lesson, you'll work on a 12-page catalog. Several pages of the catalog have already been completed. Now that the final text for the catalog has been written, you're ready to flow the article into the document and add the finishing touches to the catalog.

Note: If you have not already copied the resource files for this lesson onto your hard disk from the Adobe InDesign CS3 Classroom in a Book *CD, do so now. See "Copying the Classroom in a Book files" on page 4.*

1 To ensure that the tools and panels function exactly as described in this lesson, delete or reset the InDesign CS3 defaults preferences following the procedure in "Saving, deleting and restoring preference files" on page 2.

2   Start Adobe InDesign CS3.

Managing fonts

To begin working, you'll open an existing InDesign document. There may be fonts in this document that you do not have on your system, so you may receive an error message relating to the missing fonts.

1   Choose File > Open, and open the 04_a.indd file in the Lesson_04 folder, located inside the Lessons folder within the InDesignCIB folder on your hard disk.

Note: You may receive color profile mismatch errors. Click OK to ignore these.

When you open a file that includes fonts not installed on your system, an alert message indicates which fonts are missing. The text that uses missing fonts is also highlighted in pink. You will fix the missing font problem later in this lesson by replacing the missing fonts with an available font. This is useful because InDesign makes it clear which fonts might cause problems when printing, and provides several opportunities to correct the situation.

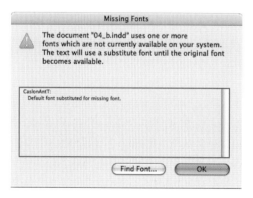

2   Click OK to close the alert message.

Navigate through the pages in the document. Pages 6 through 10 have already been completed. In this lesson, you will replace any missing fonts, complete the first five pages of the catalog, as well as pages 11 and 12.

3 Choose File > Save As and name the file **04_Catalog**, and save it in the Lesson_04 folder.

4 To see what the finished document will look like, open the 04_b.indd file in the same folder. If you prefer, you can leave the document open to act as a guide as you work. When you're ready to resume working on the lesson document, choose its name from the Window menu.

Note: You may receive color profile mismatch errors. Click OK to ignore these.

Finding and changing a missing font

When you opened the document based on the template, the CaslonAntT font may have been missing. If you have this font installed on your computer, you will not receive a warning indicator, but can follow along with the steps or skip ahead to the next section. You will now search for text containing the CaslonAntT font and replace it with the Adobe Garamond Pro font.

1 In the Pages panel, double-click the page 2 icon (you may need to scroll in the Pages panel). Choose View > Fit Page in Window. The pink highlighted text in the headlline on that page indicates that the text is formatted with a missing font.

2   Choose Type > Find Font to open the Find Font dialog box. This dialog box lists all fonts used in the document and the type of font—such as PostScript, TrueType, or OpenType. Missing fonts are indicated by an alert icon (**A**).

3   Select CaslonAntT in the list.

4   For Replace With, choose Adobe Garamond Pro from the Font Family menu, and Regular from the Font Style menu.

5   Click Change All. Click Done to close the dialog box and see the replaced font in the document.

Note: For your own projects, you may need to add the missing font to your system instead of replacing the missing font. You can fix missing fonts by installing the font on your system, by activating the font using font management software, or by adding the font files to the InDesign Fonts folder. For more information, see Installing Fonts in InDesign Help.

Creating and entering text

You can use InDesign to enter text into your documents, or you can import text created in other programs, such as word processing software.

Creating a headline and applying a style

In the gold area beneath the logo, "Expedition Tea Company" on page 1, you'll create a text frame for the catalog title, "2007 Premium Tea Catalog." This headline text frame will span the first column. You'll then apply the Catalog Headline style to this headline.

1   While viewing page 1, double-click the Zoom tool (🔍) to change the magnification to 100%.

2   To mark the location of the top of your headline frame, drag down from the horizontal ruler to create a guide at the 39p0 location. To help you position the guide, watch the Y value in either the Control or Transform panels as you drag. Hold down the Shift key to constrain the position of the guide to the increments visible on the ruler.

3   Using the Type tool (T), position the type cursor next to the left margin at the 39p0 guide. The horizontal crossbar on the type cursor should be at 39p0.

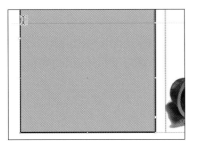

4   Drag to create a text frame in the blank area below the guide down to the bottom of the gold box. The text frame should span the first column, and the top of the frame should snap to the 39p0 guide.

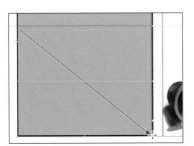

💡 *If you need to resize the frame, choose the Selection tool and drag the handles of the frame to snap to the guides. Then select the Type tool and click inside the frame.*

After you draw a text frame using the Type tool, an insertion point appears, ready for you to begin typing.

5   In the text frame you just created, type **2007 Premium Tea Catalog**.

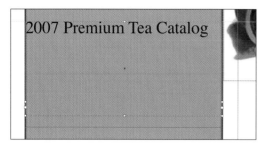

To format this type, you will apply the Catalog Title style. When you apply a paragraph style, you can place the insertion point anywhere in the paragraph or select any part of the paragraph.

6   Choose Window > Type & Tables > Paragraph Styles. With the insertion point anywhere in the headline text you just typed, select Catalog Title in the Paragraph Styles panel.

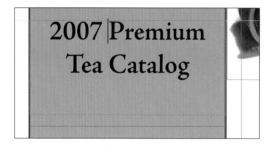

7   Save the file.

Vertically aligning text

To evenly distribute the space on the top and bottom of the text frame, you will center the text vertically using vertical justification.

1   With the insertion point anywhere in the text frame you just created, choose Object > Text Frame Options.

2   Under Vertical Justification, for Align, choose Center, and then click OK.

3   Choose File > Save.

Flowing text

The process of taking imported text, such as that from a word processing program, and placing it across several linked text frames is called flowing text. InDesign lets you flow text manually for greater control, or automatically to save time.

Flowing text manually

To flow text manually, you first select a word processing file to import. You can then drag to create a frame, or you can click anywhere on the page to create a text frame in a column. In this exercise you will use both methods to flow the text into the columns on the first page of the catalog.

1   In the Pages panel, double-click the page 1 icon to center the first page in the document window. Click on a blank part of the page to deselect all items.

2   Drag a guide down from the horizontal ruler to approximately the 7p3 position to indicate where the bottom of your first text frame will extend.

3   Choose File > Place. In the Place dialog box, make sure that Show Import Options is selected, locate and select 04_c.doc in the Lesson_04 folder, and click Open.

4   Make certain that Remove Styles and Formatting from Text and Tables is not selected in the Import Options dialog box. Deselecting this option causes the text to be imported with the same formatting that was applied in the word-processing application. Selecting this option would remove any formatting that was applied to the text. You want to keep the formatting, so you will keep this option deselected, and click OK.

You will now create a text frame spanning columns 2 and 3 to hold the text "Welcome to Expedition Tea Company."

5 Position the loaded text icon (⊞) at the upper left corner of column two and drag to create a text box across the width of columns 2 and 3 and down to the guide at 7p3.

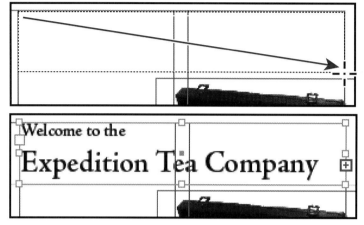

Dragging to create a text frame.

Notice that the text frame includes an out port in the lower right corner. The red plus sign indicates that there is overset text, meaning that there is more text than fits into the existing text frame. You will now flow this text into another text box in the second column on page 1.

6 Using the Selection tool (↖), click the out port of the frame you just created.

If you change your mind and decide you don't want to flow overset text, you can click any tool in the Tools panel to cancel the loaded text icon. No text will be deleted.

7 Position the loaded text icon just below the text box you just created, and click.

The text flows into a new frame from where you clicked to the bottom of the second column. The out port in the new column contains a red plus sign, again indicating that there is still overset text.

8 Repeat steps 6 and 7 above to flow the rest of the text into the third column, clicking just under the image of the wooden tea box.

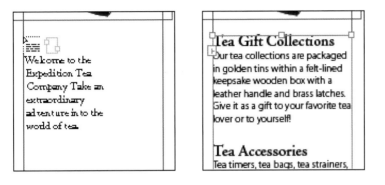

Note: While you can create separate, linked frames for each column, it is also possible to work with one large column that is divided into multiple columns using Object > Text Frame Options. Each method has its advantages in certain types of documents.

Working with styles

Styles make it easy to apply repetitive formatting across an entire document. For example, to keep all headlines formatted consistently through your document, you can create a headline style that contains the necessary formatting attributes. Styles can save time when you apply and revise text formatting and can help provide a consistent look to your documents.

Applying a style

To make the appearance of the article consistent with the other articles in the catalog, you will apply a paragraph style called Body. This style has already been created for formatting the body text of the main articles in the catalog.

1 Open the Paragraph Styles panel (or choose Window > Type & Tables > Paragraph Styles) to make the panel visible, if it is not already open.

The Paragraph Styles panel for this document now includes eight styles: Body, Catalog Title, Headline 1, Headline 2, Headline 3, Tab, Headline Reverse. and Normal. The Normal style has a disk icon (▤) next to it, indicating that the style was imported from a different application. In this case, Normal is a Microsoft Word style that was imported when you placed the article. You'll now apply the InDesign style, Body, to the text.

Note: The Basic Paragraph style is the only paragraph style available when you first create a document with InDesign. You can create new styles or add styles from other InDesign documents. Styles are also added to InDesign documents when you import text with styles from Microsoft Word.

2 In the Pages panel, double click the page 1 icon to center the first page in the Document window. Click on a blank part of the page to deselect all items.

Using the Type tool (T), click an insertion point into the first paragraph beginning "Take an extraordinary…."

3 Select Body in the Paragraph Styles panel. This paragraph is now formatted in a different font.

Take an extraordinary adventure into the world of tea. Expedition Tea Company carries an extensive array of teas from all the major tea growing regions with some of the very best these estates have to offer. Choose from our selection of teas, gift collections, teapots, or read up on information to make your tea drinking experience more enjoyable.

Take an extraordinary adventure into the world of tea. Expedition Tea Company carries an extensive array of teas from all the major tea growing regions with some of the very best these estates have to offer. Choose from our selection of teas, gift collections, teapots, or read up on information to make your tea drinking experience more enjoyable.

Before and after style is applied.

4   Repeat steps 2 and 3 above, except click an insertion point into each paragraph following the four headlines.

5   Choose File > Save.

Flowing text automatically

You will use autoflow to place text on the next two pages. When you autoflow text, InDesign creates new text frames within column guides on subsequent pages until all the overset text is flowed. If there are not enough pages in your document when you use autoflow, InDesign adds new pages until all the text is placed.

Note: A connected series of text frames is called a story.

1   Choose File > Place. In the Place dialog box, make sure that Show Import Options is turned off. Locate and select 04_d.doc in the Lesson_04 folder, and click Open.

2   In the Pages panel, double click the page 2 icon to center the second page in the Document window.

While the loaded text icon is active (⊞), you can still navigate to different document pages, or create new pages. This allows you to continue flowing text onto other pages in your document—even if these pages have not yet been created at the time you click on the out port of a text frame.

3 Holding down the Shift key, position the loaded text icon in the first column of page 2 at the guide below the Black Tea masthead, and click. Release the Shift key.

Holding down the Shift key lets you autoflow text into your document.

Notice that new text frames are added to pages 2, 3, and 4 within the column guides. This is because you held down the Shift key to autoflow text. All the text in the story is now placed.

Resizing a text frame

When you create a text frame by clicking the loaded text icon, InDesign creates the new text frame as wide as the column where you click. Although these frames are placed within the column margins, you can move, resize, and reshape any of these text frames if necessary.

1 In the Pages panel, double-click the page 2 icon to center page 2 in the Document window. (You may need to scroll down the panel to find the icon for page 2.)

Notice that the text frame in the right column covers the teapot image that was placed on this page. When you autoflow text, the text frames are created within the column settings regardless of whether objects appear in those columns. You can fix this overlap by adding a text wrap to the image or by resizing the text frame. In this exercise you will resize the text frame, so that the "Estate Teas" headline begins properly on page 3.

2 Using the Selection tool (➤), click the text frame in the right column on page 2 to select the text frame, and then drag the lower middle handle of the text frame above the image to approximately the 32p location (you can look at the vertical ruler as you drag, or in the Transform panel).

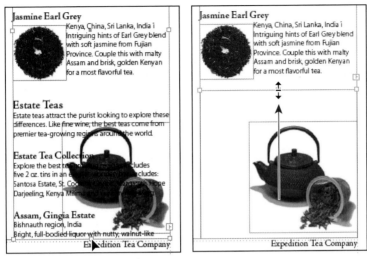

Before and after resizing text frame.

3 Choose File > Save.

Adding a column break

Sometimes you will not want to resize a frame to control the flow of text in your story. Instead you will want to add a column break which forces all the text after the break into the next column. You will now add a column break on page 3.

1 In the Pages panel, double click the page 3 icon to center the third page in the document window. Click on a blank part of the page to deselect all items.

2 Using the Type tool (T), insert your type cursor in front of "Keemun Panda" near the bottom of the first column.

3 Choose Type > Insert Break Character > Column Break. The text after the column break moves into the second column.

Note: You can also insert a column break by inserting your type cursor and pressing the Enter key on the number pad.

4 Choose File > Save.

Adding a page continuation note

Because the black tea category continues from page 3 to page 4, you can let readers know where they can resume reading when they get to the bottom of the page. To do this you will add a "(Continued on page x)" frame. You can add an automatic page number that will automatically reflect the number of the next page in the text flow.

1 Center page 3 in the document window by scrolling or using the Pages panel.

2 Drag a guide from the horizontal ruler down to the 46p6 location. Zoom in so that you can read the text in the columns easily.

3 Using the Selection tool (▶), click the text frame in the right column on page 2, and then drag the lower middle handle up to the 46p6 guide.

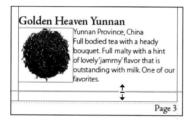

4 Select the Type tool (T), and then drag to create a text frame that fills the space at the bottom of the right-most column on page 3.

5 With a text insertion point active in the new text frame, type (**Black tea continued on page**), including the space and the parentheses. Then use the left arrow key to move the insertion point to the left of the close parenthesis.

6 Right-click (Windows) or Ctrl+click (Mac OS) the text frame, and in the context menu that appears, choose Insert Special Character > Markers > Next Page Number. The text now reads "(Continued on page 4)."

Note: The text frame containing the continued on line must touch or overlap the frame linked text for the "Next Page Number" character to work properly.

7 If necessary, select the Selection tool, and then drag the top of the new text frame up so that it snaps to the text frame above it.

Before text boxes touch   After text boxes touch

Changing horizontal and vertical text alignment

The continuation line text is probably formatted with a different paragraph style than you want to use. Next, you'll reformat that text.

1   Select the Type tool (T), and then triple-click "(Black tea continued on page 4)" to select the text.

2   In the Paragraph Styles panel, click Body.

3   In the Character section of the Control panel, choose Italic from the Style menu.

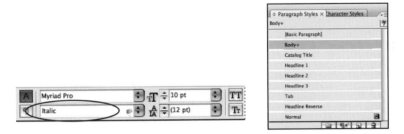

Notice that the Body style has a plus sign next to it in the Paragraph Styles panel. The plus sign next to a style indicates that the current text has formats applied to it in addition to the style.

4   In the Control panel, click the Paragraph Formatting Controls button (¶), then click the Align Right (≣) button.

Now you will align the text at the bottom of the frame.

5 Choose Object > Text Frame Options.

6 In the Align pop-up menu under Vertical Justification, select Bottom. Then click OK.

7 With the Selection tool, click the text frame containing the "Black tea continued on page" text, and then Shift+click to select the text frame immediately above it. Then choose Object > Group. This keeps the story and its jump line together if you move them.

8 Press Shift+Ctrl+A (Windows) or Shift+Command+A (Mac OS) to deselect the text. Then save the file.

Using semi-autoflow to place text frames

Now you will use semi-autoflow to place a text file into multiple columns on pages 4 and 5. Semi-autoflow lets you create text frames one at a time, without having to reload the text icon.

1 In the Pages panel, double click the page 4 icon to center the fourth page in the Document window. Click on a blank part of the page to deselect all items.

2 Choose File > Place to open the Place dialog box, and then deselect Replace Selected Items. Locate and double-click 04_f.doc in the Lesson_04 folder.

3 Holding down Alt (Windows) or Option (Mac OS), position the semi-autoflow loaded text icon in the left column at the 6p7 guide, and click.

Flowing text semi-automatically.

The text flows into the left column. Because you held down Alt or Option, the pointer is still a loaded text icon, ready for you to flow text into another frame.

4   Holding down Alt or Option, position the loaded text icon in the second column at the 6p7 guide, and click.

5   Continue to hold down the Alt or Option key and position the loaded text icon at 6p7 position in the first column of page 5, and click. Release the Alt or Option key.

Now you will create the final column. You won't hold down Alt or Option since there will only be four frames in this story.

6   Position the loaded text icon in the second column on page 5, and click. You should now have text in all four columns.

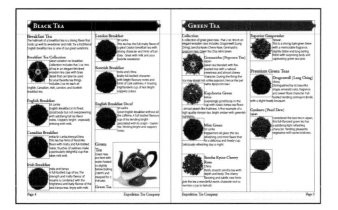

The headline "Green Tea" appears in the second column of page 4.

7   Insert your text cursor in front of "Green Tea" and select Type > Insert Break Character > Column Break, to push the text into the first column of page 5.

8   Choose File > Save.

Changing the number of columns on a page

You can change the number of columns in a text box, as opposed to creating two separate text boxes for your type. You will now change the number of columns on page 11.

1 In the Pages panel, double-click the page 11 icon to center the page in the Document window. Make sure that only page 11 in the Pages panel is highlighted so that the column change will affect only page 11. If necessary, click another page icon, and then click the page 11 icon.

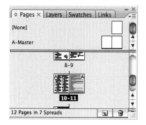

2 Choose Layout > Margins and Columns. Under Columns, type **2** for Number and click OK.

Even though the number of columns changed, the widths of the existing text frames did not change.

Notice that the text frames are independent of the number of columns. Column margins can determine how text frames are created, but the text frame widths do not change when you redefine columns. One exception to this rule is when Layout Adjustment is turned on—you can learn more about Layout Adjustment in "Exploring on your own" at the end of this lesson.

3   Using the Selection tool (↖), select the text frame on page 11 and select Object > Text Frame Options, and change the number of columns to 2 and click OK.

The text will now flow into two columns.

4   If the "Shipping Information" headline appears at the bottom of the first column, insert your text cursor in front of that line and select Type > Insert Break Character > Column Break to push it into the second column.

5   Save the file.

Loading styles from another document

Styles appear only in the document in which you create them. However, it's easy to share styles between InDesign documents by loading, or importing, styles from other InDesign documents. In this exercise, you will take styles from another document. This other document has a style that will work well for some text in this catalog. Instead of re-creating the style, you'll load the style from the other document and apply it to text in the catalog.

1   Open the Paragraph Styles panel. From the Paragraph Styles panel menu, click the Panel menu button (▾≡) and choose Load Paragraph Styles... from the Paragraph Styles panel menu.

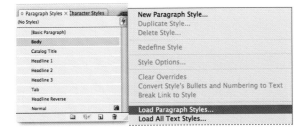

2   In the Open a File dialog box, double-click styles.indd from the Lesson_04 folder. Uncheck the Basic Paragraph style, as we only want to import the Tab with Leader style. Click OK.

3   In the Paragraph Styles panel, notice the new style Table with Leader appears. You may need to scroll through the list or resize the panel to see this additional style.

4   In the Pages panel, double click the page 11 icon to center that page in the document window, if it is not already. Click on a blank part of the page to deselect all items.

5   Using the Type tool (T), select through the three lines of type in the second column starting with "For orders up to."

6   In the Paragraph Styles panel, click to select the Tab with Leader style. The new style is applied to the selected text.

Shipping Information	Shipping Information
Expedition Tea Company uses the US Postal Service to ship our products. Shipping rates are as follows: Free shipping for orders $75 and over	Expedition Tea Company uses the US Postal Service to ship our products. Shipping rates are as follows: Free shipping for orders $75 and over
For orders up to $9.99 $3.85	For orders up to $9.99 . . . .$3.85
For orders up to $39.99 $6.85	For orders up to $39.99 . . . .$6.85
For orders up to $74.99 $10.85	For orders up to $74.99 . . . . $10.85
Orders are typically shipped the next day, ensuring a prompt and timely delivery of all your packages.	Orders are typically shipped the next day, ensuring a prompt and timely delivery of all your packages.

Before and after applying the Tab with Leader paragraph style.

Flowing text into an existing frame

When you place text, you can flow text into a new frame or an existing frame. To flow text into an existing frame, click an insertion point to flow text at that point, or click the loaded text icon in an existing frame, which replaces that frame's contents.

The last page of the catalog includes a placeholder frame for the address. You'll place a new text story in this frame.

1   In the Pages panel, double click the page 12 icon to center the last page in the Document window. Click on a blank part of the page to deselect all items.

2   Choose File > Place. In the Place dialog box, turn off Show Import Options if it is selected. Locate and double-click 04_e.doc in the Lesson_04 folder. The pointer becomes a loaded text icon (🖹), previewing the first few lines of text in the story you are placing. When you move the loaded text icon over an empty text frame, parentheses enclose the icon (🖹).

3   Position the loaded text icon over the placeholder frame below the logo, and click.

Placing a text file into an existing frame.

4   Choose File > Save.

Finding and changing

Like most popular word processors, InDesign lets you find text and replace it. You can also search for and change formatting and special characters.

Finding text and changing formatting

You will search for occurrences of the word "Expedition Tea Company" in this document. Make sure that your view-magnification level is set so that you can easily read the text and see the formatting on the page. You do not have to have anything selected for this procedure.

You will want to change all instances of "Expedition Tea Company" to include the trademark symbol at the end (™) and change the case to small capital letters.

1   Choose Edit > Find/Change. For Find What, type **Expedition Tea Company**.

2   Press Tab to move to the Change To box, and type the same words, but add the trademark symbol. This is located under Special characters for replace icon (@)next to the Change to box. Select Symbols > Trademark Symbol.

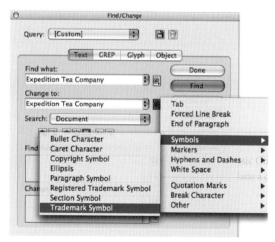

You will see that a ^d (a caret and the letter d) will be inserted after the company name. This is the search code for the trademark symbol. For Search, make sure Document is selected. In the small icon row below the Search pop-up menu, select the Include Master Pages icon (▥), since the company name also appears on these pages.

These settings tell InDesign to search all text frames throughout the document, including the Master Pages, for the word "Expedition Tea Company" and replace it with "Expedition Tea Company™." Next we will tell InDesign to change the format of the words it locates.

3   Click More Options to display additional formatting options in the dialog box.

4   Leave the area in the Find Format unchanged, but select the specify attributes to change icon (⬚) next to the Change Format box.

5   In the left side of the Change Format Settings dialog box, select Basic Character Formats. Then, in the right side, choose Small Caps from the Case pop-up menu.

6   Leave the other options blank. Click OK to return to the Find/Change dialog box. Notice the alert icon (ⓘ) above the Change to box. This icon indicates that InDesign will change text to the specified formatting.

7   Click Change All. A message appears, telling you how many instances that InDesign found and changed.

8   Click OK to close the message, and then click Done to close the Find/Change dialog box. Then save the file.

Before and after finding and changing attributes.

Checking spelling of a story

InDesign includes a utility much like those used in word processing programs for checking spelling. You can check the spelling in selected text, an entire story, all stories in a document, or all stories in several open documents at once.

1   In the Pages panel, navigate to page 1. Select the Type tool and click the cursor before the word "Welcome" in the first paragraph. Notice in the character options of the Control panel, that English: USA is selected. If you were working in a different language, you could select a different dictionary from this pop-up menu.

2   Choose Edit > Spelling > Check Spelling to open the Check Spelling dialog box.

3   From the Search pop-up menu, choose Document to check the spelling in the entire catalog document.

4   Click Start to find the first misspelled word in the document. The word "oolong" will appear in the Not in Dictionary field.

5 Note the choices offered in the Suggested Corrections list. If you wanted to replace the word, you'd select an alternate spelling from this list or simply type the corrected spelling into the Change To field. Then you'd decide whether you want to change just this instance of the word (by clicking the Change button), or all instances of the word (by clicking the Change All button).

Note: If you get a "Cannot find match" message, you may not have typed the text properly, you may have selected Whole Word or Case Sensitive, or you may not have cleared formatting used in a previous search. Another possibility is that you selected Story for Search while the text you're looking for is in a different story. Finally, you may be searching for text that does not exist in your document.

6 Because "oolong" is the correct name for a type of tea, click the Skip button to ignore this assumed misspelling. However, this will skip only the first instance of the word, and "oolong" will come up again as misspelled, as InDesign continues to check the spelling in the document. To avoid this, click the Ignore All button when the next instance is found.

If you choose to Ignore All instances of a word, it will ignore the misspelling only until InDesign is restarted.

7 Click Done to close the Check Spelling dialog box.

8 Choose File > Save.

Adding words to a dictionary

To avoid a word being repeatedly identified as misspelled in other InDesign documents, you can add the word to an external user dictionary.

1 Close your catalog document, and then quit and restart InDesign.

2 Choose File > Open, and open 04_Catalog from the Lesson_04 folder.

3 On page 1, click the cursor before the word "Welcome" in the first paragraph. Choose Edit > Spelling > Check Spelling to open the Check Spelling dialog box.

4 From the Search pop-up menu, choose Document to check the spelling in the entire catalog document.

5 Click Start to find the first misspelled word in the document. The word "oolong" will appear in the Not in Dictionary field.

6 Click the Add button to add this word to the external user dictionary file, ENG. UDC. Because this dictionary is application-wide, InDesign will recognize "oolong" as correctly spelled in all future documents.

7 Click Done to close the Check Spelling dialog box.

Adding words to a document-specific dictionary

You may want to link the specific spelling of a word to a single document only. Storing a word in an open InDesign document's internal dictionary restricts it to that document.

1 Choose Edit > Spelling > Dictionary. Note that the target dictionary is the default English language and "oolong" is listed under Dictionary List: Added Words. To remove the word from the external user dictionary, select it in the list, and then click on the Remove button.

2   From the Target pop-up menu, scroll down to select your file's name, 04_Catalog.

3   Type the word **oolong** into the Word field, and click the Add button. The word is added to the Dictionary List for this document only. This spelling of the word will be recognized only within this document, and subsequent InDesign documents will continue to list the word as misspelled. Click Done.

Checking spelling dynamically

It's not necessary for you to wait until a document is finished before checking the spelling. InDesign incorporates a Dynamic Spelling utility that allows you to see misspelled words as they are entered. If you turn on Dynamic Spelling after text has been entered, all misspellings will be highlighted.

1   Before activating this feature, choose Edit > Preferences > Spelling (Windows) or InDesign > Preferences > Spelling (Mac OS). Make sure that the Enable Dynamic Spelling box is checked. Then decide which errors you want highlighted (in the Find section), and how you want them highlighted (in the Underline Color section). Choose OK to close the Preference dialog box and return to your document. (Misspelled words, according to the default user dictionary, are immediately highlighted with a red underline.)

Note: To disable Dynamic Spelling, choose Edit > Spelling > Dynamic Spelling.

Loose Leaf Teas
Browse our wide selection of premium loose leaf teas from around the world including black, green, oolong white, rooibos and chai. Try a few samples or stock up on your favorite.

2   If you add a misspelled word to the document with Dynamic Spelling activated, the word becomes highlighted with an underline as you type it. Try typing the word **snew** into the first column on page 1 to see this feature in action.

Automatically correcting misspelled words

InDesign's Autocorrect utility takes the concept of checking spelling dynamically to the next level. With this function activated, InDesign automatically corrects misspelled words as you type them. Changes made are based on an internal list of commonly misspelled words and their correct spellings. This list can also be changed to include commonly misspelled words in other languages.

1   Before activating this feature, choose Edit > Preferences > Autocorrect (Windows) or InDesign > Preferences > Autocorrect (Mac OS). Make sure that the Enable Autocorrect box is checked. You can also choose to automatically correct capitalization errors by checking this option.

2   Note that the list of commonly misspelled words, and the Language listed by default is English: USA. Change the language to French and note the commonly misspelled words in that language. Change the language back to English: USA before proceeding.

3   Click the Add button to bring up the Add to Autocorrect List dialog box. Type the word **snew** in the Misspelled Word field, and **snow** into the Correction field. Click OK and then click OK on the Preferences dialog box.

4   Now type the word **snew** into the first column on page 1 again to see the Autocorrect feature in action.

Drag and drop text editing

For misplaced words in your document, InDesign offers a Drag and Drop Text feature that allows you to move text within and between frames, layout windows, and documents. You'll now use this utility to move text from one paragraph to another in your catalog.

1 Before attempting to move this type, choose Edit > Preferences > Type (Windows) or InDesign > Preferences > Type (Mac OS). In the Drag and Drop Text editing section, make sure that the Enable in Layout View box is checked. This allows you to move text into and out of open document windows, and within documents in the Layout View. Click OK.

Note: Layout View is the default view for InDesign where the full layout of text and graphics is visible. Alternately you can view only the text in the separate story editor window. See the next section for more information about the story editor.

2 In your Document window, navigate to page 11. Change your view so that you can comfortably read the paragraphs at the top of the first column.

3 The sentence "Tea is more than just a great beverage. " was mistakenly placed at the beginning of the first paragraph titled "More than Just the Tea." Using the Type tool (T), drag to select this sentence.

4 Without changing tools, rest your cursor on the highlighted word. You should see the cursor change to a new icon (▶T). Click and drag the word to its correct location, to the end of the paragraph, after the word "well."

5 When you release the mouse, the sentence will have moved to the new location. (If you wanted to copy the word instead of moving it, you would have simply pressed the Alt/Option key while dragging).

Using the story editor

If you're more comfortable working with an editing interface that focuses solely on the text being edited, InDesign includes a feature called the Story Editor.

1 With page 11 of the catalog in the Document window, select the Type tool (T) and click inside the first column to place your insertion point there.

2 Choose Edit > Edit in Story Editor. The Story Editor window opens, showing raw text with no formatting applied. Any graphics and other non-text elements have been omitted to make editing easier.

3 In the Story Editor window, insert your text cursor and add the word "accessories" in the first paragraph after "teapots," and before "and." If necessary, move the Story Editor window aside, so you can see that the corresponding text has also been changed in the Document window.

Note: The Story Editor displays line numbers for reference purposes, and that misspelled words are highlighted by dynamic spelling, just as they are in the Document window. If the Enable in Story Editor option is selected in the Type Preferences, you can also drag and drop type in the Story Editor, just as you did in the last lesson.

4 To make viewing and editing type easier, the display characteristics of the Story Editor window can be changed by choosing Edit > Preferences > Story Editor Display (Windows) or InDesign > Preferences > Story Editor Display (Mac OS). Change the font size to 14 points and the Line Spacing to Doublespace to see if it makes editing easier for you.

5   While type isn't displayed in the actual paragraph styles you selected in the Story Editor window, the names are listed in the column on the left, and can be applied (but not seen) in this window. For more information on applying styles in InDesign, see Lesson 7, "Working with Styles."

6   Close Story Editor.

Congratulations. You have finished the lesson.

Exploring on your own

In this lesson, we covered only the basics of creating and applying styles. If you do a significant amount of writing in InDesign, you'll want to learn how Next Style works and how to apply styles using shortcut keystrokes.

Note: In Windows, Num Lock must be on for the following shortcut keystrokes to work.

1   With no text selected, double-click the Headline 3 style in the Paragraph Styles panel.

2   Click an insertion point in the Shortcut text box. Using numbers from only the numeric keypad, press Ctrl+Alt+3 (Windows) or Command+Option+3 (Mac OS).

3   For Next Style, select Body. Click OK to close the dialog box. Now practice applying the Headline style using your keyboard shortcut. Notice that when you press Enter or Return at the end of a Headline 3 paragraph, the next paragraph automatically has the Body style.

Note: If text does not appear in the Shortcut text box, make sure that you use the numbers from the numeric keypad. In Windows, make sure that Num Lock is on. If you are using a laptop computer that does not include a numeric keypad, choose the style names from the Paragraph Styles menu.

Review

▶ **Review questions**

1   How do you autoflow text? How do you flow text one frame at a time?

2   How can using styles save time?

3   While checking the spelling of your document, InDesign flags words used in other languages. How can you fix this problem?

▶ **Review answers**

1   When the loaded text icon appears after using the Place command or clicking an out port, hold down the Shift key and click. To flow text one frame at a time, you can hold down Alt (Windows) or Option (Mac OS) to reload the text icon after you click or drag to create a frame.

2   Styles save time by letting you keep a group of formatting attributes together that you can quickly apply to text. If you need to update the text, you don't have to change each paragraph formatted with the style individually. Instead, you can simply modify the style.

3   Before you check the spelling of your document, select any phrase from a different language and use the Character panel to specify the language for that text.

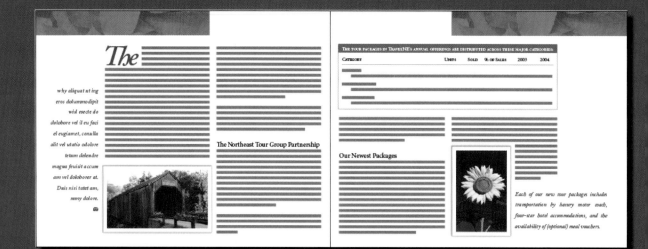

The

why aliquat at ing eros doluurono dipit wisl esecte do dolobore vel il eu faci el eugiamet, conulla alit vel utatio odolore tetum delendre magna feuisit accum am vel doloborer at. Duis nisi tatet am, nimy dolore.

The Northeast Tour Group Partnership

THE TOUR PACKAGES IN TRAVELNE'S ANNUAL OFFERINGS ARE DISTRIBUTED ACROSS THESE MAJOR CATEGORIES:

CATEGORY	UNITS	SOLD	% OF SALES	2003	2004

Our Newest Packages

Each of our new tour packages includes transportation by luxury motor coach, four-star hotel accommodations, and the availability of (optional) meal vouchers.

With InDesign you can precisely control the type and formatting of your document. You can easily change font and type styles, modify the alignment, add tabs and indents, and apply colors and strokes to text.

5 | Working with Typography

In this lesson, you'll learn how to do the following:

- Create and use a baseline grid.

- Change type spacing and appearance.

- Create special characters.

- Create a tabbed table with tab leaders and hanging indents.

- Insert special characters in text using Open Type fonts.

Getting started

In this lesson, you'll create a two-page spread for the annual report of the TravelNE company. Your work in this sample file will involve using one of the Open Type fonts that shipped on the application CD with Adobe InDesign CS3.

Note: If you have not already copied the resource files for this lesson onto your hard disk from the Adobe InDesign CS3 Classroom in a Book *CD, do so now. See "Copying the Classroom in a Book files" on page 4.*

1 To ensure that the tools and panels function exactly as described in this lesson, delete or reset the InDesign CS3 defaults preferences following the procedure in "Saving, deleting and restoring preference files" on page 2.

2 Start Adobe InDesign CS3.

To begin working, you'll open an existing InDesign document.

3   Choose File > Open, and open the 05_a.indd file in the Lesson_05 folder, located inside the Lessons folder within the InDesignCIB folder on your hard disk.

4   Choose File > Save As, rename the file **05_report.indd**, and save it in the Lesson_05 folder.

5   If you want to see what the finished document will look like, open the 05_b.indd file in the same folder. You can leave this document open to act as a guide as you work. When you're ready to resume working on the lesson document, choose its name from the Window menu.

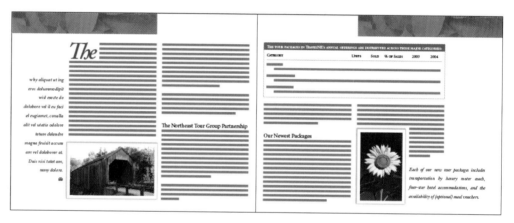

Adjusting vertical spacing

InDesign provides several options for customizing and adjusting the vertical spacing in your document. You can:

- Set the space between all lines of text using a baseline grid.
- Set the space between each line using the Leading option in the Control panel.
- Set the space between each paragraph separately using the Space Before/Space After options in the Control panel.
- Use the Vertical Justification options in the Text Frame Options dialog box to align text within a frame.

In this section of the lesson, you will use the baseline grid to align text.

Using a baseline grid to align text

Once you've decided on the font size and leading for your document's body text, you may want to set up a baseline grid (also called a leading grid) for the entire document. Baseline grids represent the leading for your document's body text and are used to align the baseline of type in one column of text with the baseline of type in neighboring columns.

Before you set the baseline grid, you'll want to check the margin value for the top of your document and the leading value for the body text. These elements work together with the grid to create a cohesive design.

1   To view the top margin value for the page, choose Layout > Margins and Columns. The top margin is set to 6p0 (6 picas, 0 points). Click Cancel to close the dialog box.

2   To determine the leading value, select the Type tool (T) in the Tools panel and click in a body-text paragraph. Check the Leading value (⁑) in the Control panel. The leading is set to 14 pt (14 points).

3 Choose Edit > Preferences > Grids (Windows) or InDesign > Preferences > Grids (Mac OS) to set your grid options. In the Baseline Grid section, type **6** for Start to match your top margin setting of 6p0. This option sets the location of the first grid line for the document. If you use InDesign's default value of 3p0, the first grid line would appear above the top margin.

4 For Increment Every, type **14pt** to match your leading. When you select another option, InDesign automatically converts the points value to picas (to 1p2).

5 Choose 100% for View Threshold.

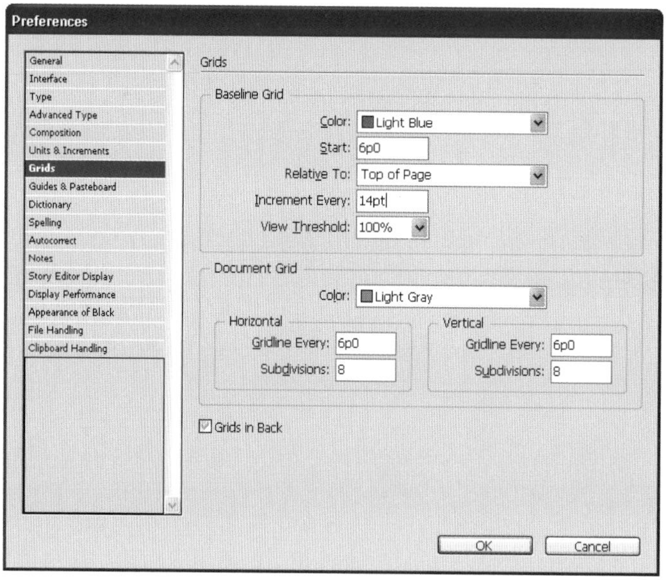

The View Threshold option sets the minimum value at which you can see the grid on-screen. At 100%, the grid appears in the document window only at magnifications of 100% or higher.

6 Click OK to close the dialog box.

Viewing the baseline grid

Now you'll make the grid you just set up visible on-screen.

1   To view the grid in the Document window, choose View > Grids & Guides > Show Baseline Grid. The grid does not appear because the document view is lower than the grid's View Threshold value. Choose 100% from the magnification menu at the lower left corner of the Document window—the grid now appears on-screen.

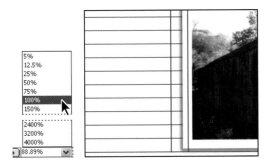

Now you'll use the Control panel to align all the text to the grid. You can align multiple stories independently of one another, or all at once. You'll align all the stories in this spread simultaneously.

2   If the Control panel isn't visible, click Window > Control to make it visible.

3   With the Type tool (T), click an insertion point anywhere in the first paragraph on the spread, and then choose Edit > Select All to select all the text in the main story.

 When applying paragraph attributes, it is not necessary to select an entire paragraph with the Type tool. Just select a portion of the paragraph or paragraphs you want to format. If you are formatting only one paragraph, you can simply click in the paragraph to make an insertion point.

4 In the Control panel, make sure the Paragraph Formatting Controls button is active (¶), and click the Align to baseline grid button (≡≡). The text shifts so that the baselines of the characters rest on the grid lines.

Before and after aligning the text to the baseline grid.

5 If necessary, scroll to the left side of the spread so you can see the pull-quote on the side of the page; then click an insertion point in the pull-quote.

6 In the Control panel, click the Align to Baseline Grid button. Because this text is formatted using 18 point leading, not the baseline grid leading value of 14pt or 1p2, aligning to the grid causes the text to expand to every other grid line (using 28 point leading).

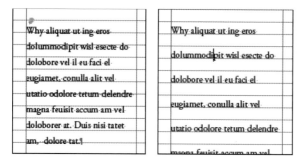

Before and after aligning the pull-quote to the baseline grid.

7 Save the file.

Changing the spacing above and below paragraphs

When you apply a space before or after a paragraph that you have previously aligned to the grid, the space automatically adjusts to the next highest multiple of the grid value. For example, if your grid is set to 14 points (1p2) and you specify Space After of any value under 14, InDesign automatically increases the space value to 14; if you specify a value over 14, such as 16, InDesign increases it to the next higher multiple, or 28. You can use the Space Before or Space After value instead of the Baseline Grid value, by selecting the Do Not Align to Baseline Grid option (≡≡) for the affected paragraph.

No space (left), space adjusted to fit grid at 28 pt (right).

Here you'll increase the space below the second paragraph of the main story. All other paragraphs in the spread have already been formatted with a 1p2 Space After value.

1 Using the Type tool (T), click anywhere in the second paragraph on the page on the left (page 1).

2 In the Control panel, type **1p2** for Space After (⬚≡) and press Enter or Return. The text in the next heading shifts automatically to the next grid line.

Ure tet voloreet nim ipit init, vel ullam aliqui bla am vel er in elit ullut praestie ex exerit verat iureetum zzril iriusting estions equat, quis autpat am quipit lore dolobore mincidunt vulla feugiat. Sustis vulputem dunt lutet, volore feuissi.

The Northeast Tour Group Partnership

Molenis sendre magnim nonsed te do consectet, vel delent wis nonse con er sum irit, voloborem eliquiscilla faccum venis niarue feugue verciliquam quis niatis dip er inim dip ex eniat at am quat. Ut utet acidunt acilla faci tat iriuscillan velit ut lutem zzrit la feu-

Before and after applying a Space After value to the upper paragraph.

Now you'll increase the space before the heading "The Northeast Tour Group Partnership" to give it even more space.

3 Click an insertion point in the heading "The Northeast Tour Group Partnership." In the Control panel, type **0p6** for Space Before (⁻≡) and then press Enter or Return. Because you previously aligned the heading to the baseline grid, the Space Before jumps to 14 points instead of 6 points.

To use the 0p6 value instead of 14, and to add more space between the heading and the following paragraph, you'll unalign the heading from the grid.

4   With an insertion point still in the heading "The Northeast Tour Group Partnership," click the Do not align to baseline grid button (≣≣) in the Control panel. The heading shifts upward a bit, away from the body text below.

Before and after unaligning the heading from the baseline grid.

This heading and the heading on the page on the right (page 2) are formatted using the Head 1 style. To automatically update the second heading so that it uses the same spacing values as the heading you just edited, you'll redefine the style.

5   Click the Paragraph Styles panel tab (or choose Type > Paragraph Styles) to make the panel visible.

6   Click an insertion point in the heading "The Northeast Tour Group Partnership." Notice that a plus sign appears after the Head 1 style name in the panel. This sign indicates that the formatting of the selected text has been modified from the original formatting for the style.

7   Click the Panel menu (▾≣), and choose Redefine Style from the Paragraph Styles panel menu. The Head 1 style now takes on the formatting of the current text.

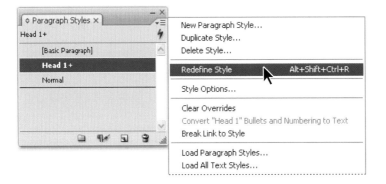

Notice that the plus sign disappears and that space is added above the heading on page 2.

8 To apply the same alignment characteristics to another heading, click the Type tool in the "Our Newest Packages" heading on page 2, and then select the Head 1 style in the Paragraph Styles panel to apply the redefined style.

9 Save the file.

Changing fonts and type style

Changing the fonts and type styles of text can make a dramatic difference in the appearance of your document. Here you'll change the font family, type style, and size for the text in one of the pull-quotes along the border of the spread. You'll make these changes using the Control panel.

1 Make sure the Control panel is visible. (If it's not, click Window > Control to make it visible).

2 Using the Type tool (T), click inside the pull-quote on the left side of page 1, and then choose Edit > Select All to select the entire paragraph.

3 In the Control panel, make sure the Character Formatting Controls button is active (A). Select Adobe Caslon Pro from the Font Family menu and Semibold Italic from the Type Style menu.

4   In Font Size, type **15,** and press Enter or Return.

5   Choose Edit > Deselect All to deselect the text. Notice how the text stays aligned to the grid even after changing these attributes.

Because Adobe Caslon Pro is an OpenType font, you can use the Glyphs panel to select alternatives for many characters.

6   Select the first character (the "W") of the pull-quote, and then choose Type > Glyphs.

7   In the Glyphs panel, choose Alternates for Selection from the Show pop-up menu, just to see the alternates for "W." You'll notice that there are many filtering options including Punctuation and Ornaments to more quickly find desired characters. Then double-click the more script-like "W" alternate to replace the original character in the pull-quote.

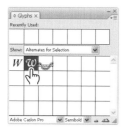

8   Close the Glyphs panel.

💡 *Some of the more commonly used glyphs, such as the copyright and trademark symbols, are also available from the context menu by right-clicking (Windows) or Ctrl+clicking (Mac OS) at the text insertion point.*

9 You won't be using the baseline grid for the remainder of the lesson, so you can hide it from view. To hide it, choose View > Grids & Guides > Hide Baseline Grid. Then save the file.

Changing paragraph alignment

You can easily manipulate how a paragraph fits in its text frame by changing the horizontal alignment. You can align text with one or both edges of a text frame or text-frame inset. Justifying text aligns both the left and right edges. In this section, you'll justify the pull-quote.

1 Using the Type tool (T), click an insertion point in the pull-quote on page 1.

2 In the Control panel, make sure the Paragraph Formatting Controls button is active (¶), and then click the Justify All Lines button (≣).

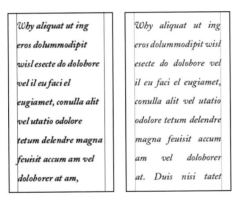

Before and after justifying text.

Adding a decorative font and special character

Now you'll add a decorative font character and a flush space (special character) to the end of the pull-quote. Used together, a decorative font and flush space can make a dramatic difference in the look of a justified paragraph.

1 Using the Type tool (T), click an insertion point in the pull-quote, just after the final period.

2 If the Glyphs panel is not still open, choose Type > Glyphs.

3 In the Glyphs panel, choose Ornaments from the Show menu.

4 From the scrollable list, select the ❀ character and double-click to insert the character. The character appears at the insertion point in the document. You're finished with the Glyphs panel for this lesson, so you can close it now, and then save your work.

Note: This font may display many more glyphs than you are accustomed to seeing because it is an OpenType font. OpenType fonts are able to carry many more characters and glyph alternates than earlier PostScript typefaces. Adobe's OpenType fonts are built on the same foundation as PostScript. For more information about OpenType fonts, visit Adobe.com/type.

Notice how the last line of the pull-quote has overly large spaces between the words. You can address this by adding a flush space to the end of the paragraph. A flush space adds a variable amount of space to the last line of a fully justified paragraph. You'll insert the flush space between the period and the decorative end-of-story character you just added.

You could add a flush space using the Type menu, but this time you'll use the Context menu to do the job.

5 Using the Type tool, click an insertion point between the final period and the ornamental character.

6 Right-click (Windows) or Ctrl+click (Mac OS) and choose Insert White Space > Flush Space.

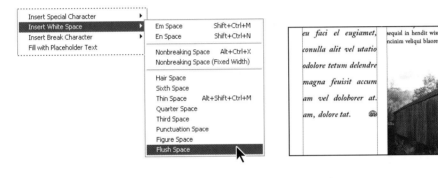

Creating a drop cap

You can add creative touches to your document using the special InDesign font features. For example, you can make the first character or word in a paragraph a drop cap, or apply a gradient or color fill to text, create superscript and subscript characters, along with ligatures and old-style numerals for font families with these features. Here you'll create a three-letter drop cap in the first paragraph of the document.

1 Using the Type tool (T), click an insertion point anywhere in the first paragraph on page 1.

2   In the Control panel, type **3** for Drop Cap Number of Lines to make the letters drop down three lines. Then type **3** for Drop Cap One or More Characters (⯆) to enlarge the first three letters. Press Enter or Return.

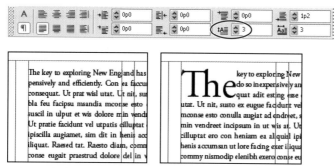

Before and after applying the drop cap.

3   Select the Character Formatting controls in the Control panel (**A**). With the Type tool (**T**), select the drop cap characters on page 1. Choose Adobe Caslon Pro from the Font Family menu and Semibold Italic from the Type Style menu.

4   Now select just the "Th." Choose Type > Glyphs to display the Glyphs panel. In the Glyphs panel, choose Alternates for Selection from the pop-up menu, just to see the alternates for "Th." Double-click the more ornate "Th" alternate to replace the original characters in the drop cap. Close the Glyphs panel.

Applying a fill and stroke to text

Next, you'll add a fill and stroke to the drop cap letters you just created.

1   With the Type tool (**T**) still selected, select the drop cap characters on page 1.

2   If necessary, select the Fill box (⯆) in the Swatches panel.

3   In the Swatches panel, select Pantone Reflex Blue. InDesign fills the letters with blue, though you can't see it yet because the text is still selected.

Note: If you don't see Reflex Blue in the panel, click the Show All Swatches button (⯆).

4   Select the Stroke box (⯆) in the Tools panel.

5   In the Swatches panel, select Black. A stroke appears around each of the letters. The default size of the stroke is 1 point. You'll change the stroke to 1.5 point.

6   Choose Window > Stroke to open the Stroke panel.

7   In the Stroke panel, type 1.5 pt for Weight and press Enter. Then, press Shift+Ctrl+A (Windows) or Shift+Command+A (Mac OS) to deselect the text to view the fill and stroke effect.

Original drop cap (left), drop cap with color fill (middle), and drop cap with fill and stroke (right).

8   Close the Stroke panel, and then save the file.

Adjusting the drop cap alignment

You can adjust the alignment of the drop cap letters as well as the scale the size of the drop cap if there is a descender such as a "y" using the Drop Cap options. In this section, you'll adjust the drop cap so that it aligns better to the left hand margin.

1   With the Type tool (T)selected, click an insertion point anywhere in the first paragraph with the drop cap. In the Control panel, at the far right, click the panel menu pop-up ( ), and choose Drop Caps and Nested Styles.

2   Click Align Left Edge to move the drop cap so that it aligns better to the left edge. Then click OK.

Before and after left alignment

Adjusting letter and word spacing

You can change the spacing between words and letters using InDesign's kerning and tracking features. You can also control the overall spacing of text in a paragraph by using the single-line or paragraph composers.

Adjusting the kerning and tracking

With InDesign, you can control the space between letters by using the kerning and tracking features. Kerning is the process of adding or subtracting space between specific letter pairs. Tracking is the process of creating an equal amount of spacing across a range of letters. You can use both kerning and tracking on the same text.

Here you'll manually kern some letters in the drop cap. Then you'll track the heading "Northwest Tour Group Partnership."

1   To distinguish the amount of space between letters more easily and to see the results of the kerning more clearly, select the Zoom tool (🔍) in the Tools panel and drag a marquee around the word with drop caps.

2   If necessary, increase the zoom level in the magnification menu in the lower left corner of the Document window.

3   Select the Type tool (T) and click an insertion point between the "h" and "e" in the drop cap word.

4   Press Alt+Left Arrow (Windows) or Option+Left Arrow (Mac OS) to move the letter "e" to the left. Press this key combination repeatedly until the two adjacent letters look visually pleasing to you. We pressed it twice.

Now we'll add additional space between the drop cap and the four lines of the paragraph next to it.

5   Click an insertion point on the first line in front of the word "key." Press Alt+Right Arrow (Windows) or Option+Right Arrow (Mac OS) to move the top four lines of text to the right. Press this key combination repeatedly until the space looks visually pleasing to you. We pressed it six times.

Before and after kerning changes.

Now you'll set a tracking value for the entire heading "The Northeast Tour Group Partnership" to condense the overall spacing. To set tracking, you must first select the entire range of characters you want to track.

6 Choose View > Fit Page in Window to view the whole page on-screen.

7 With the Type tool (T), click four times on "The Northeast Tour Group Partnership" to select the entire heading.

8 In the Control panel, click the Character Formatting Controls button (A), then enter **-15** for Tracking (A V) and press Enter or Return.

The heading after tracking is applied.

Now you'll use a keyboard shortcut to deselect the text.

9 Press Shift+Ctrl+A (Windows) or Shift+Command+A (Mac OS).

10 Press Ctrl+1 (Windows) or Command+1 (Mac OS) to return to a 100% view.

Note: The characters on the number pad do not always mirror the numbers at the top of the keyboard, especially when used in keyboard shortcuts. For instance, in the above step, Ctrl+1 or Command+1 from the number pad does nothing.

11 Save the file.

Applying the paragraph and single-line composers

The density of a paragraph (sometimes called its color) is determined by the composition method used. When composing text, InDesign considers the word spacing, letter spacing, glyph scaling, and hyphenation options you've selected, and then evaluates and chooses the best line breaks. InDesign provides two options for composing text: the paragraph composer, which looks at all the lines in the paragraph, or the single-line composer, which looks separately at each individual line.

When you use the paragraph composer, InDesign composes a line by considering the impact on the other lines in the paragraph; in the end, the best overall arrangement of the paragraph is established. As you change type in a given line, previous and subsequent lines in the same paragraph may break differently, making the overall paragraph appear more evenly spaced. When you use the single-line composer, which is the standard for other layout and word-processing programs, only the lines following the edited text are recomposed.

The text in this lesson was composed using the default, the Adobe Paragraph Composer. To see the difference between the two, you'll recompose the pull-quote text using the single-line composer.

1   Using the Type tool (T), click an insertion point in the pull-quote text on page 1.

2   Choose Type > Paragraph, then choose Adobe Single-line Composer from the Paragraph panel menu (▾≡).

The single-line composer looks at each line individually and, consequently, can make some lines in a paragraph appear more dense or sparse than others.

Because the paragraph composer looks at multiple lines at once, it makes the density of the lines in a paragraph more consistent.

3 From the Paragraph panel menu, choose Adobe Paragraph Composer. Notice that the lines of text now have a consistent density and all the text fits neatly in the text frame.

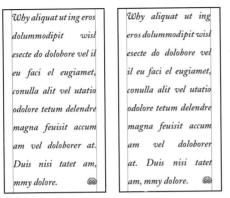

Pull-quote formatted using the Adobe Single-line Composer (left), and the Adobe Paragraph Composer (right).

4 Choose File > Save to save your file.

Working with tabs

You can use tabs to position text in specific horizontal locations in a frame. Using the Tabs panel, you can organize text and create tab leaders, indents, and hanging indents. Here you'll format the information at the top of page 2 using the Tabs panel. The tab markers have already been entered in the text, so all you will be doing is setting the final location of the text.

1 If necessary, scroll to the top of page 2 until the table appears on-screen.

2 To view the tab markers in the table, choose Type > Show Hidden Characters, and make sure that Normal View Mode (⊞) is selected in the Tools panel. If you decide not to keep them showing as you work, choose Type > Hide Hidden Characters.

3 Using the Type tool (T), click in the word "Category" at the top of the table.

4 Choose Type > Tabs to open the Tabs panel. When an insertion point is in a text frame and there is enough space at the top of the frame, the Tabs panel snaps to the border of the frame so that the measurements in the panel's ruler exactly match the text.

5   To center the page on your screen, double-click the page 2 icon in the Pages panel. Because the Tabs panel moves independently of the table, the two may no longer be aligned.

6   If the tabs panel is not aligned to the text frame, Ccick the magnet icon ( ) in the Tabs panel to realign the panel with the text.

Clicking the magnet icon in the Tabs panel aligns the ruler with the selected text.

Note: *If the Tabs panel did not snap to the text frame, part of the text block may be hidden from view, or there may not be enough room for the Tabs panel between the text frame and the top of the document window. Scroll as necessary, and then click the magnet icon ( ) again.*

7   Using the Type tool, select all of the text in the table's text frame, from the word "Category" to the number "$110,000."

8   In the Tabs panel, click the Center-Justified Tab button ( ) so that when you set the new tab positions, they will align from the center.

9   In the Tabs panel, position the pointer in the top portion of the ruler, just above the numbers, and then click to set tab markers at the following locations: 24, 29, 34, 40, and 45. You can view the location of the pointer on the ruler in the X: text box (above the left side of the ruler). To precisely set the value, drag in the ruler while watching the X value before releasing the mouse button, or type the value directly into the X value of the Tabs panel.

The value in the X: text box indicates the location of the selected tab.

Note: *If you don't get the tab locations correct the first time, you can select the tab in the ruler and type the location in the X value. You can also click on a tab in the Tabs panel and drag up to remove a tab.*

10 Press Shift+Ctrl+A (Windows) or Shift+Command+A (Mac OS) to deselect the text and view the new tab settings.

THE TOUR PACKAGES IN TravelNE's ANNUAL OFFERINGS ARE DISTRIBUTED ACROSS THESE MAJOR CATEGORIES:						
CATEGORY		UNITS	SOLD	% OF SALES	2003	2004
Fall Foliage ME, NH, VT, MA, CT, RI		400	350	47	$175,000	$185,000
Winter Wonderland ME, NH, VT, MA, CT		250	225	35	$120,0000	$122,000
Romantic Getaway ME, NH, VT		187	135	18	$81,000	$110,000

Now you'll set a tab leader for some of the tabs.

11 Select all the text in the table from "Fall" to "$110,000."

12 In the Tabs panel, click the first tab arrow along the ruler to select it so that the leader you create will affect any selected tabs at that tab marker.

13 In the Leader text box, type ._ (period, space) and press Enter or Return. You can use any character as a tab leader. We used a space between periods to create a more open dot sequence.

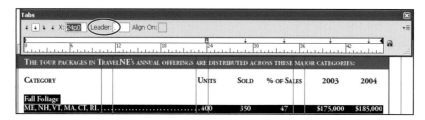

14 Deselect the table text and view the leaders.

Creating a hanging indent

Now you'll use the Tabs panel to create hanging indents. The text frame for this table has an inset value of 6 points at the top and 9 points on the sides and bottom. (To see the inset values, select the text and choose Object > Text Frame Options.) An inset sets the text apart from the frame; now you'll set it apart even more by indenting the three categories in the table.

You can set an indent in the Tabs panel or the Control panel. You'll keep the Control panel visible so you can see how the values change there, too.

1 Make sure that the Control panel is visible. If necessary, select Window > Control.

2 In the table, use the Type tool (T) to select all the text from "Fall" to "$110,000."

3 Make sure that the Tabs panel is still aligned directly above the table. If it has moved, click the magnet icon (🧲).

4 In the Tabs panel, drag the bottom indent marker on the left side of the ruler to the right until the X value is 2p0. Dragging the bottom marker moves both at once. Notice how all the text shifts to the right and the indent option in the Paragraph panel changes to 2p0. Keep the text selected.

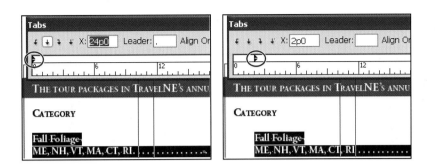

Now you'll bring just the category headings back to their original location in the table to create a hanging indent.

5   In the Tabs panel, drag the top half of the indent marker to the left until the X value is -2p0. Deselect the text and view the hanging indent.

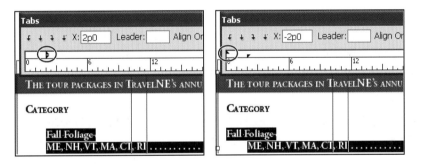

6   Close the Tabs panel and save the file.

Note: You can also create tables of information using the Table menu and Table panel. For more information, see Lesson 9, "Creating Tables."

Adding a rule below a paragraph

You can also add a rule, or line, above or below a paragraph. Here you'll add a rule under the table headings.

1   Using the Type tool (T), click an insertion point in the word Category in the table.

2   Click the Paragraph Formatting Controls button (¶) in the Control panel. From the Panel menu (▾≡) at the far right side of the Control panel, choose Paragraph Rules.

3   In the Paragraph Rules dialog box, choose Rule Below from the menu at the top of the dialog box, and then select Rule On to activate the rule.

4   To view the rule as you select your options, select Preview and move the dialog box so that it is not obstructing your view of the heading.

5   For Weight, choose 1 pt; for Color, choose Reflex Blue; for Width, choose Column; and for Offset, type **0p9**. Then click OK.

You see a blue rule under the type.

THE TOUR PACKAGES IN TravelNE's ANNUAL OFFERINGS ARE DISTRIBUTED ACROSS THESE MAJOR CATEGORIES:						
CATEGORY			UNITS	SOLD	% OF SALES	2003	2004
Fall Foliage ME, NH, VT, MA, CT, RI 400				350	47	$175,000	$185,000
Winter Wonderland ME, NH, VT, MA, CT 250				225	35	$120,0000	$122,000
Romantic Getaway ME, NH, VT. 187				135	18	$81,000	$110,000

6 Save the file.

Congratulations, you have finished the lesson.

Exploring on your own

Now that you have learned the basics of formatting text in an InDesign document, you're ready to apply these skills on your own. Try the following tasks to improve your typography skills.

1   Click your cursor within various paragraphs and experiment with enabling and disabling hyphenation from the Paragraph panel. Select a hyphenated word and choose No Break from the Character panel menu to individually stop a word from hyphenating.

2   Click your cursor within the body copy and choose Edit > Edit in Story Editor. Make some edits to the text and then select Edit > Edit in Layout. Notice how the edits made in the story editor are reflected back in the layout. Explore the formatting and editing commands that are available while working in the Story Editor.

3   Apply Optical Margin Alignment to each paragraph in the main story (everything except the pull-quotes and tables). You can access the Optical Margin Alignment feature by choosing the Story command in the Type menu. Optical Margin Alignment—the text visually aligns along the edges of the text frame, allowing some of the text, such as punctuation and quotation marks, to be positioned outside of the text frame.

Review

▶ **Review questions**

1   How do you view a baseline grid?

2   When and where do you use a flush space?

3   What is the difference between the paragraph composer and the single-line composer?

▶ **Review answers**

1   To view a baseline grid, choose View > Grids & Guides > Show Baseline Grid. The current document view must be at or above the View Threshold set in the Baseline Grid preferences. By default, that value is 75%.

2   You use a flush space on justified text. For example, if used with a special character or decorative font at the end of a paragraph, it absorbs any extra space in the last line.

3   The paragraph composer evaluates multiple lines at once when determining the best possible line breaks. The single-line composer looks at only one line at a time when determining line breaks.

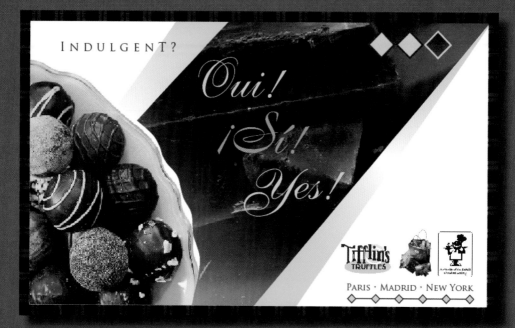

INDULGENT?

Oui!
¡Si!
Yes!

Tifflin's TRUFFLES

PARIS · MADRID · NEW YORK

You can create, save and apply process and spot colors, including tints, mixed inks, and blended gradients.

When your document must meet color standards set by clients and designers, viewing and editing color consistently becomes critical, from scanning source images to creating final output. A color management system reconciles color differences among devices so that you can be reasonably certain of the colors your system ultimately produces.

6 | Working with Color

In this introduction to working with colors and color management, you'll learn how to do the following:

- Add colors to the Swatches panel.
- Apply colors to objects.
- Create dashed strokes.
- Create and apply a gradient swatch.
- Adjust the direction of the gradient blend.
- Create a tint.
- Create a spot color.
- Specify a color management engine.
- Specify default source ICC profiles.
- Assign ICC profiles in InDesign CS3.
- Embed ICC profiles in graphics created in other Adobe programs.

Getting started

In this lesson, you'll work on and set up color management for an advertisement for a fictitious chocolate company called Tifflins Truffles. Color management is important in environments where you must evaluate image color reliably in the context of your final output. Color correction is a different issue that involves images with tonal or color-balance problems, and is usually handled in the original graphics application, such as Photoshop CS3.

The ad will run in a variety of publications, so getting consistent and predictable color is your goal. You will set up the color management system using a CMYK press-oriented workflow, build the document using graphics from other Adobe products, and specify ICC profiles for individual graphics to ensure color integrity.

The ad consists of graphics created in InDesign CS3 and other Adobe applications. You will color-manage those graphics to achieve consistent color output from InDesign CS3.

Note: If you have not already copied the resource files for this lesson onto your hard disk from the Adobe InDesign CS3 Classroom in a Book *CD, do so now. See "Copying the Classroom in a Book files" on page 4.*

1   To ensure that the tools and panels function exactly as described in this lesson, delete or reset the InDesign CS3 defaults preferences following the procedure in "Saving, deleting and restoring preference files" on page 2.

2   Start Adobe InDesign CS3.

3   Choose File > Open, and open the 06_a.indd file in the Lesson_06 folder, located inside the Lessons folder within the InDesignCIB folder on your hard disk

4   Choose File > Save As, rename the file **06_Color.indd**, and save it in the Lesson_06 folder.

Note: This lesson is designed for users who work with InDesign CS3 in environments that also involve Adobe Illustrator (version 9 or later) and Adobe Photoshop (version 5 or later). If you do not have those programs installed on your computer, you will skip some of these step-by-step instructions for color-managing graphics from Illustrator and Photoshop.

5 If you want to see what the finished document will look like, open the 06_b.indd file in the same folder. You can leave this document open to act as a guide as you work. When you're ready to resume working on the lesson document, choose its name from the Window menu.

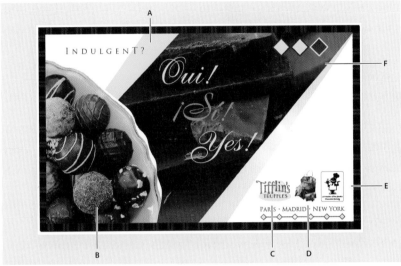

A. InDesign CS3 object. B. Legacy (archived) CMYK file.
C. Illustrator file exported as a bitmap. D. Legacy (archived) CMYK file
E. Adobe Illustrator file F. Photoshop PSD file.

Note: As you work through the lesson, feel free to move panels around or change the magnification to a level that works best for you. For more information, see "Changing the magnification of a document" and "Using the Navigator panel" in Lesson 1.

Defining printing requirements

It's a good idea to know printing requirements before you start working on a document. For example, meet with your prepress service provider and discuss your document's design and use of color. Because your prepress service provider understands the capabilities of their equipment, they may suggest ways for you to save time and money, increase quality, and avoid potentially costly printing or color problems. The magazine article used in this lesson was designed to be printed by a commercial printer using the CMYK color model.

Adding colors to the Swatches panel

You can add color to objects using a combination of panels and tools. The InDesign CS3 color workflow revolves around the Swatches panel. Using the Swatches panel to name colors makes it easy to apply, edit, and update colors for objects in a document. Although you can also use the Color panel to apply colors to objects, there is no quick way to update these colors, called unnamed colors. Instead, you'd have to update the color of each object individually.

You'll now create most of the colors you'll use in this document. Because this document is intended for a commercial press, you'll be creating CMYK process colors.

1   Make sure that no objects are selected, and then click the Swatches panel tab. (If the Swatches panel is not visible, choose Window > Swatches.)

The Swatches panel stores the colors that have been preloaded into InDesign CS3, as well as the colors, tints, and gradients you create and store for reuse.

2   Choose New Color Swatch from the Swatches panel menu (▾≡).

3   Deselect Name With Color Value, and for Swatch Name, type **Brown**. Make sure that Color Type and Color Mode are set to Process and CMYK, respectively.

The Name With Color Value option names a color using the CMYK color values that you enter, and automatically updates the name if you change the value. This option is available only for process colors and is useful when you want to use the Swatches panel to monitor the exact composition of process-color swatches. For this swatch, you deselected the Name With Color Value option, so that you can use a name (Brown) that's easier to read for this lesson.

4   For the color percentages, type the following values: C = **0**, M = **76**, Y = **76**, K = **60**, and then click Add to keep the dialog open and make two more colors.

5   Repeat the previous three steps to name and create the following colors:

	C	M	Y	K
Blue	60	20	0	0
Tan	2	13	29	0

If you forget to type the name for a color or if you type an incorrect value, double-click the swatch, change the name or value, and then click OK.

New colors added to the Swatches panel are stored only with the document in which they are created. You'll apply these colors to text, graphics, and frames in your document.

Applying colors to objects

There are three general steps to applying a swatch color: (1) selecting the text or object, (2) selecting the stroke or fill in the Tools panel, depending on what you want to change, and (3) selecting the color in the Swatches panel. You can also drag swatches from the Swatches panel to objects.

1   Choose the Selection tool (➤), and click in any one of the diamond shapes at the top right of the page to select it.

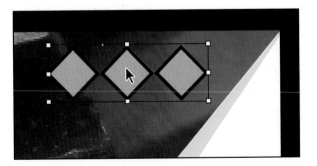

Notice that these three objects are grouped, so all are now selected. You will ungroup these objects and lock them in place. Locking objects prevents you from accidentally moving them.

2   With the group of objects still selected, choose Object > Ungroup and then choose Object > Lock Position.

3   Deselect the objects. To deselect an object, you can choose Edit > Deselect All, you can click a blank area in your document window, or you can press Shift+Ctrl+A (Windows) or Shift+Command+A (Mac OS).

4   Choose the Zoom tool (🔍) in the Tools panel and drag to draw a marquee around the diamonds. The view magnification changes so that the area defined by the marquee now fills the document window. Make sure that you can see all three diamond shapes.

💡 *To fine-tune the zoom magnification, you can press Ctrl+= (Windows) or Command+= (Mac OS). To zoom out, you can press Ctrl+- (Windows) or Command+- (Mac OS).*

5   Choose the Selection tool (▶), and click in the middle diamond to select it. Select the Stroke box (⬚) in the Tools panel, and then click the Green swatch in the Swatches panel (you may need to scroll down the list of swatches).

The stroke of the diamond shape is now green.

6   Deselect the object.

7   Click the left diamond to select it. Select Brown in the Swatches panel to apply a brown stroke.

8   With the left diamond still selected, choose the Fill box (◼) in the Tools panel, and select Green in the Swatches panel (you may need to scroll down the list of swatches).

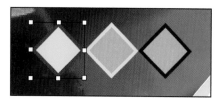

The right diamond requires the same Brown stroke and Green fill. You'll use the eyedropper to copy the stroke and fill attributes from the left diamond in one quick step.

9 Select the Eyedropper tool (✐), and click the left diamond. Notice that the eyedropper is now filled (🖋), indicating that it picked up the attributes from the clicked object.

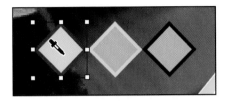

10 With the filled Eyedropper tool, click the gray background of the rightmost diamond. The right diamond takes on the left diamond's fill and stroke attributes.

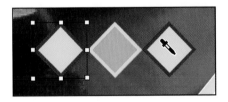

Now you'll change the color of the middle diamond.

11 Choose the Selection tool, and then deselect the objects.

12 Using the Selection tool, click the middle diamond to select it. Select the Fill box in the Tools panel, and then click [Paper] in the Swatches panel.

[Paper] is a special color that simulates the paper color on which you're printing. Objects behind a paper-colored object won't print where the paper-colored object overlaps them. Instead, the color of the paper on which you print shows through.

13 Choose Edit > Deselect All.

Now you'll stroke the 6 small diamonds and line at the bottom of the ad with brown.

14 Using the Selection tool, hold down the Shift key and select the six small diamonds on the bottom of the ad as well as the line behind them.

15 In the swatches panel, select the Stroke box (◳) and click the Brown swatch in the Swatches panel.

Creating dashed strokes

You'll now change the black line that borders the ad to a custom dashed line. Because you will be using the custom dashed line on only one object, you will create it using the Stroke panel. If you need to save a stroke for repetitive use throughout a document, you can easily create a stroke style. For more information about saving Stroke styles, including dashes, dots, and stripes, see InDesign Help, "To define custom stroke styles."

1 Deselect any selected objects and Zoom out to fit window. Choose the Selection tool (➤) and select the black outline that borders the ad.

2 If the Stroke panel is not already visible, choose Window > Stroke or click on it's tab in the dock.

3 For Type, select Dashed.

Six dash and gap boxes appear at the bottom of the Stroke panel. To create a dashed line, you specify the length of the dash, and then the gap, or spacing, between the dashes.

4   Type the following values in the Dash and Gap boxes: **16**, **4**, **2**, **4** (press Tab after you type each value to move to the next box). Leave the last two dash and gap boxes empty.

5   Select Brown from the Gap Color to fill the gap with brown.

6   Deselect the line and close the Stroke panel. Then choose File > Save.

Working with gradients

A gradient is a graduated blend between two or more colors, or between tints of the same color. You can create either a linear or a radial gradient.

A. Linear gradient.   *B. Radial gradient.*

Creating and applying a gradient swatch

Every InDesign CS3 gradient has at least two color stops. By editing the color mix of each stop and by adding additional color stops in the Gradient panel, you can create your own custom gradients.

1   Make sure no objects are selected, and choose New Gradient Swatch from the Swatches panel menu (⯯☰).

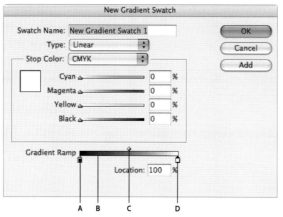

A. Left stop. B. Gradient bar. C. Ramp slider. D. Right stop.

Gradients are defined by a series of color stops in the gradient bar. A stop is the point at which a gradient changes from one color to the next and is identified by a square below the gradient bar.

2   For Swatch Name, type **Brown/Tan Gradient**.

3   Click the left stop marker (⬠). For Stop Color, select Swatches, and then scroll down the list of color swatches and select Brown.

Notice that the left side of the gradient ramp is brown.

4   Click the right stop marker. For Stop Color, select Swatches, and then scroll down the list and select Tan.

The gradient ramp shows a color blend between brown and tan.

5   Click OK.

Now you'll apply the gradient to the fill of the middle diamond in the upper right hand corner.

6   Zoom in on the upper right hand corner, bringing the three diamond shapes into view.

7   Use the Selection tool (▸), to select the middle diamond.

8   Select the Fill box (■) in the Tools panel, and then click Brown/Tan Gradient in the Swatches panel.

Adjusting the direction of the gradient blend

Once you have filled an object with a gradient, you can modify the gradient by using the Gradient tool to "repaint" the fill along an imaginary line you drag. This tool lets you change the direction of a gradient and change the beginning point and endpoint of a gradient. You'll now change the direction of the gradient.

1 Make sure the middle diamond is still selected, and then select the Gradient Swatch tool (□) in the Tools panel.

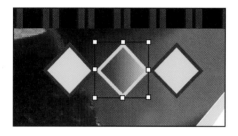

Now you'll experiment with the Gradient tool to see how you can change the direction and intensity of the gradient.

2 To create a more gradual gradient effect, place the pointer outside the selected diamond and drag across and past it.

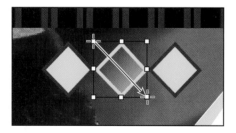

When you release the mouse button, you'll notice that the blend between brown and tan is more gradual than it was before you dragged the Gradient tool.

3 To create a sharper gradient, drag a small line in the center of the diamond. Continue to experiment with the Gradient tool so that you understand how it works.

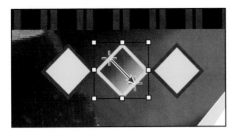

4 When you have finished experimenting, drag from the top corner of the diamond to the bottom corner. That's how you'll leave the gradient of the middle diamond.

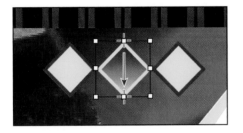

5 Choose File > Save.

Creating a tint

In addition to adding colors, you can also add tints to the Swatches panel. A tint is a screened (lighter) version of a color. You'll now create a 30% tint of the brown swatch you saved earlier in this lesson.

Tints are helpful because InDesign CS3 maintains the relationship between a tint and its parent color. For example, if you changed the brown color swatch to a different color, the tint swatch you create in this procedure would become a lighter version of the new color.

1 Deselect all objects.

2 Choose View > Fit Page in Window to center the page in the document window.

3   Click Brown in the Swatches panel. Choose New Tint Swatch from the Swatches panel menu (▾☰). For Tint percentage, type **30** and then click OK.

The new tint swatch appears at the bottom of the list of swatches. The top of the Swatches panel displays information about the selected swatch, with a Fill/Stroke box showing that the brown tint is currently the selected fill color and a Tint option showing that the color is 30% of the original Brown color.

4   Use the Selection tool (▸), to click the outlined text "¡Sí!" in the center of the page to select it.

5   Make sure the Fill box (■₁) is selected, and then click the Brown tint that you just created in the Swatches panel; notice the color change.

About spot and process colors

A spot color is a special premixed ink that is used instead of, or in addition to, CMYK process inks, and that requires its own printing plate on a printing press. Use spot color when few colors are specified and color accuracy is critical. Spot color inks can accurately reproduce colors that are outside the gamut of process colors. However, the exact appearance of the printed spot color is determined by the combination of the ink as mixed by the commercial printer and the paper it's printed on, not by color values you specify or by color management. When you specify spot color values, you're describing the simulated appearance of the color for your monitor and composite printer only (subject to the gamut limitations of those devices).

A process color is printed using a combination of the four standard process inks: cyan, magenta, yellow, and black (CMYK). Use process colors when a job requires so many colors that using individual spot inks would be expensive or impractical, as when printing color photographs.

- For best results in a high-quality printed document, specify process colors using CMYK values printed in process color reference charts, such as those available from a commercial printer.

- The final color values of a process color are its values in CMYK, so if you specify a process color using RGB (or LAB, in InDesign), those color values will be converted to CMYK when you print color separations. These conversions differ based on your color-management settings and document profile.

- Don't specify a process color based on how it looks on your monitor, unless you are sure you have set up a color-management system properly, and you understand its limitations for previewing color.

- Avoid using process colors in documents intended for online viewing only, because CMYK has a smaller color gamut than that of a typical monitor.

Sometimes it's practical to use process and spot inks in the same job. For example, you might use one spot ink to print the exact color of a company logo on the same pages of an annual report where photographs are reproduced using process color. You can also use a spot color printing plate to apply a varnish over areas of a process color job. In both cases, your print job would use a total of five inks—four process inks and one spot ink or varnish.

—From InDesign Help

Creating a spot color

This ad will be printed by a commercial printer using the standard CMYK color model, which requires four separate plates for printing—one each for cyan, magenta, yellow, and black. However, the CMYK color model has a limited range of colors, which is where spot colors come in handy. Because of this, spot colors are used to create additional colors beyond the range of CMYK or to create consistent, individual colors such as those used for company logos.

In this ad, the design calls for a spot ink not found in the CMYK color model. You'll now add a spot color from a color library.

1   Deselect all objects.

2   In the Swatches panel menu (▾☰), select New Color Swatch.

3   In the New Color Swatch dialog box, select Spot on the Color Type pop-up menu.

4   In Color Mode, select PANTONE solid coated.

5   In the PANTONE C text box, type **567** to automatically scroll the list of Pantone swatches to the color you want for this project, which is PANTONE 567 C.

6   Click OK. The spot color is added to your Swatches panel. Notice the icon (◉) next to the color name in the Swatches panel. This icon indicates that it is a spot color.

Note: The color you see on your monitor does not reflect the actual printed color. To determine the color you want to use, look at a chart provided by the color system, such as a PANTONE Color Formula Guide, or an ink chart obtained from your printer. Each spot color you create generates an additional spot-color plate for the press. In general, commercial printers typically produce either 2-color, using black and one spot color, or 4-color CMYK work with the possibility of adding one or more spot colors. Using spot colors generally increases your printing costs. It is a good idea to consult with your printer before using spot colors in your document.

Applying color to text

As with graphics, you can apply a stroke or fill to text itself. You'll apply colors to the text on the top and bottom of the document.

1   Choose the Selection tool (➤), click the word "Indulgent?" then hold down the shift key and click the text "Paris • Madrid • New York" to select.

2   In the Tools panel, make sure the Fill box (▇) is selected and then click the small "T" icon (the Formatting affects text button) in the row below the Fill box.

3   In the Swatches panel, click PANTONE 567 C, and then click a blank area to deselect. The text now appears in the spot color.

4   Choose File > Save.

Applying colors to additional objects

Now you'll apply the same color used by the outlined text "Yes!" to color the outlined text "Oui!" First you'll magnify the view of the outlined text "Yes!" to see which color is used.

1   In the Tools panel, choose the Zoom tool (🔍), and then drag to place a marquee around the outlined text in the middle of the page.

2 Select the Direct Selection tool ( ), and then click on the outlined text "Yes!" to select. Notice that the corresponding swatch in the Swatches panel becomes highlighted when you select the object to which the swatch is applied.

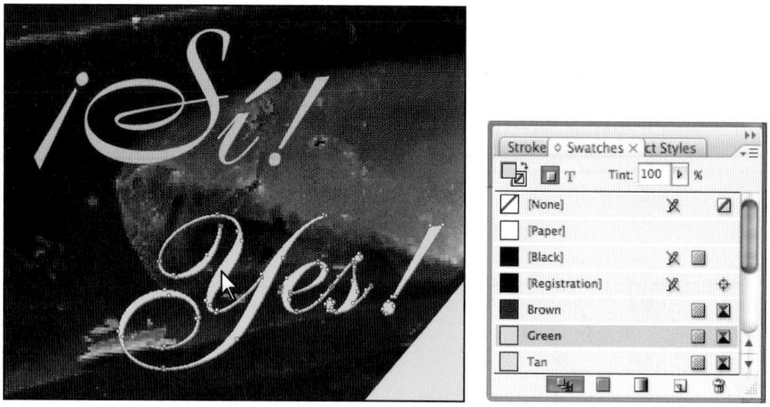

Now you'll apply this color to the outlined text "Oui!"

3 Drag the Green fill swatch from the Swatches panel to the outlined text "Oui!" Be sure to drop it inside the object and not on the object's stroke. The cursor will change to an arrow with a black box ( ) when you drop the swatch onto the fill of the outlined text. An arrow with a line to the right ( ) will appear if you drag the swatch onto the stroke of the outlined text. Make sure that the Tint in the Swatches panel is 100%.

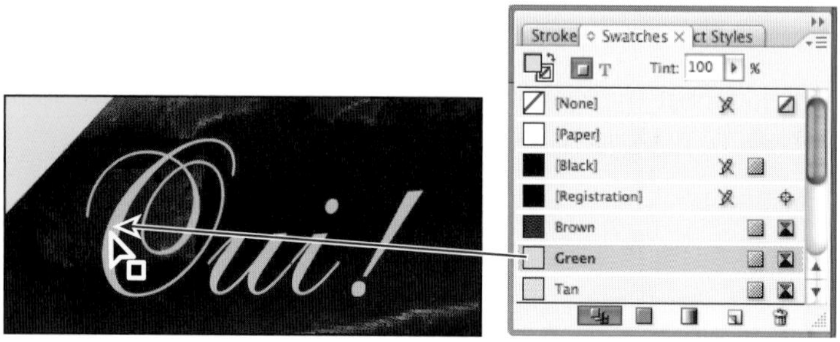

Dragging and dropping can be a more convenient way to apply color, because you don't have to select the object first.

If you applied the color to the wrong object, choose Edit > Undo Apply Attribute and try again.

Creating another tint

You'll now create a tint based on the Blue color. When you edit the Blue color, the tint that is based on the color will also change.

1 Deselect all objects.

2 Click Blue in the Swatches panel. Choose New Tint Swatch from the Swatches panel menu (▾☰). Type **40** in the Tint box, and then click OK.

3 Choose the Selection tool (➤) and select the outlined text "¡Si!" shown below and apply the Blue 40% fill.

Next you'll change the Blue color. Blue 40% is based on the Blue swatch, so the tint will also change.

4 Deselect all objects.

5 Double-click Blue (not the Blue tint) to change the color. For Swatch Name, type **Violet Blue**. For the color percentages, type the following values: C = **59**, M = **80**, Y = **40**, K = **0**. Click OK.

Notice that the color change affects all objects to which Blue and Blue 40% were applied. As you can see, adding colors to the Swatches panel makes it easy to update colors in multiple objects.

6 Choose File > Save.

Using advanced gradient techniques

Earlier you created and applied a gradient and adjusted its direction using the Gradient tool. InDesign CS3 also lets you create gradients of multiple colors, and control the point at which the colors blend. In addition, you can apply a gradient to individual objects or to a collection of objects.

Creating a gradient swatch with multiple colors

Earlier in this lesson, you created a gradient with two colors—brown and tan. Now you'll create a gradient with three stops so that a yellow/green color on the outside will fade to white in the middle. Make sure that no objects are selected before you begin.

1   On the Swatches panel menu (▾≡), choose New Gradient Swatch, and then type **Green/White Gradient** for Swatch Name.

The colors from the previous blend appear in the dialog box.

2   Click the left stop marker (▲), select Swatches for Stop Color, and select the Green swatch in the list box. Click the right stop marker (▲), select Swatches for Stop Color, and select the Green swatch in the list box.

3   With the right stop marker still selected, choose CMYK from the Stop Color pop-up menu. Holding the Shift key down, drag the Yellow slider until the % value for Yellow is 40% and let go. The gradient ramp is now made up of light Green and Green. Now you'll add a stop marker to the middle so that the color fades toward the center.

4   Click just below the center of the gradient bar to add a new stop. For Location, type **50** to make sure the stop is centered.

5   For Stop Color, select CMYK and then drag each of the four color sliders to 0 (zero) to create white. You could also select Swatches and choose the Paper color to create a white color stop.

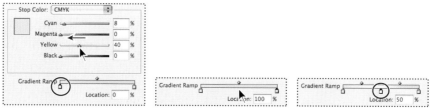

Edit Green stop on left.   Click to add new stop.   Change stop to white.

6   Click OK, and then choose File > Save.

Applying the gradient to an object

Now you'll apply the new gradient fill you just created. First, change the view size so that you can see the entire page.

1 Choose View > Fit Page in Window or double-click on Hand tool (🖑) in the Tools panel to achieve the same result.

2 With the Selection tool (⬏) chosen, click on the yellowish-green stripe on the right side of the chocolate picture to select it. Select the Fill box (◼) in the Tools panel, and then select Green/White Gradient in the Swatches panel. Select the Stroke box (◻) in the Tools panel, and then click the None button (⊘) at the bottom of the Tools panel.

3 To create a sharper gradient, select the Gradient Swatch tool (◼) in the Tools panel and drag up across the center of the gradient.

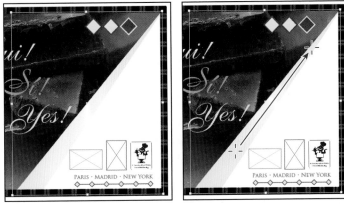

The Green/White gradient applied   *Edit the gradient with the Gradient tool.*

4 Choose Edit > Deselect All, then choose File > Save.

Applying a gradient to multiple objects

Previously in this lesson, you used the Gradient tool to change the direction of a gradient, and to change the gradient's beginning point and end point. You'll now use the Gradient tool to apply a gradient across multiple objects in the three diamond shapes on the bottom of the page.

1 Double-click the Hand tool (🖑) to fit page to window.

2   Choose the Selection tool (➤), and then click on the left diamond shape below the "Paris • Madrid • New York" text to select it, then while holding the Shift key, select the other five diamond shapes.

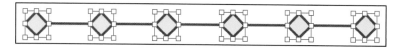

Now you'll apply the Green/White Gradient to the six different diamond objects.

3   Confirm that the Fill box (◖▮) is selected in the Swatches panel, then click on the Apply last used gradient button in the Tools panel.

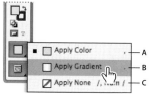

A. Apply last-used color.
B. Apply last-used gradient.
C. Remove color or gradient.

Now that the Fill box is set to the gradient and the Stroke box is set to none, the next object you draw will contain the gradient fill with no stroke.

Notice that the gradient affects each object on an individual basis. Now you'll use the Gradient tool to apply the gradient across the six selected objects as one.

4   With the six objects still selected, select the Gradient Swatch tool (◪) in the Tools panel. Drag an imaginary line as shown.

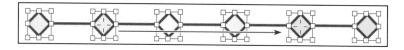

Now the gradient runs across all three selected objects.

5   Save the file by choosing File > Save.

Ensuring consistent color

Color management is important in environments where you must evaluate image color reliably in the context of your final output. Color correction is a different issue that involves images with tonal or color-balance problems, and is usually handled in the original graphics application, such as Photoshop.

Do you need color management?

You will benefit from a color management system if you need to accomplish any of the following:

• Get predictable and consistent color output on multiple output devices including color separations, your desktop printer, and your monitor. Color management is especially useful for adjusting color for devices with a relatively limited gamut, such as a four-color process printing press.

• Accurately soft-proof (preview) a color document on your monitor by making it simulate a specific output device. (Soft-proofing is subject to the limitations of monitor display, and other factors such as room lighting conditions.)

• Accurately evaluate and consistently incorporate color graphics from many different sources if they also use color management, and even in some cases if they don't.

• Send color documents to different output devices and media without having to manually adjust colors in documents or original graphics. This is valuable when creating images that will eventually be used both in print and online.

• Print color correctly to an unknown color output device; for example, you could store a document online for consistently reproducible on-demand color printing anywhere in the world

If you decide to use color management, consult with your production partners—such as graphic artists and prepress service providers—to ensure that all aspects of your color management workflow integrate with theirs.

Note: Don't confuse color management with color correction. A color management system won't correct an image that was saved with tonal or color balance problems. It provides an environment where you can evaluate images reliably in the context of your final output.

—From InDesign Help

Note: See also the "Color Management" section in the Contents in InDesign Help.

Color management: An overview

Devices and graphics have different color gamuts. Although all color gamuts overlap, they don't match exactly, which is why some colors on your monitor can't be reproduced in print or online. The colors that can't be reproduced in print are called out-of-gamut colors because they are outside the spectrum of printable colors. For example, you can create a large percentage of colors in the visible spectrum using programs such as InDesign CS3, Photoshop CS3, and Illustrator CS3, but you can reproduce only a subset of those colors on a desktop printer.

The printer has a smaller color space or gamut (the range of colors that can be displayed or printed) than the application that created the color.

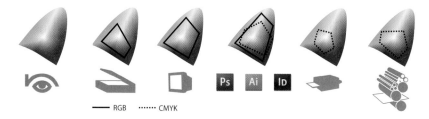

Visible spectrum containing millions of colors (far left) compared with color gamuts of various devices and graphics.

To compensate for these differences and to ensure the closest match between on-screen colors and printed colors, applications use a color management system (CMS). Using a color management engine, the CMS translates colors from the color space of one device into a device-independent color space, such as CIE (Commission Internationale d'Éclairage) LAB. From the device-independent color space, the CMS fits that color information to another device's color space by a process called color mapping, or gamut mapping. The CMS makes any adjustments necessary to represent the color consistently among devices.

A CMS uses three components to map colors across devices:

• A device-independent (or reference) color space.

• ICC profiles that define the color characteristics of different devices and graphics.

• A color management engine that translates colors from one device's color space to another's.

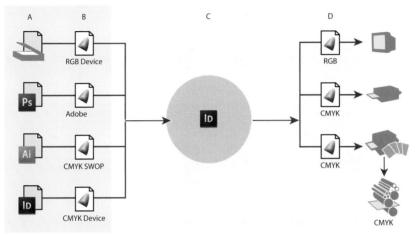

A. Scanners and software applications create color documents.
B. ICC source profiles describe document color spaces.
C. A color management engine uses ICC source profiles to map document colors to a device-independent color space through supporting applications.
D. The color management engine maps document colors from the device-independent color space to output-device color spaces using destination profiles.

About the device-independent color space

To successfully compare gamuts and make adjustments, a color management system must use a reference color space—an objective way of defining color. Most CMS use the CIE LAB color model, which exists independently of any device and is big enough to reproduce any color visible to the human eye. For this reason, CIE LAB is considered device-independent.

About ICC profiles

An ICC profile describes how a particular device or standard reproduces color using a cross-platform standard defined by the International Color Consortium (ICC).

ICC profiles ensure that images appear correctly in any ICC-compliant applications, and on color devices. This is accomplished by embedding the profile information in the original file or assigning the profile in your application.

At a minimum, you must have one source profile for the device (such as a scanner or digital camera) or standard (such as SWOP or Adobe RGB) used to create the color, and one destination profile for the device (such as monitor or contract proofing) or standard (SWOP or TOYO, for example) that you will use to reproduce the color.

About color management engines

Sometimes called the color matching module (CMM), the color management engine interprets ICC profiles. Acting as a translator, the color management engine converts the out-of-gamut colors from the source device to the range of colors that can be produced by the destination device. The color management engine may be included with the CMS or may be a separate part of the operating system.

Translating to a gamut—particularly a smaller gamut—usually involves a compromise, so multiple translation methods are available. For example, a color-translation method that preserves correct relationships among colors in a photograph will usually alter the colors in a logo. Color Management engines provide a choice of translation methods, known as rendering intents, so that you can apply a method appropriate to the intended use of a color graphic. Examples of common rendering intents include Perceptual (Images) for preserving color relationships the way the eye does, Saturation (Graphics) for preserving vivid colors at the expense of color accuracy, and Relative and Absolute Colorimetric for preserving color accuracy at the expense of color relationships.

Components of a CMYK press-oriented workflow

In a CMYK workflow, you work with CMYK images prepared for a specific printing press or proofing device, or legacy (archived) CMYK images. You generate a source profile based on your press or contract-proofing standard and embed it into the CMYK images or assign the profile in InDesign CS3. The profile enables consistent CMYK printing at other color-managed sites, such as when printing a widely distributed magazine on presses in many different cities. Because you use color management, the reliability and consistency of color display improves across all your workstations.

For final printed output, you select a printer profile in the Print dialog box that describes your contract-proofing standard or your printing press.

Setting up color management in InDesign CS3

No mechanical device can produce the full range of color visible to the human eye: no monitor, film, printer, copier, or printing press. Each device has a specific capability, so that different devices make different kinds of compromises in reproducing color images. The unique color-rendering abilities of a specific output device are known collectively as its gamut or color space.

InDesign CS3 and other graphics applications, such as Adobe Photoshop CS3, Adobe Illustrator CS3, and others, use color numbers to describe the color of each pixel in an image. The color numbers correspond to the color model, such as the familiar RGB values for red, green, and blue or the CMYK values for cyan, magenta, yellow, and black.

Color management is simply the designation of a consistent way of translating the color numbers for each pixel from the source (the document or image stored on your computer) to the output device (such as your monitor, color printer, or high-resolution printing press, each with its own specific gamut).

In an ICC workflow—that is, one that follows the conventions of the ICC—you specify a color management engine and a color profile. The color management engine is the software feature or module that does the work of reading and translating colors between different color spaces. A color profile is the description of how the color numbers map to the color space (capabilities) of output devices.

Adobe Creative Suite 3 applications give you easy-to-use color management features and tools that help achieve good, sellable color without the need to become a color management expert. With color management enabled out-of-the-box, you'll be able to view colors consistently across applications and platforms while ensuring more accurate color from edit to proof to final print.

A look at the Adobe Bridge

The Adobe Bridge application in Adobe Creative Suite 3 is a central location where users can select a color settings file with preset color management policies and default profiles. Selecting a Color Settings File (CSF) in Adobe Bridge ensures that color is handled consistently and that color displays and prints the same way from all Adobe Creative Suite 3 applications.

When users select a CSF, the file's preset values determine the color management behavior in all applications, such as how embedded profiles are handled, what the default RGB and CMYK working spaces are, and whether to display warning dialogs when embedded profiles don't match the default working space. Selecting the correct CSF depends on your workflow. For more information on the Adobe Bridge application, visit the Help and search for, "Adobe Bridge."

Specifying the Adobe ACE engine

Different companies have developed various ways to manage color. To provide you with a choice, you use a color management system to designate a color management engine that represents the approach you want to use. Remember that the color management engine translates colors from the source. InDesign CS3 offers the Adobe ACE engine as one of your choices. This engine uses the same architecture as in Photoshop and Illustrator, so that your color management choices are integrated across these Adobe graphics applications.

1   Choose Edit > Color Settings.

The color management engine and other settings you choose in the Color Settings dialog box are saved with InDesign CS3 and apply to all InDesign CS3 documents you work on in the future.

By default, color management in InDesign CS3 is enabled.

2 Select the North America Prepress 2 from the Settings pop-up menu if it's not chosen already.

3 Select the Advanced Mode check box.

4 Under Conversion Options in the lower part of the dialog box, select Adobe (ACE) in the Engine pop-up menu if it's not already chosen.

5 For Intent, select Perceptual from the pop-up menu. Later in this lesson, you'll explore the Intent options in more detail.

6 From the Color Management Policies, CMYK settings, choose Preserve Embedded Profiles from the pop-up menu.

7 Leave the dialog box open so you can use it in the next section.

Choose Adobe ACE unless your prepress service provider recommends another engine. Use the same engine throughout your workflow in Photoshop CS3, Illustrator CS3, Acrobat 8 and InDesign CS3.

Setting up default working spaces

To complete the application-wide color management setup, you'll choose profiles for the devices you will use to reproduce the color, including your monitor, composite proofing device, and final separations standard. InDesign CS3 refers to these preset profiles as working spaces. These working spaces are also available in other Adobe graphics applications, including Illustrator CS3 and Photoshop CS3. Once you designate the same working space in all three applications, then you've automatically set up consistent color for illustration, digital images, and document layouts.

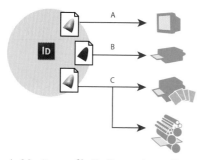

A. Monitor profile. B. Composite profile.
C. Separations profile (which can be an
output device or press standard, such as
SWOP or TOYO).

First, you'll select a monitor profile. If the Color Settings dialog box is not still open from the previous procedure, reopen it now.

1 Under Working Spaces, for CMYK select U.S. Web Coated (SWOP) v2 if it's not already chosen.

In a later section, you'll set the on-screen display of images to full resolution so that InDesign CS3 can color-manage all available image data.

2 Move the dialog box out of your way and study the colors in the ad.

Notice the heavy use of brown. You'll see a noticeable difference in the browns when you apply color management by closing the dialog box in the next step.

3 Click OK.

4 Choose View > Proof Colors. This will show soft-proof colors on your monitor. Depending upon your viewing conditions, this can give you a more accurate preview of how your image will print.

Several colors change in the ad, but most noticeably the browns; they appear to have more detail. It's important to note that although the images look better than they did when you opened the document, the images themselves have not been altered—only the display of the images has changed. Specifically, what you see now represents the color characteristics of the following devices:

- The program or scanner that saved the image, using the source profile embedded in the image.

- The final output device for the document, using the destination profile you set up earlier in the lesson.

It's easy to see that the success of color management ultimately depends on the accuracy of your profiles.

Assigning source profiles

Source profiles describe the color space InDesign CS3 uses when you create colors in InDesign CS3 and apply them to objects, or when you import an RGB, CMYK, or LAB color graphic that wasn't saved with an embedded profile. When you import an image with embedded profiles, InDesign CS3 will color-manage the image using the embedded profiles rather than the profiles you choose here, unless you override the embedded profiles for an individual image.

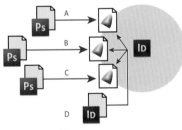

A. *LAB profile.*
B. *RGB profile.*
C. *CMYK profile.*
D. *InDesign CS3 document applying a profile that matches the color model of each image that lacks a profile.*

1   Choose Edit > Assign Profiles. In both the RGB Profile and CMYK Profile areas of the dialog box, select the Assign Current Working Space options which should be set to Adobe RGB (1998) and U.S. Web Coated (SWOP) v2, as shown.

Notice that the text following the words "working space" contains the same working-space information that you entered in the Color Settings dialog box. With these settings, the Adobe ACE engine won't unnecessarily convert colors for which you've already specified a profile.

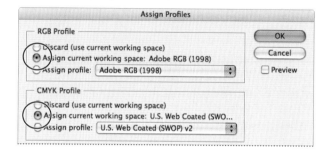

2   Leave the dialog box open so you can use it in the next section.

Specifying the rendering intent

The rendering intent determines how the color management engine converts colors, based on the source and destination profiles you specify in InDesign CS3. You'll specify the color-translation method for the InDesign CS3 color management engine to apply to the graphics in the advertisement.

1   In the lower area of the Assign Profiles dialog box, leave Relative Colorimetric selected for the Solid Color Intent option. This option preserves individual colors at the expense of color relationships, so it's appropriate for business logos and other such graphics.

Solid Color Intent:	Relative Colorimetric
Default Image Intent:	Use Color Settings Intent
After-Blending Intent:	Use Color Settings Intent

2   Make sure that Use Color Settings Intent is selected in both the Default Image Intent and After-Blending Intent options. These options are appropriate for this photo-intensive page spread.

3   Click OK to close the Assign Profiles dialog box, and then save your work.

Using full-resolution display with color management

When you use image-display resolutions lower than High Quality so that screen redraw is faster, image-color display is also made faster by displaying their colors less precisely. Image colors display most precisely when you view images at the fullest resolution (in addition to turning on color management).

Choose View > Display Performance > High Quality Display.

It's especially important to view color-managed images at full resolution when you work with duotones.

When color management is on, image display is set to full resolution, and you use accurate profiles that are applied properly, you see the best possible color representation that your monitor is capable of showing.

Note: To save disk space, the sample files for this lesson are 150 pixels per inch (ppi), so the colors are not as precise as they would be using a higher resolution.

Color-managing imported graphics in InDesign CS3

When you import a graphic, you can control its color management in your document. If you know that an imported graphic contains an accurate embedded profile with an appropriate rendering intent, you just import it and continue working. InDesign CS3 will read and apply the embedded profile to the graphic, integrating it into the CMS for the document. If an imported bitmap image does not include an embedded profile, InDesign CS3 applies the default source profile (CMYK, RGB, or LAB) to the image.

InDesign CS3 also applies a default source profile to InDesign CS3-drawn objects. You can assign a different profile within InDesign CS3—using Edit > Assign Profiles to open the Assign Profiles dialog box—or open the graphic in the original application and embed the profile there.

The ad already includes two images that were saved without embedded profiles. You'll integrate those images into the document CMS using two different methods: assigning a profile within InDesign CS3 and opening the original image so that you can embed the profile. Later in the lesson, you'll import two additional graphics and practice two methods of assigning a profile before you place them in the ad.

Assigning a profile after importing an image

When you import images that were saved without embedded profiles into InDesign CS3, InDesign CS3 applies its default source profile to the image. If an imported image was not created in the default color space, you should assign the profile that describes the image's original color space.

InDesign CS3 applies its default source profile to any bitmap image without embedded profiles.

You'll work with an image that was imported into InDesign CS3 before you turned on color management. First, you'll confirm the default profile InDesign CS3 is using to color-manage the image. Then, within InDesign CS3, you'll assign a new profile because the image's original color space is different from the default color space.

1 Using the Selection tool (➤), select the plate of truffles on the left side of the ad.

2 Choose Object > Image Color Settings.

Notice that Use Document Default is selected for Profile. InDesign CS3 enables color management for each imported image and assigns the default source profile you set up earlier in this lesson. You can also assign a new profile here. Because you are assigning the profile within InDesign CS3, the change will apply only to the selected image in this document.

3   For Profile, choose U.S. Sheetfed Coated v2 to match the image's original color space. This profile represents the color-lookup tables used by the scanner operator who originally scanned this as a CMYK image.

4   Leave the Rendering Intent set as Use Document Image Intent, and click OK. The colors deepen noticeably.

InDesign CS3 will color-manage the image using the newly assigned profile.

Embedding a profile in a Photoshop image

As a general rule, you should embed ICC profiles in files before importing the files into another document that uses color management. That way, images with embedded profiles will more likely appear as intended in InDesign CS3 or other color-managed programs without requiring any additional work.

In this section, you'll work with a previously imported, color bitmap image that does not contain an embedded profile.

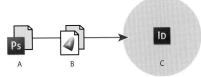

A. Image's working CMYK color space.
B. Image with embedded ICC profile.
C. InDesign CS3 uses embedded profile.

Note: *If you don't have Photoshop installed on your system, you can use the Photoshop files provided in the lesson folder. The steps indicate when to do so.*

Setting up color management in Photoshop CS3

First, you'll define the working color spaces (used for viewing and editing) for the image's RGB and CMYK color modes.

1   Start Photoshop, and choose Edit > Color Settings.

2   For Settings, select North America Prepress 2 on the pop-up menu. Click More Options to view all the selections available.

3   For the CMYK option under Working Spaces, select U.S. Web Coated (SWOP) v2, if it is not already selected, so that the embedded profile matches the default separations profile you specified in InDesign CS3.

4   Leave the other settings as they are, and click OK.

Embedding the profile

Now that you have specified the working color spaces for the Photoshop image, you'll embed the specified profile.

1 From Photoshop, choose File > Open and select 06_d.psd inside the Lesson_06 Folder.

2 In Photoshop, if the Missing Profile dialog box appears, select Assign Working CMYK. Notice that it is already set to U.S. Web Coated (SWOP) v2, which is the profile you selected in the previous procedure, "Setting up color management in Photoshop." Click OK. If you do not receive a Missing Profile warning, choose Image > Mode > Convert to Profile and choose U.S. Web Coated (SWOP) v2 as the Destination Profile and click OK.

3 To embed the profile, choose File > Save As. Select your Lesson_06 folder in your InDesignCIB folder, and then choose TIFF from the Format drop down menu. Type **06_dprof.tif** for File Name. Make sure that the ICC Profile: U.S. Web Coated (SWOP) v2 check box (Windows) or the Embed Color Profile: U.S. Web Coated (SWOP)v2 check box (Mac OS) is selected, and click Save.

4 In the TIFF Options dialog box, click OK to accept the default.

5 Close the image, exit Photoshop and return to InDesign CS3.

Updating the image within InDesign CS3

Now that you've embedded the ICC profile in the Photoshop file, you can update the image in InDesign CS3. InDesign CS3 will color-manage the image using the embedded profile.

1   In InDesign CS3, with the Selection tool (▶) double-click to select the large chocolate image.

2   Do one of the following:

• If you followed Photoshop instructions in the previous sections, click the Relink button (✸) at the bottom of the Links panel. Locate the 06_dprof.tif file you just saved in the Lesson_06 folder. Double-click the file.

Note: When relinking to a file using a different file format, you need to select All Files under the Files of Type pop-up menu when browsing for the file on the Windows operating system.

• If you don't have Photoshop, or skipped the previous two sections, click the Relink button (✸) at the bottom of the Links panel. Locate 06_dprof.psd in the Final folder. Double-click the file.

Note: You may need to select All Files for Files of Type.

3   To confirm that the embedded profile is being used, open the Links panel menu (choose Window > Links if the Links panel is not visible), select a file, and choose Link Information. In the Link Information dialog box, make sure that the Profile says U.S. Web Coated (SWOP) v2, and then click Done.

💡 *A quick way to check profiles for all graphics in a document is by using the Preflight feature to view document components. Another way to check for the profile is to select the graphic and open the Info panel.*

Now that you have fixed existing graphics in the document, you will finish the ad by importing two additional graphics and setting options as you import.

Assigning a profile while importing a graphic

If you know that a color-managed image uses a color space that is different from the color space described by the default source profile, you can assign a profile to it while you're importing the image into InDesign CS3. In this section, you'll import a legacy (archived) CMYK image scanned without a profile, and assign a profile before you place it in the ad.

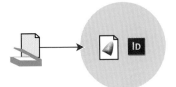

You can assign a profile while you import an image.

1   In InDesign CS3, choose View > Show Frame Edges to show the outline of the frame for the graphic you're about to place—and the outlines for all the graphics frames in the ad.

2   If necessary, adjust your view so that you can easily see the frames in the lower right area of the spread. Using the Selection tool (➤), select the tallest of these three frames.

3   Choose File > Place to open the Place dialog box, and do the following:

•   Open Lesson_06 folder in the InDesignCIB folder and select the 06_e.psd file.

•   Select the Show Import Options check box, so that you'll have an opportunity to specify a profile.

- Click Open.

4   In the Image Import Options dialog box, select the color button in the middle of the dialog box.

5   Select the following options:

- For Profile, select U.S. Sheetfed Coated v2 to match the image's original color space.

Note: If you selected a different profile in "Assigning a profile after importing an image," select the same profile here.

- For Rendering Intent, select Perceptual (Images).

- Click OK.

The image appears in the selected frame. InDesign CS3 will color-manage the image using the profile you assigned.

6   Choose Object > Fitting > Fit Content Proportionally if the image doesn't fit.

Embedding a profile in an Illustrator graphic

In this lesson, you'll set up Illustrator (version 9 or later) so that its color-management settings match InDesign CS3. You'll then save a color-managed Illustrator graphic and place it in an InDesign CS3 document.

InDesign CS3 can color-manage vector graphics created in Illustrator 9 or later when you save them in formats that embed profiles, such as PDF or TIFF. In this lesson, you'll save a file as PDF and then place the graphic in InDesign CS3.

Note: If you don't have Illustrator 9 or later installed on your system, you can read the information in the next two sections, and then skip to step 2 in "Placing a color-managed Illustrator file into InDesign CS3" later in this lesson to use the Illustrator file provided in the Lesson_06 folder.

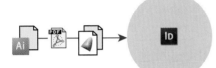

InDesign CS3 color-manages a PDF file using the profiles saved with the PDF version of the file.

Setting up color management in Illustrator CS3

Now you'll set up color management in Illustrator CS3 so that it matches color management settings in InDesign CS3. This ensures that the colors are consistent from Illustrator to InDesign CS3 on-screen and in print. Setting up color management in Illustrator also enables you to embed an ICC profile in an exported version of the Illustrator file. When you place the exported Illustrator file in the InDesign CS3 layout, InDesign CS3 color-manages the logo using the embedded profile.

1   Start Adobe Illustrator CS3, and choose Edit > Color Settings.

2   Select the Advanced Mode check box to expand the dialog box so that you see more options, and then in the Color Settings dialog box, select North America Prepress 2 if it is not already chosen.

3   Under Working Spaces, for RGB select sRGB IEC61966-2.1. Leave CMYK set for U.S. Web Coated (SWOP) v2.

4   Review the conversion options and make sure that the Adobe (ACE) engine, and Relative Colorimetric intent are selected.

5   Click OK.

You have finished setting up color management in Illustrator.

Embedding a profile in a graphic from Illustrator

You can embed an ICC profile in files that you create in Illustrator and export in PDF or bitmap (.bmp) formats. Then, InDesign CS3 can use the profile to color-manage the graphic. In this task, you'll export a file to PDF format, and then place the graphic in an InDesign CS3 document.

1 In Illustrator, choose File > Open. Locate and double-click the 06_f.ai file in the Lesson_06 folder inside the InDesignCIB folder.

2 When the Missing Profile dialog box opens, select Assign current working space: U.S. Web Coated (SWOP) v2, and click OK.

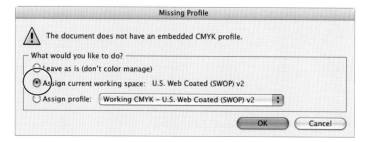

3 Choose File > Save As.

4 Name the file **06_Logo.pdf**, and choose Adobe PDF from the Save as Type (Windows) or Format (Mac OS) menu. Make sure that the Lesson_06 folder is targeted, and then click Save to close the Save As dialog box, and the Adobe PDF Format Options dialog box will appear next.

5 Make sure that the PDF compression options are appropriate for your final print production by clicking General on the left side of the dialog box.

6   For Compatibility, choose Acrobat 5, if it is not already selected, and match the settings shown below. This setting ensures that the profile is saved with the PDF file. Then click Save PDF.

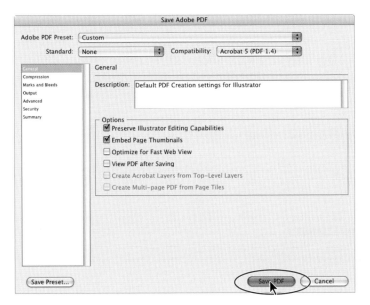

7   Close the file and quit Illustrator.

Placing a color-managed Illustrator file into InDesign CS3

Now that you have created a PDF file of the Illustrator document, you'll place it in InDesign CS3.

1   In InDesign CS3, select the remaining empty frame in the bottom right area of the ad.

2   Do one of the following:

•   If you followed Illustrator instructions in the previous sections, choose File > Place and select the 06_Logo.pdf file that you created. Make sure that Show Import Options is checked when you place the graphic.

•   If you don't have Illustrator, or skipped the previous two sections, choose File > Place and select the 06_Logo.pdf file in the Final folder in the Lesson_06 folder, located inside the Lessons folder within the InDesignCIB folder on your hard disk. Make sure that Show Import Options is selected before you click Open.

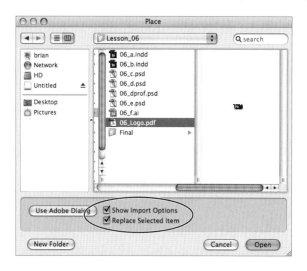

3   In the Place PDF dialog box, for Crop To, choose Bounding Box. This option places only the logo's bounding box—the minimum area that encloses the logo.

4 Make sure that Transparent Background is selected so that you can see any text or graphics behind the bounding box, and then click OK.

Place PDF (06_Logo.pdf)

General | Layers

Preview

Pages
- Previewed Page
- All
- Range: 1

Options
Crop to: Bounding Box

☑ Transparent Background

◄ ◄ 1 ► ►

Total pages: 1

☑ Show Preview   Cancel   OK

The logo appears in the selected frame. InDesign CS3 will color-manage the PDF file using the embedded profile.

5 If the graphic is not fitting into the frame, choose Object > Fitting > Fit Content Proportionally.

6 Choose File > Save to save the file.

In this lesson, you have learned how to set up color management across three Adobe applications—an admirable achievement. You have learned several methods for incorporating graphics so that they can be color-managed when placed in InDesign CS3 documents. Because you described your color environment to the other Adobe applications whose graphics you imported, you can expect predictable, consistent color for those graphics across the applications.

At this time, you could either hand off the native InDesign CS3 file with all the linked files, or export the InDesign CS3 file as PDF, embedding the ICC profiles you assigned. If you create a PDF file of the document, the colors in the ad will look the same across all publications that use the ad, regardless of the color-management settings used by the publication's layout application. Other users can preview and proof your color-managed files more accurately, and repurpose them for different print conditions when that is useful, or when it is a requirement of your project.

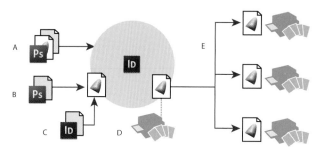

A. Image with embedded CMYK profile.
B. Image with CMYK profile assigned in InDesign CS3.
C. InDesign CS3 document using a CMYK profile based on a separation profile.
D. Separation profile.
E. Different separation profiles when targeting different presses.

Other information resources for color management

You can find additional information on color management on the web and in print. Here are a few resources that are available as of the date of publication of this book:

• At the Adobe web site (Adobe.com), search for color management.

• At the Apple web site (Apple.com), search for ColorSync.

• At your local library or bookstore, look for *Real World Color Management* (ISBN 0321267222).

Exploring on your own

Follow these steps to learn more about importing colors and working with gradients.

1   To create a new document, choose File > New > Document, and then click OK in the New Document dialog box.

2   To import the colors from a different InDesign CS3 document, use the following procedure:

- Use the Swatches panel menu and choose New Color Swatch.

- In the Color Mode pop-up menu, select Other Library and browse to find the Lesson_06 folder.

- Double-click 06_Color.indd (or 06_b.indd). Notice that the colors you created earlier in this lesson appear in this dialog box list for the new document.

- Select the Brown/Tan Gradient and click OK to close the dialog box and add the color to the Swatches panel.

- Repeat this entire process a few more times to add other colors to the Swatches panel.

3   Using the lesson files or your own InDesign CS3 document, double-click the color swatch Paper and change its composition. Notice how the color of the document changes to reflect the color of the paper on which the document will be reproduced.

Review

▶ ## Review questions

1   What is the advantage of applying colors using the Swatches panel instead of the Color panel?

2   What are the pros and cons of using spot colors versus process colors?

3   After you create a gradient and apply it to an object, how do you adjust the direction of the gradient blend?

4   What does the color management engine do?

5   What do source profiles describe?

6   What are three ways to attach an ICC profile to a graphic so that InDesign CS3 can color-manage the graphic?

7   Why would you embed an ICC profile in a graphic?

8   Which file formats embed ICC profiles for use in both Windows and Mac OS?

▶ ## Review answers

1   If you use the Swatches panel to apply a color to several objects, and then decide you want to use a different color, you don't need to update each object individually. Instead, change the color in the Swatches panel and the color of all the objects will be updated automatically.

2   By using a spot color, you can ensure color accuracy. However, each spot color requires its own plate at the press, so using spot colors is more expensive. Use process colors when a job requires so many colors that using individual spot inks would be expensive or impractical, such as when printing color photographs.

3   To adjust the direction of the gradient blend, use the Gradient swatch tool to repaint the fill along an imaginary line in the direction you want.

4   The color management engine translates colors from the color space of one device to another device's color space by a process called color mapping.

5   Source profiles selected in the Assign Profiles dialog box describe the color space InDesign CS3 assigns to objects you create using the drawing tools, or when you import an RGB, CMYK, or LAB color graphic that wasn't saved with an embedded profile.

6   You can embed the profile in the original file, assign a profile within InDesign CS3, or use the default profile you specified when you set up color management in InDesign CS3.

7   Embedding an ICC profile ensures that the graphic displays correctly in any application that uses ICC-compliant color management. The application that uses the graphic honors the embedded profile rather than applying a default one.

8   A growing number of formats can contain an embedded ICC profile, but the most widely supported formats to use with embedded ICC profiles at this time are bitmap image formats such as Photoshop (PSD), TIFF, and JPEG.

With Adobe InDesign CS3 you can create styles, or sets of bundled formatting attributes, that can be applied in multiple instances. Applying styles to a document allows you to change the look and feel of its graphics and text with a single action.

7 | Working with Styles

In this introduction to working with InDesign styles, you'll learn how to do the following:

- Create and apply Object styles.
- Create and apply Character styles.
- Create and apply Paragraph styles.
- Create and apply Table styles.
- Nest Character styles inside Paragraph styles.
- Globally update Object, Character, and Paragraph styles.
- Create Style groups.
- Import and apply styles from other InDesign documents.

Getting started

In this lesson, you'll work on a three page document for Expedition Tea Company. Several items in the document, including text and graphics, have already been placed for you. Your objective is to apply styles, or grouped attributes, to these items.

Note: If you have not already copied the resource files for this lesson onto your hard disk from the Adobe InDesign CS3 Classroom in a Book *CD, do so now. See "Copying the Classroom in a Book files" on page 4.*

1 To ensure that the tools and panels function exactly as described in this lesson, delete or reset the InDesign CS3 defaults preferences following the procedure in "Saving, deleting and restoring preference files" on page 2.

2 Start Adobe InDesign CS3.

To begin working, you'll open an existing InDesign document.

3   Choose File > Open, and open the 07_a.indd file in the Lesson_07 folder, located inside the Lessons folder within the InDesignCIB folder on your hard disk.

4   Choose File > Save As, rename the file **07_etc.indd**, and save it in the Lesson_07 folder.

5   If you want to see what the finished document will look like, open the 07_b.indd file in the same folder. You can leave this document open to act as a guide as you work. When you're ready to resume working on the lesson document, choose its name from the Window menu.

Creating and applying paragraph styles

Paragraph styles allow you to apply and globally update formatting to your text. They allow you to speed up production and create a more consistent overall design. Paragraph styles incorporate all elements of text formatting, and can include character attributes like font, size, style, and color, combined with paragraph attributes like indents, alignment, tabs, and hyphenation. They are different than character styles, which you'll do later in this document, in that they are applied to entire paragraphs at once, not just to selected characters.

Creating a paragraph style

In this exercise you'll apply additional text formatting to your document by creating and applying a paragraph style to selected paragraphs that have already been placed in the document.

1   With 07_etc.indd open, double-click on page 1 in the Pages panel to center the page in your document window.

The easiest way to create a paragraph style is to format an example paragraph using local (i.e., not style-based) formatting, then create a new style based on that example paragraph. Again, this allows you to effectively "see" the style before you build it. In this case, you'll style the text in the first part of the document locally, and then have InDesign pick up this existing formatting and build it into a new paragraph style. The new style can then be reused efficiently throughout the rest of the document.

2   Choose the Type tool (T) from the Tools panel and drag to select "Loose Leaf Teas" in the first column of the document.

3   In the Control panel, click on the Character formatting button (A), and specify the following:

- Font: Adobe Caslon Pro

- Style: Semibold

- Size: 18 pt

Leave all other settings at their defaults.

4   In the Control panel, click on the Paragraph formatting button (¶), and increase the Space Before ( ) to 0p9.

Now you'll create a paragraph style using this formatting so you can use it to format the other sections of the document. Make sure that you leave your text insertion point in the text you just formatted.

5   If it's not already visible, open the Paragraph Styles panel by choosing Window > Type & Tables > Paragraph Styles. There are a few styles already in the panel that have been provided for you including the default, [Basic Paragraph].

6   In the Paragraph Styles panel, create a new paragraph style by choosing "New Paragraph Style" from the panel menu. The New Paragraph Style window opens, displaying the formatting you used in the Style Settings section.

7   First assign a name to the style by typing it into the Style Name field at the top of the window. Name this style **Head2** since this will be the second largest headline.

8 In the General section of this window, note that you can base a new style on a previously created style. Since you're creating a new style, leave this setting at the default.

9 You can also have InDesign switch to another style automatically when you press Return or Enter after entering text. Select Body Text for the Next Style, as this is the style used for the text following each Head2 headlines.

10 You can also create a keyboard shortcut for easy application of this style. Click inside the Shortcut field, hold down Ctrl (Windows) or Command (Mac OS), and type the number **9** from the numeric keypad on your keyboard. (InDesign requires the use of a modifier key for style shortcuts.)

11 Click Apply Style to Selection in order to apply this new style to the text you just formatted. Otherwise, the style will appear in your Paragraph Style panel but will not automatically be applied to the text you formatted and will not be updated should you need to globally update the Head2 style.

12 You have now created your first paragraph style. Click OK to close the New Paragraph Style window. You should see the new Head2 style appear in the Paragraph Styles panel.

Applying a paragraph style

Now you'll apply your paragraph style to selected text in the other sections of the document.

1 In the Pages panel, double-click on Page 1 to center it in your document window.

2 Using the Type tool (T), click to insert an insertion point in "Tea Gift Collections."

3 Then click once on the Head2 style in the Paragraph Styles panel to apply the style to the text. You should see the text attributes change to reflect the paragraph style you've just created.

4   Repeat steps 2 and 3 to apply the Head2 style to "Teapots and Tea Accessories" in the second column.

5   Next you will go to page 2 and then to page 3 to style two more headlines with the Head2 style. Repeat steps 2 and 3 above to apply the Head2 style to "Premium Loose Leaf Tea Selections" on page 2 and then to "About Tea and Training" on page 3.

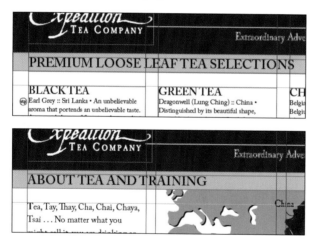

Note: You also could have used the keyboard shortcut you defined earlier (Ctrl/Command+9) to apply the Head2 style.

6   Choose File > Save.

Creating and applying character styles

In the previous exercise, paragraph styles allowed you to apply paragraph formatting to text with a single click or a key press. Similarly, character styles are a way to apply multiple attributes to text using a single action. Unlike paragraph styles, character styles apply formatting to ranges of text smaller than a paragraph (i.e., a character, a word, or a group of words). Because of this, character styles are best used for character formatting you use over and over again when creating a document.

Creating a character style

The text for items listed on the Expedition Tea Company document was previously created in a word processing application and imported into the lesson file for you. The object of this exercise is for you to create and apply a character style to selected text in the document, and to recognize the advantages in efficiency and consistency that character styles have to offer.

1   With 07_etc.indd open, double-click on Page 1 in the Pages panel to center the page 1 in your document window.

2   If it's not already visible, open the Character Styles panel by choosing Window > Type & Tables > Character Styles. Note that the only style listed in this panel is the default, [None].

As you did with the paragraph styles in the previous section, you'll build your character style based on existing text formatting. This approach allows you to effectively "see" the style before you build it. In this case, you'll format the Expedition Tea Company name and build it into a character style, so that it can be reused efficiently throughout the document.

3   Choose the Type tool (T) from the Tools panel, and select the words "Expedition Tea Company™" in the first column of page 1.

> **Teapots & Gift Collections**
>
> Expedition Tea Company™ carries an extensive array of teas from all the major tea growing regions and tea estates. Choose from our selection of teas, gift collections, teapots, or learn how to make your tea drinking experience more enjoyable from our STI Certified Tea Specialist, T. Elizabeth Atteberry.

4   In the Control panel, click the Character formatting button (A) and select Small Caps.

5   Now that the text is formatted, you will create a new character style by choosing New Character Style from the Character Styles panel menu (▾≡). The New Character Style window opens, displaying the formatting you applied to the text in the Style Settings box.

6   Assign a name to the style by typing it into the Style Name field at the top of the window. Name this style **Company** to define the text to which it is to be applied.

7   In the General section of this window, note that you can base a new character style on a previously created style. Since you're creating a new style, leave this setting at the default [None].

8 You can create a keyboard shortcut for easy application of this style. Click inside the Shortcut field, hold down Ctrl (Windows) or Command (Mac OS), and type the number **8** from the numeric keypad on your keyboard. (InDesign requires the use of a modifier key for style shortcuts.)

9 Click Apply Style to Selection in order to apply this new style to the text you just formatted. Otherwise, the style will appear in your Character Style panel but will not automatically be applied to the text you formatted and will not be updated should you need to globally update the Company style.

10 You have now created (and edited) your first character style. Click OK to close the New Character Style window. You should see the new Company style appear in the Character Styles panel.

Applying a character style

Now you'll apply your character style to selected text already placed in the document. As with paragraph styles, using character styles prevents you from having to manually apply multiple type attributes to each run of text individually.

1 If you aren't already there, double click on Page 1 in the Pages panel to center the first page of the document in your document window.

At the bottom of the page, you'll see the words "Expedition Tea Company" at the bottom of the second column. To maintain a consistent look for the company name, you'll apply the Company character style.

2 Choose the Type tool (T) from the Tools panel, and select the words "Expedition Tea Company."

3   In the Character Styles panel, click once on the Company style to apply it to this text. You should see the font change to reflect the character style you've just created.

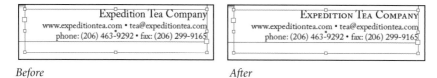

Before   *After*

Note: You also could have used the keyboard shortcut you defined earlier (Ctrl/Command+8) to apply the Logo style.

4   Using either method described above, apply the Company character style to the words "Expedition Tea Company" which also appear twice on page 3.

5   Choose File > Save.

Nesting character styles inside paragraph styles

To make the use of styles more convenient and powerful for you, InDesign provides for the nesting of character formatting within paragraph styles. These nested styles allow you to apply character formatting to portions of a paragraph, whether it's the first character, the second word, or the third sentence. This makes nested styles ideal for applying to run-in headings (where the first portion of a line or paragraph is styled differently from the rest of the line or paragraph), structured paragraphs, or drop caps.

Creating character styles for nesting

The two prerequisites for using nested styles are that you have first created a character style, and that you then have built a paragraph style in which to nest it. In this section, you'll create two characters styles and then nest them within the paragraph style Tea Body which already exists.

1   With 07_etc.indd open, double-click on Page 2 in the Pages panel to center the second page in your document window.

If the body copy is too small to view, zoom in to the first paragraph beginning with "Earl Gray." In this exercise, you'll create two nested styles to distinguish the tea name and the region where it was grown. You'll notice that a set of semi-colons (::) separate the name and region, and then a bullet (•) after the region. These will be important in creating our nested styles later in this section.

2   Choose the Type tool (T) and select the words "Earl Gray" in the first column. In the Control panel, format this text with Style: Bold. Leave all other settings at their defaults.

3   Your locally formatted text should now be ready to serve as the basis for a new character style. If it's not already visible, open the Character Styles panel by choosing Window > Type & Tables > Character Styles.

4   In the Character Styles panel, select New Character Style from the panel menu (▾≡). The New Character Style window opens, displaying the formatting you applied.

5   Assign a name to the style by typing it into the Style Name field at the top of the window. Name this style **Name** to define the text to which it will be applied.

6 To make the tea name stand out a little more, you'll now change the color from black to burgundy. From the list on the left, click Character Color.

7 In the Character Color settings that appear to the right, select the burgundy color (C=43 M=100 Y=100 K=30).

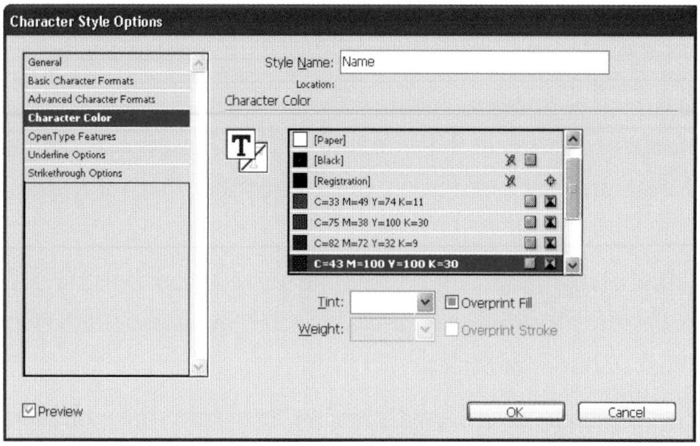

8 Click OK to close the New Character Style window. You should see the new Name style appear in the Character Styles panel.

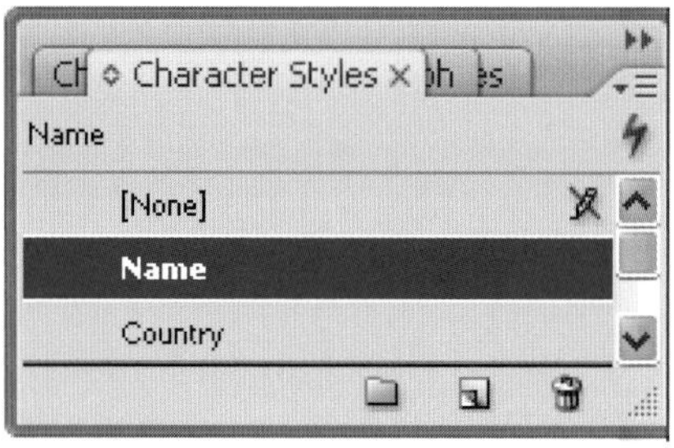

9 Now you'll create a second character style for nesting. Select the text "Sri Lanka" right after the Earl Gray you just formatted. Format this as Adobe Caslon Pro Italic.

10 Repeat steps 3 – 5 above to create a new character style called Country. When finished, click OK to close the Character Styles Option window. You should see the new Country style appear in the Character Styles panel.

You have successfully created two new character styles, and, together with the paragraph style Tea body that already exists, you are ready to create and apply your nested style.

Creating a nested style

When you create a nested style within an existing paragraph style, you're essentially building a secondary set of rules for InDesign to follow while formatting a paragraph. In this exercise, you'll build a nested style into the Tea body style using the two characters styles you created in the last exercise.

1   If it's not already centered on your screen, double-click on Page 2 in the Pages panel to center page 2 in your document window.

2   If the Paragraph Styles panel is not visible, select Window > Type & Tables > Paragraph Styles.

3   In the Paragraph Styles panel, double-click on the Tea body style to open the Paragraph Style Options dialog box.

4   From the categories on the left, select Drop Caps and Nested Styles. You'll see options for applying drop caps and nested styles appear on the right.

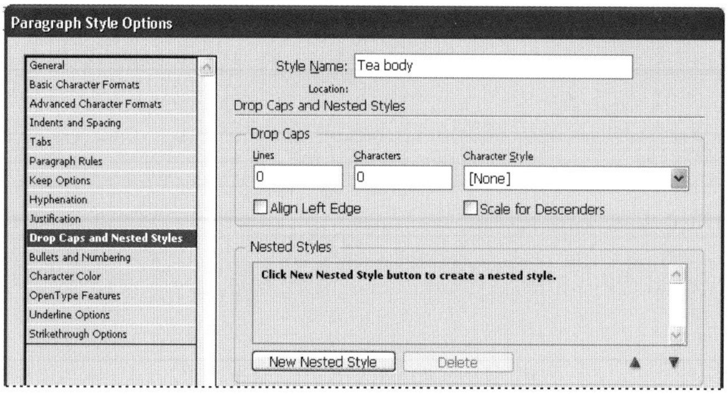

5   In the Nested Styles section below, click on the New Nested Style button to create a new nested style.

6   When it appears below, click on the [None] style to reveal a pop-up menu. Click and hold on the arrow to the right to expand the pop-up menu, exposing your choices of the character styles available for nesting.

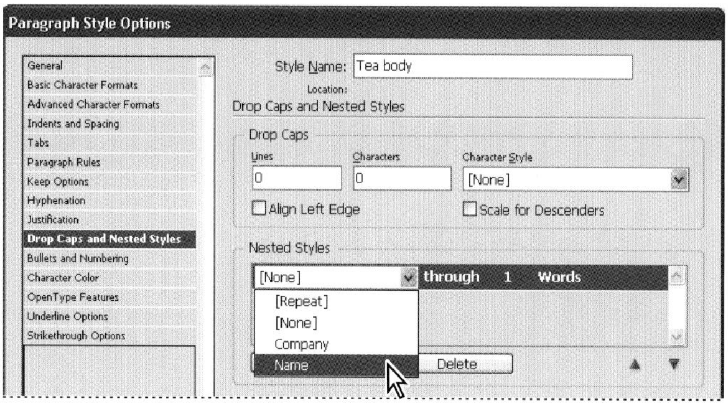

7   Select Name, as this will be the first nested style in the sequence.

8   Click on the word "through" to expose another pop-up menu. This menu contains only two choices: through and up to. You will be setting this style up to the first semi-colon (:) after Earl Gray, so select "up to."

9   Click on the number "1" next to "up to" to expose a text field into which you can type a number. The number defines how many elements the style will apply through or up to. Although there are two semi-colons, you only need to reference the first semi-colon, so leave this as the default "1."

10   Click on "Words" to expose another pop-up menu. This menu contains many choices of elements to which the style will be applied, including sentences, characters, and spaces. In this case, you don't want any of the listed items, and will instead type a semi-colon in the field. Click back in the field to dismiss the pop-up and type : in the field.

11   If it is not already selected, click Preview and move the Paragraph Style Options window. You should now see that the name for each tea is bold and burgundy up to (but not including) the semi-colon. Click OK.

Now we'll add another nested style. But first we need to copy a bullet from the page.

12   Navigate to a bullet on the page, select one and choose Edit > Copy.

13   In the Paragraph Styles palette, double-click the Tea body style. In the Nested Styles section, click on the New Nested Style button to create another new nested style.

14   You will now repeat steps 7 – 11 to create your new nested style with the following formatting:

- First pop-up menu: Select Country

- Second pop-up menu: Select "up to"

- Third pop-up menu: Leave as the default "1"

- Fourth pop-up menu, enter the bullet character by pasting the bullet we copied.

15   If not already visible, move the Paragraph Style Options window so you can see the country for each tea is italicized. However, the two semi-colons are also italicized. For that we'll one to add one additional nested style, [None], between the other two styles for the semi-colons.

16 In the Nested Styles section, click on the New Nested Style button to create another new nested style.

17 You will now repeat steps 7 – 11 to create your new nested style with the following formatting:

• First pop-up menu: Select [None]

• Second pop-up menu: Select "through"

• Third pop-up menu: Type "2"

• Fourth pop-up menu: Type another semi-colon.

18 You now have a nested style, but it needs to be between the Name and Country nested styles to be in the proper position sequentially. With the [None] style selected, click the up arrow once to move the style between the other two.

19 Click OK to accept these changes. You have now finished creating a nested style that will apply the Name and Country character styles to any paragraph styled with the Tea Body paragraph style.

BLACK TEA

Earl Grey :: *Sri Lanka* • An unbelievable aroma that portends an unbelievable taste. A correct balance of flavoring that results in a refreshing true Earl Grey taste.

English Breakfast :: *Sri Lanka* • English Breakfast at its finest. Good body with satisfying full tea flavor. Enticing with milk.

Assam, Gingia Estate :: *Bishnauth region, India* • Bright, full-bodied liquor with nutty, walnut-like character. Try with milk and a dash of sweetener.

GREEN TEA

Dragonwell (Lung Ching) :: *China* • Distinguished by its beautiful shape, emerald color, and sweet floral character. Full-bodied with a slight heady bouquet.

Genmaicha (Popcorn Tea) :: *Japan* • Green tea blended with fire-toasted rice with a natural sweetness. During the firing the rice may "pop" not unlike popcorn.

Sencha Kyoto Cherry Rose :: *China* • Fresh, smooth sencha tea with depth and body. The cherry flavoring and subtle rose

20   Select File > Save.

Creating and applying object styles

Object styles allow you to apply and globally update formatting to graphics, text, and frames. These formatting attributes, including fill, stroke, transparency, and text wrap options, create a more consistent overall design, and speed up tedious production tasks.

Creating an object style

In this section, you'll be creating and applying an object style to the black circle of the etp symbols on page 2. The etp symbol stands for Ethical Tea Partnership.

1   Double-click on page 2 in the Pages panel to center page 2 in the window.

2   Select the Zoom tool (🔍) from the Tools panel and increase the magnification to better view the etp symbol near Earl Gray.

You'll apply an Inner Bevel effect to the circle and fill it with burgundy. To make this task easier, the type and circle for all the etp symbols have been placed on separate layers—the circles on a layer called etp circle and the type on the layer called etp type.

4   Select Window > Layers to view the layers panel. Click the lock (🔒) next to etp type to lock the type in the center of the circle.

5   With the Selection tool, click the black circle next to Earl Gray.

6   From the Swatches panel, change both the stroke and fill color to burgundy (C=43 M=100 Y=100 K=30).

7   Choose Object > Effects > Bevel and Emboss. If it isn't already selected, choose "Inner Bevel" from the Style pop-up menu under Structure. Make sure the Preview box is checked and move the Effects window to view the circle.

8   In the Size field, type 0p2 to change the shape of the bevel. Leave the other defaults the same.

9   Click OK. The symbol should now be embossed.

Before and after Bevel and Emboss effect

10   In the Object Styles panel, create a new object style by choosing New Object Style from the panel menu (▾☰). The New Object Style window opens, offering you formatting options to be built into the style.

11   Assign a name to the style by typing it into the Style Name field at the top of the window. Name this style **etp circle** to describe the attributes to be applied.

12   Click Apply Style to Selection in order to apply this new object style to the circle you just formatted. Otherwise, the style will appear in your Object Style panel but will not automatically be applied to the circle you formatted and will not be updated should you need to globally update the etp circle style.

13   In the General section of this window, note that you can base a new object style on a previously created style. Since you're creating a style from scratch, leave this setting at the default [None].

14   If you were creating this style based on existing formatting in the document, you'd see those settings displayed in the Style Settings section of this window. Because this style is created from scratch, clicking on the triangles next to each setting shows the defaults for that attribute.

15 The check boxes to the left of this window show the attributes that will be applied when this style is used. To add a drop shadow to the style, click on the words Drop Shadow to both select this option and view the Drop Shadow settings on the right hand side of the window.

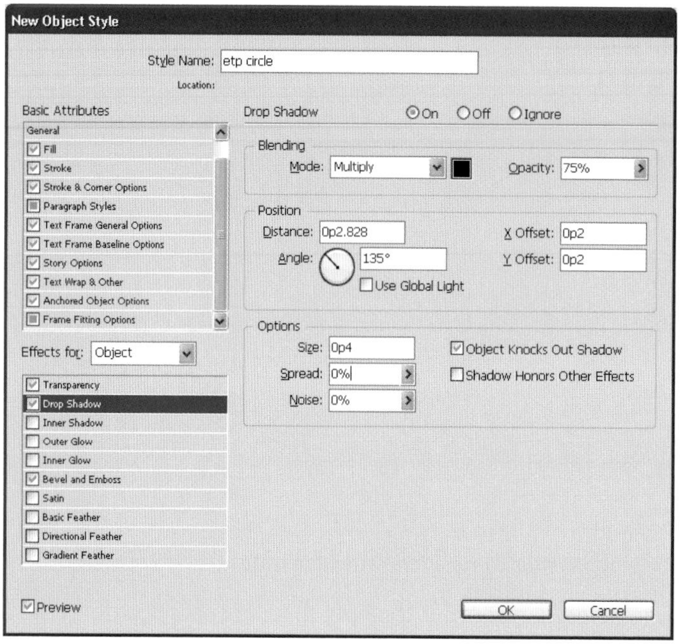

16 In the Drop Shadow settings that appear to the right, specify the following:

- Change the X and Y Offset values to 0p2.

- Set the Size value to 0p4.

- Leave all other settings at their defaults, making sure Black is chosen as the shadow color.

17 You have now created your first object style. Click OK to close the New Object Style window, and you should see the new etp circle style appear in the Object Styles panel.

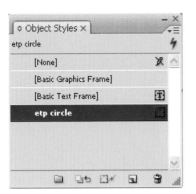

Applying an object style

Now you'll apply your object style to the other circles on page 2. The use of an object style prevents you from having to manually apply the shadow and text wrap attributes to each image individually.

1 In the Pages panel, double-click on page 2 to center it in the window.

2 Using the Selection tool (↖), select the second circle and then click the etp circle style in the Object Styles panel. The circle should appear exactly as the first circle you originally formatted.

3 To speed up the process, press the Shift key and then click to select each of the circles on page 2. Then apply the etp circle style.

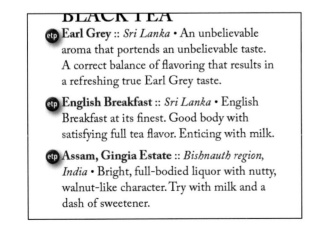

4 Choose File > Save.

Creating and applying table and cell styles

Tables are a great way to easily organize content in rows and columns. Table and cell styles allow you to format tables with the same convenience and consistency you get from styling text with paragraph and character styles. Table styles allow you to control the visual attributes of the table including the table borders, space before and after the table, rows and column strokes as well as alternating fill patterns. Cell styles allow you to control text inset, vertical justification, individual cell strokes and fills, as well as diagonal lines. You'll learn more about creating tables in Lesson 9.

In this section, you'll create and apply a table and two cell styles to tables in your document.

Creating cell styles

You'll begin by creating a cell style for both the header row and body rows for the table at the bottom of page 2. These two styles will be nested inside the Table style later, much as character styles were nested within paragraph styles earlier in this lesson.

1   If you aren't already there, double-click on page 2 in the Pages panel to center the page in your window. Double-click the Zoom tool (🔍) to increase the magnification to 100% and then scroll, if necessary, to view the table at the bottom of the page.

2   Using the Type tool, select the first two cells in the Header row containing the words "Tea" and "Finished Leaf." Then choose Table > Cell Options > Strokes and Fills. For Cell Fill, select the pale yellow color (C=4 M=15 Y=48 K=0). Click OK.

3   With the cells still selected, bring up the Cell Styles panel by selecting Window > Type and Tables > Cell Styles.

4   From the Cell Styles panel menu (▾≡), select New Cell Style. The cell formatting you applied is displayed in the Style Settings box. Notice the additional cell options on the left side of the dialog box. In this section, however, we are just going to set the desired paragraph style to use for the Header row.

5   Assign a name for this style in the Style Name field. Name this **Table Head**.

6   From the Paragraph Style pop-up menu, select Head4. This paragraph style was already created for you in the document. Click OK.

Now you will create a new Cell Style for the body rows.

7   Select the first two cells of the second row of the table including "White" and "Soft, grayish white."

8   From the Cell Styles panel menu (▾≡), select New Cell Style.

9   Assign a name for this style in the Style Name field. Name this **Table Body Rows**.

10 From the Paragraph Style pop-up menu, select Table Body. This paragraph style was already created for you in the document.

11 Click OK. You should now see your two new cell styles in the Cell Styles panel.

Now you have your two cell styles, you can create a Table style that uses both.

Creating a table style

The Table style allows you to control the cell styles you want for your table as well as format the overall look of the table including the table border, space before and after the table, and alternating row strokes, column strokes, and fill patterns.

1 If you aren't already there, double-click on page 2 in the Pages panel to center the page in your window. Double-click the Zoom tool (🔍) to increase the magnification to 100% and then scroll, if necessary, to view the table at the bottom of the page.

2 Using the Type tool, click to create an insertion point anywhere in the table.

3 Choose Window > Type and Tables > Table Styles. From the Table Styles panel menu (▾≡), select New Table Style.

4 In the Style Name field, assign a name for your new table style. Enter **Tea Table**.

Now you will choose the two cell styles you created to format the header and body rows.

5   In the Cell Styles section, select Table Head from the Header Rows pop-up ;menu.

6   In the same section, select Table Body Rows from the Body Rows pop-up menu.

Now you will format the table to have alternating rows of color in the body rows.

7   Select Fills from the left hand menu. Choose Every Other Row from the Alternating Pattern pop-up menu. The options for Alternating rows will appear.

8   For Color, select the pale yellow color (C=4 M=15 Y=48 K=0).

9   For Tint, enter 30%.

10   Click OK. You should now see the new table style Tea Table in your Table Styles panel.

Applying a table style

Now you'll apply the table style you just created to the two tables in your document.

1   If you aren't already there, double-click on page 2 in the Pages panel to center the page in your window. Double-click the Zoom tool ( ) to increase the magnification to 100% and then scroll, if necessary, to view the table at the bottom of the page.

2   Using the Type tool (T), click to create an insertion point anywhere in the table.

3   From the Tables Styles panel, click the Tea Table style. The table should format with the table and cell styles you created.

TEA	FINISHED LEAF	LIQUOR	CAFFEINE
White	Soft, grayish white	Pale yellow or pinkish	15 mg
Green	Dull to brilliant green	Green or yellowish	20 mg
Oolong	Blackish or greenish	Green to brownish	30 mg
Black	Lustrous black	Rich red or brownish	40 mg

4   Now double-click on page 3 from the Pages panel. Click to place an insertion point anywhere in the table in the third column.

5   From the Table Styles panel, click the Tea Table style. The table should format with the table and cell styles you created.

TEA TASTING OVERVIEW
An overview and tasting of the white, green, oolong and black, and how each are grown and processed, and how to best prepare each.
BLACK TEA TASTING
Learn to distinguish the various types of black tea including Assams, Ceylons, Darjeelings, Yunnans and other regional blacks.
GREEN TEA TASTING
An overview and tasting of Japanese and Chinese greens including Dragonwell, Gyrokuro, Matcha and Genmaicha.
OOLONG TEA TASTING
The complexities of oolong teas come alive in this tasting overview, including Ti Kuan Yin, Quangzhou Milk and Phoenix Iron Goddess oolong teas.
WHITE TEA TASTING
Learn of these delicate, rare teas that many believe is the purist, healthiest tea to drink.

You will notice that it looks a little different as there was no header row created in this table, so the Table Head style has been ignored. You will learn more about creating tables in Lesson 9: Creating Tables.

6   You have successfully create and applied cell and table styles. Click File > Save.

Globally updating styles

There are two ways to update object, character, or paragraph styles in InDesign. The first is simply to open the style itself and make changes to the formatting options, as you just did when you created cell and table styles. Because there's a parent-child relationship between the style and the instance(s) in which it's applied, all instances are updated to reflect a modified style.

The other way to update object, character, or paragraph styles is to use local formatting to change an instance, and then redefine the style based on that instance. In this exercise, you'll make a change to the Head3 style to include a rule below it.

1   With 07_etc.indd open, double-click on page 2 in Pages panel to center the page in your window. Then double-click on the Zoom tool (🔍) to increase the magnification to 100%.

2   Using the Type tool (**T**), click to place an insertion point in "Black Tea" in the first column.

3   If it's not already visible, choose Window > Type & Tables > Paragraph Styles to access the Paragraph Styles panel. Note that the Paragraph Styles panel shows the Head3 style you applied to this text earlier in the lesson.

4   In the Control panel, at the far right, select Paragraph Rules from the panel menu (▼≡).

5   Select Rule Below from the Paragraph Rules pop-up menu and click Rule On. Make sure that Preview is selected at the bottom of the dialog box and move the box so you can see "Black Tea" on your screen.

6   Create a rule below using the following settings:

- Weight: 1 pt

- Color: C=4 M=15 Y=48 K=0

- Offset: 0p2

Leave all other settings at their defaults.

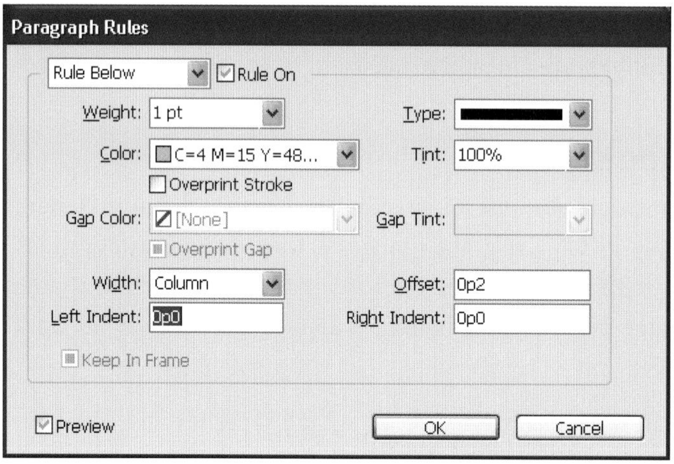

7   Click OK. A thin yellow line now appears below "Black Tea."

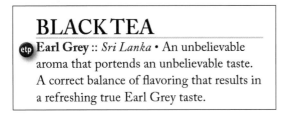

Note: You'll also see a + appear next to the style name in the Paragraph Styles panel. This indicates that local formatting has been applied (and added to the previously applied Head3 style).

8   Now you'll redefine the paragraph style so that the local change applies to all the headlines previously styled with the Head3 style. In the panel menu of the Paragraph Styles panel (⚇≡), choose Redefine Style. The + should no longer appear next to the Head3 style name. All headlines in the document that have been styled with Head3 should globally update to reflect the changes you made.

Note: The same process can be used to redefine character, object and table styles based on local formatting.

9   Select File > Save.

Loading styles from another document

Styles appear only in the document in which you create them. However, it's easy to share styles between InDesign documents by loading, or importing, styles from other InDesign documents. In this exercise, you will import and apply a new nested paragraph style from the finished document 07_b.indd to the first body paragraph on page 3, which has a nested drop cap character style.

1 With 07_etc.indd open, double-click on page 3 in the Pages panel to center this page in your window. Double-click the Zoom tool (🔍) to increase the magnification to 100%.

2 If it's not already visible, select Window > Type & Tables > Paragraph Styles to access the Paragraph Styles panel.

3 Click the panel menu button (▾☰) in the Paragraph Styles panel and choose Load All Text Styles. You will have the opportunity to pick and choose from all the text styles from the 07_b.indd document.

4 In the Open a File dialog box, double-click 07_b.indd from the Lesson_07 folder. The Load Styles dialog box appears. Click Uncheck All to avoid overwriting existing styles on import. Check the paragraph style Drop Cap Body. Notice that character style Drop Cap becomes checked further down the list, as this is a character style nested within the Drop Cap Body. Both styles will be imported. Click OK.

5 Using the Type tool (T), place an insertion point in the first paragraph starting with "Tea, Tay" and choose the new Drop Cap Body style from the Paragraph Styles panel. The initial "T" should transform into a burgundy drop cap.

6 Select File > Save.

Congratulations. You have finished the lesson.

Review

▶ **Review questions**

1   How can using object styles speed your workflow?

2   What must you have created previously in order to create a nested style?

3   What are the two ways to globally update a style you've applied to an InDesign document?

4   How would you import styles from another InDesign document?

▶ **Review answers**

1   Object styles save time by letting you keep a group of formatting attributes together that you can quickly apply to images. If you need to update the formatting, you don't have to change each image formatted with the style individually. Instead, you can simply modify the style.

2   The two prerequisites for using nested styles are that you have first created a character style, and that you then have built a paragraph style in which to nest it.

3   There are two ways to update object, character, or paragraph styles in InDesign. The first is simply to open the style itself and make changes to the formatting options. The other is to use local formatting to change an instance, and then redefine the style based on that instance.

4   Importing styles is easy. Simply choose appropriate Load style option from the Object, Character, or Paragraph panel menus and locate the InDesign document from which you want to load them. The styles are then loaded into the respective panel(s) and are immediately available for use inside your document.

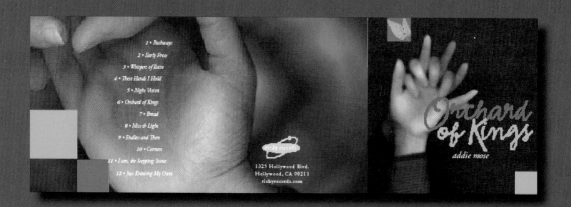

You can easily enhance your document with photographs and artwork imported from Adobe Photoshop, Adobe Illustrator, or other graphics programs. If these imported graphics change, InDesign can tell you that a newer version of a graphic is available. You can update or replace imported graphics at any time.

8 Importing and Linking Graphics

In this lesson, you'll learn how to do the following:

- Distinguish between vector and bitmap graphics.

- Place layered Adobe Photoshop and Adobe Illustrator graphics.

- Import clipping paths with graphics, and create clipping paths.

- Manage placed files using the Links panel.

- Use and create libraries for objects.

- Import graphics using Adobe Bridge.

- Import a PDF.

Getting started

In this lesson, you'll assemble a booklet for a compact disc by importing and managing graphics from Adobe Photoshop, Adobe Illustrator, and Adobe Acrobat. After printing and trimming, the insert will be folded so that it fits into a CD case.

This lesson includes a procedure that you can perform using Adobe Photoshop, if you have a copy of that program installed on your computer.

Note: If you have not already copied the resource files for this lesson onto your hard disk from the Adobe InDesign CS3 Classroom in a Book *CD, do so now. See "Copying the Classroom in a Book files" on page 4.*

1 To ensure that the tools and panels function exactly as described in this lesson, delete or reset the InDesign CS3 defaults preferences following the procedure in "Saving, deleting and restoring preference files" on page 2.

2 Start Adobe InDesign CS3.

3   Choose File > Open, and open the 08_a.indd file in the Lesson_08 folder, located inside the Lessons folder within the InDesignCIB folder on your hard disk.

4   A message appears, saying that the publication contains missing or modified links. Click Don't Fix; you will fix this later in the lesson.

5   If necessary, move the Links panel out of the way so it doesn't obscure your view of the document. The Links panel opens automatically whenever you open an InDesign document that contains missing or modified links.

6   To see what the finished document will look like, open the 08_b.indd file in the same folder. If you prefer, you can leave the document open as you work to act as a guide. When you're ready to resume working on the lesson document, select 08_a.indd from the Window menu.

7   Choose File > Save As, rename the file **08_cdbook.indd**, and save it in the Lesson_08 folder.

Note: As you work through the lesson, feel free to move panels around or change the magnification to a level that works best for you. For more information, see "Changing the magnification of your document" and "Using the Navigator panel" in Lesson 1, "Getting to Know the Work Area."

Adding graphics from other programs

InDesign supports many common graphics file formats. While this means that you can use graphics that were created using a wide range of graphics programs, InDesign works most smoothly with other Adobe professional graphics programs, such as Photoshop, Illustrator, and Acrobat.

By default, imported graphics are linked, which means that InDesign displays a graphics file on your layout without actually copying the entire graphics file into the InDesign document.

There are two major advantages to linking resource files. First, it saves disk space, especially if you reuse the same graphic in many InDesign documents. Second, you can edit a linked document in the program you used to create it and then simply update the link in the InDesign Links panel. Updating a linked file maintains the current location and settings for the resource so you don't have to redo that work.

All linked graphics and text files are listed in the Links panel, which provides buttons and commands for managing links. When you create final output using PostScript® or PDF, InDesign uses the links to produce the highest level of quality available from the original, externally stored versions of placed graphics.

Comparing vector and bitmap graphics

The drawing tools of Adobe InDesign CS3 and Adobe Illustrator create vector graphics, which are made up of shapes based on mathematical expressions. Vector graphics consist of smooth lines that retain their clarity when scaled. They are appropriate for illustrations, type, and graphics, such as logos that are typically scaled to different sizes.

Bitmap images are based on a grid of pixels and are created by image-editing applications, such as Adobe Photoshop. In working with bitmap images, you edit individual pixels rather than objects or shapes. Because bitmap graphics can represent subtle gradations of shade and color, they are appropriate for continuous-tone images, such as photographs or artwork created in painting programs. A disadvantage of bitmap graphics is that they lose definition and appear "jagged" when enlarged. Additionally, bitmap images are typically larger in file size than a similar vector file.

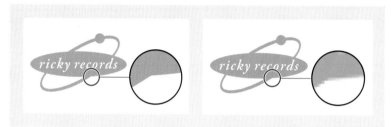

Logo drawn as vector art (left), and rasterized as bitmap art (right).

In general, use vector drawing tools to create art or type with clean lines that look good at any size, such as a logo used on a business card and also on a poster. You can create vector artwork using the InDesign drawing tools, or you might prefer to take advantage of the wider range of vector drawing tools available in Illustrator. You can use Photoshop to create bitmap images that have the soft lines of painted or photographic art and for applying special effects to line art.

Managing links to imported files

When you opened the document, you saw an alert message about problems with linked files. You'll resolve those issues using the Links panel, which provides complete information about the status of any linked text or graphics file in your document.

Identifying imported images

To identify some of the images that have already been imported into the document, you'll use three different techniques involving the Links panel. Later in this lesson, you'll also use the Links panel to edit and update imported graphics.

1 If necessary, zoom or scroll the document window so that you can see both spreads in the document. Alternatively, choose View > Entire Pasteboard.

2 If the Links panel is not visible, choose Window > Links.

3 Using the Selection tool (↖), select the Orchard of Kings logotype on page 4, the far right page of the first spread. Notice that the graphic's filename, 08_i.ai, becomes selected in the Links panel when you select it on the layout.

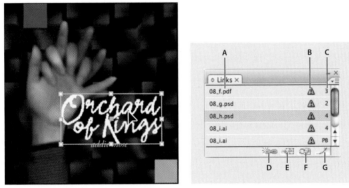

*A. Linked file name. **B.** Alert icon. **C.** Page on which linked item appears.*
*D. Relink button. **E.** Go To Link button. **F.** Update Link button. **G.** Edit Original button.*

Now you'll use the Links panel to locate a graphic on the layout.

4 In the Links panel, select 08_g.psd, and then click the Go To Link button (⬚). The graphic becomes selected and centered on the screen. This is a quick way to find a graphic when you know its file name.

If the Links panel is still in the center of the document window, you can move it now so that it doesn't block your view of the page as you work through the rest of the lesson.

These techniques for identifying and locating linked graphics are useful throughout this lesson and whenever you work with a large number of imported files.

Viewing information about linked files

You can use the Links panel to manage placed graphics or text files in many other ways, such as updating or replacing text or graphics. All the techniques you learn in this lesson about managing linked files apply equally to graphics files and text files that you place into your document.

1   If the Links panel is not visible, choose Window > Links to display it. If you cannot see the names of all the linked files without scrolling, drag the lower right corner of the panel to enlarge it so that all the links are visible.

2   Double-click the link 08_g.psd. The Link Information dialog box appears, describing the linked file.

3   Click Next to view information about the following file on the Links panel list, 08_h.psd. You can quickly examine all the links this way. Some of the other links may display an alert icon (⚠) under Content Status; this icon indicates a linking problem, which you'll address in the next topic. After you've examined the link information, click Done.

By default, files are sorted in the Links panel so that files listed first are those that may need to be updated or relinked. You can use commands in the Links panel menu to sort the file list in different ways.

4   In the Links panel, choose Sort by Page from the Links panel menu (▾≡). The panel now lists the links in numerical order by the page on which the linked item appears.

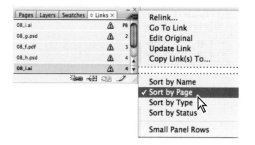

Showing files in the Explorer (Windows) or Finder (Mac OS)

Although the Links panel gives you information on the attributes and location of a specific file, it does not give you access to the file itself. You can access a file directly from your hard drive with the Reveal in Finder option.

1   Select the graphic 08_g.psd if it is not currently chosen. Right-click or Ctrl+click on the graphic and choose Graphics > Reveal in Explorer (Windows) or Graphics > Reveal in Finder (Mac OS). This opens the window where the linked file is currently stored. This feature is useful for locating documents on your hard drive and renaming them if necessary.

2   Close the window and, if necessary, click on the document to return to InDesign.

Updating revised graphics

Even after you place text or graphic files in your InDesign document, you can still use other programs to modify those files. The Links panel indicates which files have been modified outside of InDesign and gives you the choice of updating your document with the latest versions of those files.

In the Links panel, the file 08_i.ai has an alert icon (⚠), indicating that the original has recently been modified. This is the file, as well as some others, that caused the alert message when you opened this document. You'll update its link so that the InDesign document uses the current version.

Viewing link status in the Links panel

A linked graphic can appear in the Links panel in any of the following ways:

• An up-to-date graphic displays only the file name and its page in the document.

• A modified file displays a yellow triangle with an exclamation point (⚠). This alert icon means that the version of the file on disk is more recent than the version in your document. For example, this icon will appear if you import a Photoshop graphic into InDesign, and then another artist edits and saves the original graphic using Photoshop.

• A missing file displays a red hexagon with a question mark (❷). The file isn't at the location from which it was originally imported, though the file may still exist somewhere. This can happen if someone moves an original file to a different folder or server after it's been imported into an InDesign document. You can't know whether a missing graphic is up to date until its original is located. If you print or export a document when this icon is displayed, the graphic may not print or export at full resolution.

1   In the Links panel, select the second instance of the file 08_i.ai (on page 4), and
click the Go To Link button ( ). You don't have to do this step to update a link, but it's
a quick way to double-check which imported file you are about to update.

2   Click the Update Link button ( ). The appearance of the image in the document
changes to represent its newer version. However, the new image is larger than the
previous version, so the existing frame now crops the updated graphic, you will change
this in the next step. Select the other files displaying the alert icon (⚠) and click the
update button. You can hold down the Shift key to select multiple consecutive files to
be updated in a single step, or Ctrl+click (Windows) or Command+click (Mac OS), to
select non-consecutive items in the Links panel.

💡 *All the buttons at the bottom of the Links panel are also available as commands in the
Links panel menu.*

3   Select the 08_i.ai graphic on the page and choose Object > Fitting > Fit Content
Proportionally. The larger graphic is now visible.

You'll replace the image of the hands that spans the first spread (pages 2-4) with a modified image. You'll use the Relink button to reassign the link to another graphic.

4   Go to pages 2-4 (the first spread) and choose View > Fit Spread in Window.

5   Select the 08_h.psd image, which is the photograph of the interlocked hands that sits on page 4. You can tell when you've selected the right image because the filename becomes selected in the Links panel.

6   Click the Relink button (⬚) in the Links panel.

7   Browse to find the 08_j.psd file in the Lesson_08 folder, and then click Open. The new version of the image (which has a different background) replaces the original image, and the Links panel is updated accordingly.

8   Click a blank area of the pasteboard to deselect all objects in the file.

9   Choose File > Save to save your work.

Adjusting view quality

Now that you've resolved all the file's links, you're ready to start adding more graphics. But first, you will adjust the view quality of the Illustrator file 08_i.ai you updated in the last step.

As you place an image into a document, InDesign automatically creates a low-resolution (proxy) version of it, corresponding to the current settings in the Preferences dialog box. This and any other images in this document are currently low-resolution proxies, which is why the image appears to have jagged edges. You can control the degree of detail InDesign uses to display placed graphics. Reducing the on-screen quality of placed graphics displays pages faster, and doesn't affect the quality of final output.

1   In the Links window, select the image 08_i.ai file you updated in the last exercise (on page 4). Click the Go To Link button to view the document in magnified view.

2   Right-click (Windows) or Ctrl+click (Mac OS) the "Orchard of Kings" image, and then choose Display Performance > High Quality Display from the context menu that appears. The image appears at full resolution. Use this process to confirm the clarity, appearance, or position of an individual placed graphic in your InDesign layout.

On-screen display using Typical Display (left) and High Quality Display (right).

3   Choose View > Display Performance > High Quality Display. This setting changes the default display performance for this document. All graphics will be displayed at the highest quality. On older computers, or for designs with many imported graphics, this setting can sometimes tax the system, resulting in slower screen redraw. In most cases, it is advisable to set your Display Performance to Typical Display and then change the display quality of individual graphics as needed.

4   Choose File > Save.

Working with clipping paths

You can remove unwanted backgrounds from images using InDesign. You'll get some experience doing this in the following procedure. In addition to removing the background using Adobe InDesign CS3, you can also create paths or alpha channels in Photoshop, which can then be used to silhouette an image in an InDesign layout.

The image you will be placing has a solid rectangular background that blocks your view of the area behind it. You can hide unwanted parts of an image using a clipping path—a drawn vector outline that acts as a mask. InDesign can create clipping paths from many kinds of images:

• If you drew a path in Photoshop and saved it with the image, InDesign can create a clipping path from it.

• If you painted an alpha channel in Photoshop and saved it with the image, InDesign can create a clipping path from it. An alpha channel carries transparent and opaque areas and is commonly created with images used for photo or video compositing.

- If the image has a light or white background, InDesign can automatically detect its edges and create a clipping path.

The pear image you will be placing doesn't have a clipping path or an alpha channel, but it does have a solid white background that InDesign can remove.

Removing a white background using InDesign

You can use the Detect Edges option of the Clipping Path command to remove a solid white background from an image. The Detect Edges option hides areas of an image by changing the shape of the frame containing the image, adding anchor points as necessary.

1 Navigate to page 7 of your document by double-clicking on the Page 7 icon in the Pages panel. Choose File > Place and double-click the file 08_c.psd in the Lesson_08 folder.

2 In the Layers panel, make sure that the Photos layer is selected so that the image will appear on that layer.

3 Position the loaded graphics icon outside the purple square—to the left and slightly below the top edge (make sure you are not placing the cursor in the square itself), and click to place an image of a pear on a white background. If you need to reposition the image, do so now.

4 Choose Object > Clipping Path > Options. If necessary, drag the Clipping Path dialog box so that you can see the pear image.

5   In the Type pop-up menu, choose Detect Edges. If the Preview checkbox is not selected, do so now. The white background is almost entirely eliminated from the image.

6   For Threshold, drag the slider and watch the image on page 7 until the Threshold setting hides as much of the white background as possible without hiding parts of the subject (darker areas). We used a Threshold value of 20.

Note: If you can't find a setting that removes all the background without affecting the subject, specify a value that leaves the entire subject visible along with small bits of the white background. You'll eliminate the remaining white background by fine-tuning the clipping path in the following steps.

The Threshold option works by hiding light areas of the image, starting with white. As you drag to the right to choose a higher value, increasingly darker tones are included within the range of tones that become hidden. Don't try to find a setting that matches the pear perfectly. You'll learn how to improve the clipping path a little bit later.

7   For Tolerance, drag the slider slightly to the left until the Tolerance value is between about 1 and 1.8.

Clipping Path

Type: Detect Edges

OK

Cancel

Threshold: 20

Preview

Tolerance: 1.01

Inset Frame: 0p0

Invert
Include Inside Edges
Restrict to Frame
Use High Resolution Image

The Tolerance option determines how many points define the frame that's automatically generated. As you drag to the right, InDesign uses fewer points so that the clipping path fits the image more loosely (higher tolerance). Using fewer points on the path may speed up document printing, but may also be less accurate.

8   For Inset Frame, specify a value that closes up any remaining background areas. We specified a value of 0p1 (zero picas, one point). This option shrinks the current shape of the clipping path uniformly, and is not affected by the lightness values in the image. Then click OK to close the Clipping Path dialog box.

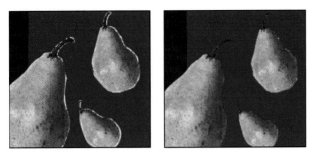

Before and after applying an inset of 1 point.

9 (Optional) You can refine the clipping path manually. Switch to the Direct Selection tool (↖) to activate it. You can then drag individual anchor points and use the Drawing tools to edit the clipping path around the pears. With images which have complex edges, you will want to magnify the document in order to effectively work with the anchor points.

10 Choose File > Save to save the file.

💡 *You can also use the Detect Edges feature to remove a solid black background. Just select the Invert option and specify a high threshold value.*

Working with alpha channels

When an image has a background that isn't solid white or black, the Detect Edges feature may not be able to remove the background effectively. With such images, hiding the background's lightness values may also hide parts of the subject that use the same lightness values. Instead, you can use the advanced background-removal tools in Photoshop to mark transparent areas using paths or alpha channels, and let InDesign make a clipping path from those areas.

Note: If you place a Photoshop file (.psd) that consists of an image placed on a transparent background, InDesign honors the transparency with no dependence on clipping paths or alpha channels. This can be especially helpful when you place an image with a soft or feathered edge.

Importing a Photoshop file and alpha channels

You imported the previous image using the Place command. This time, use an alternate method: You'll simply drag a Photoshop image directly onto an InDesign spread. InDesign can use Photoshop paths and alpha channels directly—you don't need to save the Photoshop file in a different file format. For more information search for "drag and drop graphics" in InDesign Help.

1 In the Layers panel, make sure that the Photos layer is selected so that the image will appear on that layer.

2 Go to page 2 of your document. Then resize and arrange your Explorer window (Windows) or Finder window (Mac OS), and your InDesign windows, as needed, so that you can simultaneously see the list of files on the desktop and the InDesign document window. Make sure that the lower left quarter of page 2 in your document is visible.

3 In Explorer (Windows) or the Finder (Mac OS), open the Lesson_08 folder, which contains the file 08_d.psd file.

4 Drag the file 08_d.psd to page 2 in the InDesign document and place it on the pasteboard. Then use the Selection tool (➤) to reposition the graphic so that it is in the lower left corner of the page.

Note: When you place the file, be careful to drop it onto the white pasteboard. If you drop it in an object drawn using InDesign, it will be placed inside the object. If this happens, choose Edit > Undo, and try again.

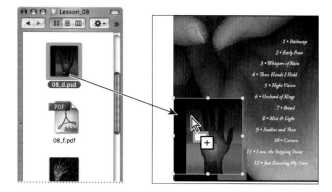

5 If necessary, you can now maximize the InDesign window to its previous size, because you've finished importing the file.

Examining Photoshop paths and alpha channels

In the Photoshop image that you just dragged into InDesign, the hand and the background share many of the same lightness values. Therefore, the background can't easily be isolated using the Detect Edges option in the Clipping Path command.

Instead, you'll set up InDesign to use a path or alpha channel from Photoshop. First you'll use the Links panel to open the image directly in Photoshop to see what paths or alpha channels it already includes.

The procedure in this topic requires a full version of Photoshop 4.0 or later, and is easier if you have enough RAM available to leave both InDesign and Photoshop open as you work. If your configuration doesn't include these two conditions, you can still read these steps to help you understand what Photoshop alpha channels look like and do, and resume your work in the next section of this lesson.

1   If necessary, use the Selection tool (k) to select the 08_d.psd image in InDesign.

2   If the Links panel is not already open, choose File > Links. The image filename appears selected in the Links panel.

3   In the Links panel, click the Edit Original button ( ). This opens the image in a program that can view or edit it. This image was saved from Photoshop, so if Photoshop is installed on your computer, InDesign starts Photoshop with the selected file.

Note: Sometimes the Edit Original button opens an image in a program other than Photoshop or the program that created it. When you install software, some installer utilities change your operating system's settings for associating files with programs. The Edit Original command uses these settings for associating files with programs. To change these settings, see the documentation for your operating system.

4   If an Embedded Profile Mismatch dialog box appears as the image opens in Photoshop, do one of the following:

•   If you are not using color management, select Use the Embedded Profile (Instead of the Working Space).

•   If you've properly configured all Photoshop and InDesign color-management settings for your workflow using accurate ICC profiles, select Convert Document's Colors to the Working Space to reproduce the image properly in Photoshop.

5   In Photoshop, choose Window > Channels to display the Channels panel, or click the Channels panel tab.

Scroll down the Channels panel if necessary to view the three alpha channels in addition to the standard RGB channels. These channels were drawn using the masking and painting tools in Photoshop.

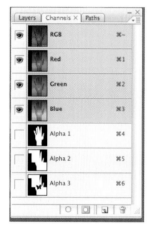

Photoshop file saved with three alpha channels.

6   In the Channels panel in Photoshop, click Alpha 1 to see how it looks, then click Alpha 2 and Alpha 3 to compare them.

7 In Photoshop, choose Window > Paths to open the Paths panel, or click the Paths panel tab.

The Paths panel contains two named paths, "Shapes" and "Circle." These were drawn using the Pen tool (✑) and other Path tools in Photoshop, although they could also be drawn in Illustrator and pasted into Photoshop.

8 In the Photoshop Paths panel, click Shapes to view that path. Then click Circle. You're finished using Photoshop, so you can now quit that program.

Using Photoshop alpha channels in InDesign

Now you'll return to InDesign and see how you can create different clipping paths from the Photoshop paths and alpha channels.

1 Switch to InDesign. Make sure that the 08_d.psd Photoshop file is still selected on the page; if necessary, select it using the Selection tool (➤).

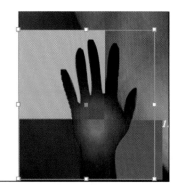

2   (Optional) Right-click (Windows) or Ctrl+click (Mac OS) the hand image, and choose Display Performance > High Quality from the context menu that appears. This step isn't necessary, but it lets you precisely preview the following steps.

3   With the hand image still selected, choose Object > Clipping Path > Options to open the Clipping Path dialog box. If necessary, move the Clipping Path dialog box so that you can see the image as you work.

4   Make sure that Preview is selected in the Clipping Path dialog box, and then choose Alpha Channel from the Type menu. The Alpha menu becomes available, listing the three alpha channels you saw in Photoshop by the names used in that program.

5   In the Alpha menu, choose Alpha 1. InDesign creates a clipping path from the alpha channel. Then choose Alpha 2 from the same menu, and compare the results.

💡 *The first clipping path you see represents the default settings for defining the edges of an alpha channel. You can fine-tune the clipping path that InDesign creates from an Alpha Channel by adjusting the Threshold and Tolerance options, as you did for the Detect Edges feature earlier in this lesson. For Alpha Channels, start with a low Threshold value, such as 1.*

6 Choose Alpha 3 from the Alpha menu, and then select the Include Inside Edges option. Notice the changes in the image.

Selecting the Include Inside Edges option makes InDesign recognize a butterfly-shaped hole painted into alpha channel 3, and adds it to the clipping path.

💡 *You can see how the butterfly-shaped hole looks in Photoshop by viewing Alpha Channel 3 in the original Photoshop file. To see the butterfly you may need to select Include inside edges in the Clipping Path dialog box.*

7 Choose Photoshop Path from the Type menu, and then choose Shapes from the Path menu. InDesign reshapes the image's frame to match the Photoshop path.

8 Choose Circle from the Path menu. Since this is the effect wanted for this design, click OK.

Placing native files

InDesign works with native Adobe files such as Photoshop, Illustrator, and Acrobat in unique ways. A document may have different requirements for graphics, and InDesign allows you to import different file types, and provides options for controlling how the file is imported. For example, a Photoshop file with layers can be imported as a complete document, or you have the option of importing one (or more) of the layers separately.

Importing a Photoshop file with layers and layer comps

In the last exercise, you worked with a Photoshop file with saved paths and alpha channels; however, the file had only a single background layer. When you work with a layered Photoshop file, you can adjust the visibility of the individual layers. Additionally, you can view different layer comps.

Layer comps were introduced with Photoshop CS and are often used when a designer wants to create multiple compositions of an image in order to compare different styles or artwork. Layer comps are created in Photoshop and saved as part of the file; when the file is placed into InDesign you have the ability to preview the different comps in relation to your entire layout.

1 In the Links panel, click on the link for 08_j.psd and click the Go To Link button (⬅️) to select the file and center it on your screen. This file, which you relinked in a previous exercise, has four layers and three layer comps.

2 Choose Object > Object Layer Options to open the Object Layer Options window. This window allows you to turn layers off and on, as well as switch between layer comps.

3 Move the Object Layer Options window to the bottom of your screen in order to see the selected image more clearly. Check the Preview checkbox. This will allow you to view changes while keeping the Object Layer Options window open.

4 Click on the eye icon (👁) to the left of the hands layer. This turns off the hands layer, leaving only the simple background layer visible. Direct your attention to the Links panel and note that in the link for the current graphic (08_j.psd) there is an eye icon. This icon appears when the visibility of a layered document is modified by the user and is a visual cue that the default state of the graphic has been changed.

5 Click on the square next to the hands layer to turn visibility back on. The eye icon disappears from the Links panel because the image's original state has been restored.

6 In the Layer Comp section of the Object Layer window, click on the pop-up menu and choose the Green Glow option. This layer comp has a different background and the hands layer has a green glow added to it. The glow was added as a layer style in Photoshop to the Green Textured layer comp.

7 From the Layer Comp section, choose the Purple Opacity option. This layer comp has a different background and the hands layer is partially transparent. Layer comps are not merely an arrangement of different layers, but are able to save Photoshop layer styles, visibility, and position values.

8 From the Layer Comp section, choose the Blue Plain option. This layer comp was the original version of the document. Click OK.

Placing inline graphics

Inline graphics are graphics that flow with the text when placed. In this exercise you will place the album logo into the paragraph text.

1   In the Pages panel double-click on the second spread and choose View > Fit Spread in Window. Scroll down if necessary. At the bottom of the pasteboard is a text frame with the logo "Orchard of Kings." You will be inserting this graphic into the paragraph above.

2   Using the Selection tool (↖), click on the logo named Orchard of Kings and choose Edit > Cut to place the graphic into your clipboard.

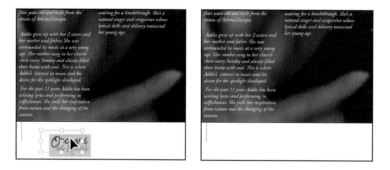

3   Click on the Zoom tool (🔍) and click on the text frame on page 6 to magnify the view; we used 150%. Choose Type > Show Hidden Characters to view the spaces and paragraph returns in the text. This will help you locate where you want to paste the inline graphic.

Note: Show Hidden Characters is not a necessary step when placing inline graphics; it is used here to help identify the structure of the text.

4   Choose the Type tool (T) and click on the second paragraph return following the words "Athens, Georgia." You will see a blinking text cursor. Choose Edit > Paste to place the graphic between the two paragraphs. Notice that the text after the graphic reflows when the image is placed.

5   You will now create space between the graphic and the surrounding text by using Space Before. At the top of your screen, in the Control panel, click on the Paragraph button (¶) to switch to the paragraph formatting options. In the Space Before property (⇥☰), click the up arrow to change the value to 0p4. As you increase the value, the inline graphic and following text shift downwards slightly.

Adding text wrap to an inline graphic

Text Wrap can be added to an inline graphic quite easily. This feature allows a designer to experiment with different layouts and see the results immediately.

1   Choose the Selection tool (↖) and click on the Orchard of Kings graphic you placed in the last exercise. Hold down the Ctrl and the Shift keys (Windows) or the Command and the Shift keys (Mac OS) on your keyboard and click and drag the top right handle of the frame up and to the right. This key combination allows you to proportionally scale the graphic and the frame simultaneously. You should scale the graphic until it is roughly 25% into the second column.

2   Choose Window > Text Wrap to access the text wrap options. Even though the graphic is inline, it is placed beneath the existing text.

3   In the Text Wrap window, click on the third option, Wrap around object shape (▦) to add text wrap to the graphic.

4   To increase space around the bounding box of the graphic, press the up arrow in the Top Offset option and change the value to 1p0.

5   Text can also wrap around the shape of the graphic rather than just the bounding box. To see this more clearly, click on the white pasteboard to deselect and then click back on the "Orchard of Kings" logo, then press the forward slash key (/) to apply no fill color.

6 In the Contour Options of the Text Wrap window, choose Detect Edges from the pop-up menu. Because this image is a vector graphic, the text wrap honors the edges of the text. To view the document clearly, click on the background to deselect the graphic and choose Type > Hide Hidden Characters to hide the paragraph returns and space.

7 Use the Selection tool (▶) to once again select the "Orchard of Kings" logo. In the Wrap To pop-up menu of the text wrap window, select Right Side. The type will move to the right side of the image, avoiding the area right below the image, even though there is space for it to display beneath the text wrap boundary.

8 Now select Both Left and Ride Sides. The type will move into all available areas around the image. You'll notice that there is a small break in the type where the text wrap boundary drops into the type area.

9 Finally, select Largest Area. The text will move into the largest area to one side of the text wrap boundary.

10 (Optional) Click on the Direct Selection tool (▶) and then click on the graphic to view the anchor points used for the text wrap. When using the Detect Edges option, you can always manually adjust the anchor points used to define the text wrap by clicking on the anchor points and adjusting them.

11 Close the Text Wrap panel.

Importing an Illustrator file

InDesign takes full advantage of the smooth lines provided by EPS (Encapsulated PostScript) vector graphics such as those from Adobe Illustrator. When you use InDesign's high-quality screen display, EPS vector graphics and type appear with smooth edges at any size or magnification. Most EPS vector graphics don't require a clipping path because most programs save them with transparent backgrounds. In this section, you'll place an Illustrator graphic into your InDesign document.

1   Select the Layers panel and click on the Graphics layer to target it. Choose Edit > Deselect All to make sure nothing is selected in your document. Then choose File > Place and select the Illustrator file 08_e.ai from the Lesson_08 folder. Make sure that Show Import Options is off. Click Open.

2   Place your loaded cursor on the top left corner of page 5 and click to add the Illustrator file. Position it as shown below. Graphics created in Illustrator are transparent in the areas where there is no artwork.

3   If you want, resize the InDesign window once you've finished importing the file.

Importing an Illustrator file with layers

If you want to import an Illustrator file with layers, you must save the original Illustrator file in layered PDF format. This will allow you to control the visibility of the layers and reposition the graphic; however, you will not be able to edit the paths, objects, or text.

1   Be sure nothing is selected by clicking in the white area of your document. Choose File > Place. In the bottom left corner of the Place window, select the checkbox Show Import Options. Select the file 08_n.pdf and click the Open button. The Place PDF window appears when Show Import Options box is checked.

2   In the Place PDF window, make sure that Show Preview is selected; in the options section, be sure Crop to: Bounding Box and Transparent Background are selected.

To create a layered PDF in Adobe Illustrator

Adobe InDesign CS3 and Adobe Acrobat both provide features for changing the visibility of layers in an Adobe PDF file. By saving a layered PDF file in Illustrator, you allow your illustration to be used in different contexts. For example, rather than creating multiple versions of the same illustration for a multilanguage publication, you can create one PDF file that contains text for all languages.

Note: Keep the layers that you want to adjust in InDesign in the top level or within a layer set at the top level. Do not place them in nested layer sets.

1 Set up your illustration so that the adjustable elements (those you want to show and hide) are in separate top-level layers, not nested within sublayers. For example, if you're creating an illustration to be repurposed for multiple languages, put the text for each language in a different top-level layer.

2 Save the file in Adobe PDF format.

3 In the Save Adobe PDF dialog box, choose Acrobat 8 (1.7) or Acrobat 7 (1.6) for Compatibility.

4 Select Create Acrobat Layers from Top-Level Layers, set additional PDF options, and click Save PDF.

—From Illustrator Help

3 Click the Layers button to view the layers in this file. This file has three layers: A background image of trees (Layer 3), a layer of text in English (English Title) and a layer of text in Spanish (Spanish Title). Although you can designate which layers you would like to import at this point, the small Preview area makes it difficult to see the results, so you will do so in the document itself. Click OK.

4 With the loaded graphic icon (⬚), place your cursor to the left of the large blue box on page 5, do not place your cursor inside the blue box or you will insert the graphic into the frame. Click once to place the graphic and then position the graphic so that it is centered over the blue box.

5   With the graphic still selected, choose Object > Object Layer Options. Move the window if necessary so you can see the graphic in the document. Select the Preview checkbox and then click the eye icon (👁) next to the English Title layer to turn it off. Now click the empty box next to the Spanish Title to turn on that layer. Click OK and deselect the graphic by clicking on the white pasteboard. Using layered Illustrator files allows you to re-purpose illustrations without having to create two separate documents.

Using a library to manage objects

Object libraries let you store and organize graphics, text, and pages that you frequently use. You can also add ruler guides, grids, drawn shapes, and grouped images to a library. Each library appears as a separate panel that you can group with other panels any way you like. You can create as many libraries as you need—for example, different libraries for each of your projects or clients. In this section, you'll import a graphic currently stored in a library, and then you'll create your own library.

1   If not currently on page 5, type **5** into the page navigation box at the bottom of the InDesign document window to go to that page, and then press Enter or Return.

2   Choose File > Open, select the file 08_k.indl in the Lesson_08 folder, and then click Open. Drag the lower right corner of the panel to reveal more of the items it contains.

3   In the 08_k.indl library panel, click the Show Library Subset button (🔍). In the last box for the Parameters option, type **tree**, and click OK.

Show Subset
⦿ Search Entire Library
◯ Search Currently Shown Items
Parameters

OK
Reset
Back
Forward

Item Name ▲▼ Contains ▲▼ tree

More Choices   Fewer Choices

4   Make sure that the Links panel is visible. In the Layers panel, make sure that the Graphics layer is targeted.

5   Out of the two objects visible in the 08_k.indl library panel, drag Tree.psd to page 5. The file is added to the page, and notice how the file name appears in the Links panel.

Note: Because you copied the Tree.psd from its original location to your hard drive, InDesign may alert you to the fact that the file is in a new location by displaying a missing link icon (●) or an alert icon (▲) in the links panel. You can remove the warning by choosing the Update Link command from the Links panel menu.

6   Using the Selection tool (▶), position the Tree.psd image as shown below.

Creating a library

Now you'll create your own library.

1 Choose File > New > Library. Type **CD Projects** as the library filename, navigate to the Lesson_08 folder, and click Save. The library appears in its own floating panel, labeled with the filename you specified.

2 Go to page 3 and, using the Selection tool (▶), drag the "ricky records" logo to the library you just created. The logo is now saved in the library for use in other InDesign documents.

3 In the CD Projects library, double-click the "ricky records" logo. For Item Name, type **Logo**, and then click OK.

4 Using the Selection tool, drag the address text block to the library you created. It appears in the CD Projects library panel.

5 In the CD Projects library, double-click the address text block. For Item Name, type **Address**, and then click OK. Now your library contains both text and graphics. As soon as you make changes to the library, InDesign saves the changes.

Note: Graphics stored using an InDesign library still require the original, high-resolution file for printing. The entire graphic file is not copied into the library; it maintains a link to the original source file.

6 Close the Library.

Using Adobe Bridge to import graphics

Adobe Bridge is a separate application which is installed with Adobe InDesign CS3. Adobe Bridge allows you to browse your local and networked computers for images and then place them into InDesign.

1 Choose File > Browse to launch Adobe Bridge.

2 In the upper left corner in the Favorites section is a list of the various locations you can browse for documents in Adobe Bridge. If you placed the Lesson_08 folder used for this lesson on your desktop, locate the folder and double-click on it to view the contents. If you placed the Lesson_08 folder in a different location, double-click on My Computer (Windows) or Computer (Mac OS) and navigate to the Lesson_08 folder, and then double-click on the folder to view its contents.

3 Adobe Bridge allows you to view the thumbnails of all your images. Click once on the graphic named Leaf.psd to select it. Then click once on the file name to select the file name field. Rename the file 08_o.psd and press the Return or Enter key to commit the change. Renaming files directly in Adobe Bridge can be very useful.

4 If necessary, resize the Adobe Bridge window so the InDesign document is visible in the background, then click and drag the 08_o.psd file into the white pasteboard area of your document. Click once in the document to return to InDesign.

5 Position the leaf graphic in the upper right corner of page 3, on top of the purple box.

6   Click on the 08_j.psd file in the Links panel to select it. Then select the Go To Link button (⊷⬚) at the bottom of the Links panel. Right-click (Windows) or Ctrl+click (Mac OS) on the graphic in the document and choose Graphics > Reveal in Adobe Bridge. You will switch from InDesign to Adobe Bridge and the 08_j.psd file will be selected.

7   Return to InDesign and save the file.

Congratulations! You've created a CD booklet by importing, updating, and managing graphics from many different graphics file formats.

Exploring on your own

Now that you've had some practice working with imported graphics, here are some exercises to try on your own.

1   Place different file formats with Show Import Options turned on in the Place dialog box, and see what options appear for each format. For a full description of all the options available for each format, see InDesign Help.

2   Place a multiple-page PDF file with Show Import Options turned on, and import different pages from it.

3   Create libraries of text and graphics for your work.

Review

▶ **Review questions**

1   How can you determine the filename of an imported graphic in your document?

2   What are the three options in the Clipping Path window, and what must an imported graphic contain for each option to work?

3   What is the difference between updating a file's link and replacing the file?

4   When an updated version of a graphic becomes available, how do you make sure that it's up to date in your InDesign document?

▶ **Review answers**

1   Select the graphic and then choose Window > Links to see if the graphic's filename is highlighted in the Links panel. The graphic will appear in the Links panel if it takes up more than 48KB on disk and was either placed or dragged.

2   The Clipping Path window in InDesign allows you to create a clipping path from an imported graphic by using:

• The Detect Edges option when a graphic contains a solid white or solid black background.

• The Photoshop Path option when a Photoshop file contains one or more paths.

• The Alpha Channel option when a graphic contains one or more alpha channels.

3   Updating a file's link simply uses the Links panel to update the on-screen representation of a graphic so that it represents the most recent version of the original. Replacing a selected graphic uses the Place command to insert another graphic in place of the selected graphic. If you want to change any of a placed graphic's import options, you must replace the graphic.

4   Check the Links panel and make sure that no alert icon is displayed for the file. If an alert icon appears, you can simply select the link and click the Update Link button as long as the file has not been moved. If the file has been moved, you can locate it again using the Relink button.

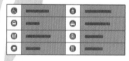

Tables are an efficient and effective way to communicate large amounts of information. With InDesign, you can easily create visually rich tables. You can either create your own tables or import tables from other applications.

9 Creating Tables

In this lesson you'll learn how to do the following:

- Import formatted tables from other applications, such as Microsoft Word and Microsoft Excel.

- Format tables with alternating row colors.

- Format cell and border strokes.

- Apply colors to individual rows.

- Delete and resize columns.

- Set precise column dimensions.

- Place single or multiple graphics within a cell.

- Format text in tables by columns and by rows.

Getting started

In this lesson you'll work on a fictional magazine spread that takes tables of information and brings them into the world of effective visual design. You'll develop tables using the Table panel which gives you complete control over table features.

Note: If you have not already copied the resource files for this lesson onto your hard disk from the Adobe InDesign CS3 Classroom in a Book *CD, do so now. See "Copying the Classroom in a Book files" on page 4.*

1   To ensure that the tools and panels function exactly as described in this lesson, delete or reset the InDesign CS3 defaults preferences following the procedure in "Saving, deleting and restoring preference files" on page 2.

2   Start Adobe InDesign CS3.

3   Choose File > Open, and open the 09_a.indd file in the Lesson_09 folder inside the Lessons folder located in the InDesignCIB folder on your hard disk. This layout contains specific information about a garden tour.

4   Choose File > Save As, name the file **09_Gardens**, and save it in the Lesson_09 folder in the InDesignCIB folder on your hard disk.

5   To see what the finished document will look like, open the 09_b.indd file in the same folder. You can leave this document open to act as a guide as you work. When you're ready to resume working on the lesson document, choose Window > 09_Gardens.indd.

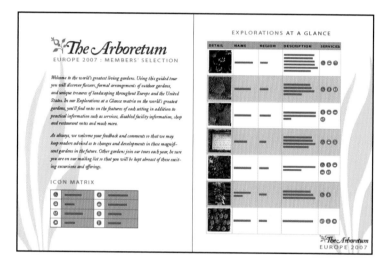

In the Pages panel of your 09_Gardens.indd document, notice that page 1 and page 2 are on different spreads. You want those pages to face each other in a single spread, so you will number them pages 2 and 3.

6 In the Pages panel, double-click to select page one. From the panel menu (▾☰), choose Numbering & Section Options, and then select the Start Page Numbering At option and type **2**. Click OK to close the dialog box.

7 From the Pages panel menu, deselect Allow Selected Spread to Shuffle. If you were to add or remove pages, doing this would keep this pair of pages together.

8   Open the Layers panel, and make the following adjustments:

•   (Optional) Click the eye icon (👁) for the Leaves layer to hide that layer. This will make it easier to keep from accidentally clicking on the leaves in the background.

•   Select the Table layer to target it.

•   Click to lock the Text layer so that you don't accidentally change it while you work on the first table.

Importing and formatting a table

Since you've worked with tables before in a previous lesson, you already know that tables are grids of individual cells set in rows (horizontal) and columns (vertical). The border of the table is a stroke that lies on the outside perimeter of the entire table. Cell strokes are lines within the table that set the individual cells apart from each other. Many tables include special rows or columns that describe the category of information they contain. Typically, these are in the top row or the first column.

InDesign CS3 can import tables from other applications, including Microsoft Word and Microsoft Excel. You can even create a link to these external files so that if you update the Word or Excel file, you can update that information in your InDesign document. In this section, you'll import a table that was created in Word. This table contains all the information about the garden tour that you want in your InDesign layout, organized into rows and columns.

1   From the Pages panel, double-click page 3 to center it in the Document window.

2   Select View > Grids & Guides, and make sure that the Snap to Guides command is selected, as indicated by a check mark. If the Show Guides command is available in the Grids & Guides submenu, select it now.

To create a link to the Microsoft Word document, so that you can update the file later, you will need to change your preferences.

3   Select Edit > Preferences > Type (Windows) or InDesign > Preferences > Type (Mac OS). Under Links, select Create Links When Placing Text and Spreadsheet Files and then click OK.

4   With the Type tool (T), click to place an insertion point in the burgundy framed text box on page 3. You want the file to be placed in this box.

5   Choose File > Place, and then navigate to the Lesson_09 folder and double-click the 09_c.doc file. If the Microsoft Word Import Options dialog box appears, click OK. If the missing fonts dialog box appears, click OK.

6   The file flows into the text box. Because it is a table, text wraps within the cells. You can edit text and make selections according to rows, columns, or the entire table.

Garden name	Location	Description	Services	1999 Tour
Anreuten-Wynne	Looten	Small gardens; outbuildings and historical ornament of note; guided tours provided Tues–Sat at noon; bookstore with publications on gardening and on Anreuten-Wynne.	disabled, bus, dining	Yes
Bilsettre Manor	Mornay	Mansion estate; unusual collection of rare peonies and topiary; open only April through October	Disabled, baby, retail	Yes
Caledonia Place	Caledonia	Former college; five buildings and reflecting pool, sculpture garden	Baby, bus, taxi, retail	No
Ducca D'bro	Arepa	Garden reflects designs of original owners, landscape designers with French formal gardening background.	Disabled, bus, lockers	Yes
Dveenolde Pilke	Denham	Unusual greenhouse and rare blooming plants.	Disabled, baby, bus, taxi, retail	No
Filbenne Grand Gardens	Sutton	Very grand garden estate currently undergoing major renovations; most areas open.	Disabled, baby	Yes
G'honoré-Wyatt	Limson	Mansion, extensive gardens.	Retail, lockers, coffee	No

EXPLORATIONS AT A GLANCE

7   You may notice a red dot in one of the columns. This indicates that the column is not wide enough to accommodate the text.

Garden name	Location
Anreuten-Wynne	Looten
Bilsettre Manor	Mornay
Caledonia Place	Caledonia

If so, adjust the column by positioning the Type tool over a column stroke and, when you see a horizontal arrow icon, drag the column wider to accommodate the text.

You are now ready to begin formatting your table.

Formatting borders and alternating row colors

InDesign CS3 includes many easy-to-use formatting options for tables. You can use these to make your tables attractive and easy for readers to understand so that they find the information they need quickly and comfortably.

1   Using the Zoom tool (🔍), click the upper left area of page 3 to increase the magnification to 100% or more. Then select the Type tool (T).

2   Move the pointer to the upper left corner of the imported table, so that the pointer appears as a heavy diagonal arrow, and click once to select the entire table.

Increase the magnification if you experience difficulty getting the diagonal arrow to appear. An alternate way to select an entire table is to click the Type tool anywhere in the table and then choose Table > Select > Table. If the Type tool is not selected, this command is not available.

3   Choose Table > Table Options > Table Setup. Or, choose the same command on the Table panel menu (▾☰). The Table Options dialog box opens at the Table Setup tab.

4   Under Table Border, set the following options:

- Weight: 1
- Type: Solid
- Color [Black]
- Tint 50%

Table Options

| Table Setup | Row Strokes | Column Strokes | Fills | Headers and Footers |

Table Dimensions

Body Rows: 8   Columns: 6
Header Rows: 0   Footer Rows: 0

Table Border

Weight: 1 pt   Type: ▼
Color: ■ [Black]   Tint: 50%   ☐ Overprint
Gap Color: ☐ [Paper]   Gap Tint: 100%   ☐ Overprint
☐ Preserve Local Formatting

Table Spacing

Space Before: 0p4   Space After: -0p4

Stroke Drawing Order

Draw: Best Joins

☑ Preview   OK   Cancel

5 Then click the Fills tab and set the following options:

• For Alternating Pattern, select Every Other Row.

• On the left side, select Color as C = 43, M = 0, Y = 100, K = 56, and then type **20%** for in the Tint field.

• On the right side, select Color as [Paper].

• In Skip First, type **1** so that the alternating colors start on row 2 (the row below the headings).

Table Options

| Table Setup | Row Strokes | Column Strokes | Fills | Headers and Footers |

Alternating Pattern: Every Other Row ▼

Alternating

First: 1 Rows   Next: 1 Rows
Color: ■ C=43 M=0 Y=100... ▼   Color: ☐ [Paper] ▼
Tint: 20% ☐ Overprint   Tint: 100% ☐ Overprint

Skip First: 1 Rows   Skip Last: 0 Rows

☐ Preserve Local Formatting

☑ Preview   OK   Cancel

6   Click OK to close the dialog box, and then choose Edit > Deselect All so that you can see the results.

The even-numbered rows now have a pale green fill color behind the black text.

Editing cell strokes

Cell strokes are the lines around individual cells. You may want edit the default black strokes, or remove the strokes altogether. In this section, we'll alter the cell strokes so they match the new table border.

1   Select the Type tool (T) and move the pointer to the upper left corner of the table until it turns into a diagonal arrow, then click to select the entire table.

2   Choose Table > Cell Options > Strokes and Fills or choose the same command from the Table panel menu (▾≡).

3   In the Cell Stroke area of the dialog box, select the following options:

- Weight: 1
- Type: Solid
- Color [Black]
- Tint 50%

4   Click OK and then select Edit > Deselect All to see the results of your formatting.

Formatting the heading cells

Another element that makes reading a table easier is to set the categories apart from the table data. By making the categories visually distinctive, your readers are more likely to comprehend the table information. In this procedure, you'll create insets so that the text doesn't run into the strokes on each cell, and then give the heading row a unique color fill.

1 Using the Type tool (T), move the pointer over the left edge of the first row until it appears as a heavy horizontal arrow (→). Then click to select the entire first row.

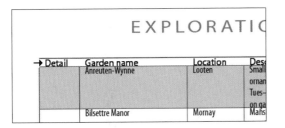

2 Choose Table > Cell Options > Text.

3 On the Text tab, set the following options:

• Under Cell Insets, type **0p3.6** for Top and then click the Make All Settings the Same icon (⚙) to autofill Bottom, Left and Right to match.

• Under Vertical Justification, for Align, select Align Center.

• For First Baseline, make sure that the Offset is set as Ascent. Leave the dialog box open.

4   Click the Strokes and Fills tab, leave the Cell Stroke value as it is (1 pt, Solid, [Black], 50%). For the Color option under Cell Fill, select C = 43, M = 0, Y = 0, K = 56. Set the Tint at 40%, and leave the dialog box open.

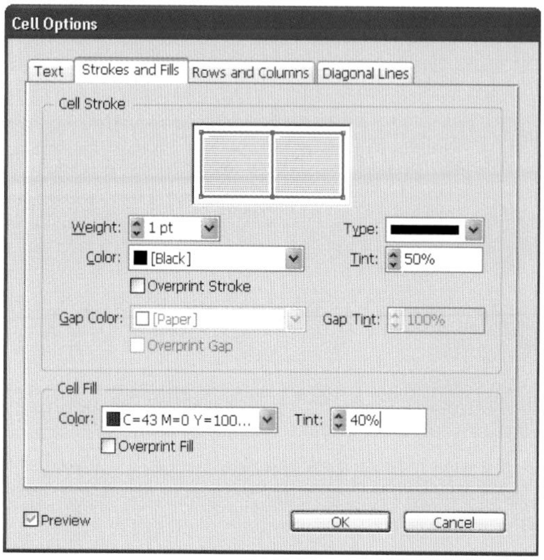

Cell Options

Text | Strokes and Fills | Rows and Columns | Diagonal Lines

Cell Stroke

Weight: 1 pt   Type: ▬▬▬
Color: ■ [Black]   Tint: 50%
☐ Overprint Stroke
Gap Color: ☐ [Paper]   Gap Tint: 100%
☐ Overprint Gap

Cell Fill
Color: ■ C=43 M=0 Y=100...   Tint: 40%
☐ Overprint Fill

☑ Preview   OK   Cancel

5   Click the Rows and Columns tab, for Row Height, choose Exactly from the pop-up menu, and then type **2p0**.

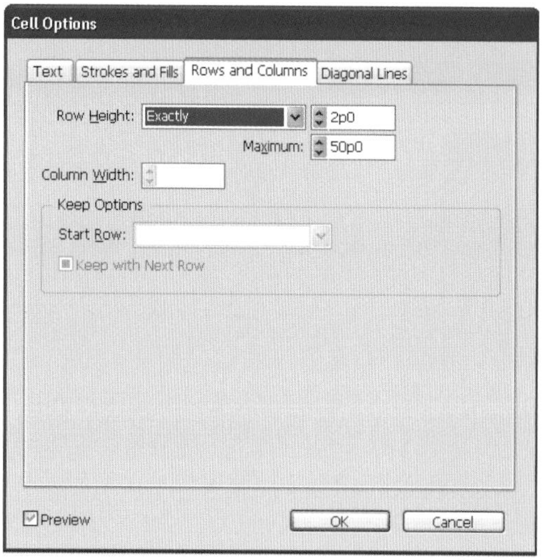

Cell Options

Text | Strokes and Fills | Rows and Columns | Diagonal Lines

Row Height: Exactly   2p0
            Maximum: 50p0
Column Width:
Keep Options
Start Row:
☐ Keep with Next Row

☑ Preview   OK   Cancel

6   Click OK to close the dialog box, and then deselect to see the results of your work.

The heading row of the table now appears formatted with white type against a green background.

Deleting a column

After you create or import a table, you can add or delete entire rows or columns to or from your table structure. Sometimes, you'll want to delete just the contents of a cell, row, or column. Other times, you'll want to delete the cell, row, or column itself, including its contents. The techniques for these two procedures differ slightly so that you make the exact edits that you intend.

The information in the column on the far right of this table is out of date and no longer relevant, so you'll delete the entire column now.

1   Using the Type tool (T), move the pointer to the top edge of column 6 (the last column, on the right) until the pointer turns into a heavy downward-pointing arrow (↓). Then click to select the entire column.

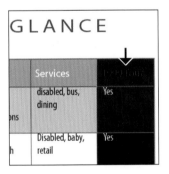

2   Choose Table > Delete > Column. Now the entire column disappears.

Note: To delete only the contents of a column, you can select the column and use the Delete key on your keyboard.

You'll find additional commands in the Table menu and Table panel menu for inserting additional columns and rows, for deleting rows and entire tables, and for selecting rows, columns, cells, and entire tables.

Using graphics within tables

You can use InDesign tables to create effective tables that combine text, photographs, and illustrations. The techniques involved are as easy as working with text.

In this section, you'll adjust your table formatting so that the cells are the correct sizes for the graphics you'll place in them. Then you'll put graphics into those cells.

Setting fixed column and row dimensions

You can define the sizes of cells, columns, or rows to fit precise measurements. In this exercise, you will adjust the size of the first column so that the one-inch photographic images fit nicely within the cells.

1   Using the Type tool (T), select the first column, either by dragging from top to bottom or by clicking the top edge of the column when the heavy downward-pointing arrow (↓) appears. Or, you can click in any cell of the column and select Table > Select > Column.

2   Choose Window > Type & Tables > Table to show the Table panel, if it is not already visible. In the Column Width option (⊞), type **6p10.8** , and press Return or Enter. Then click anywhere in the table to deselect the column.

3   Using the Type tool, drag down from the second cell in the first column. Select all the cells except the heading cell at the top of the column.

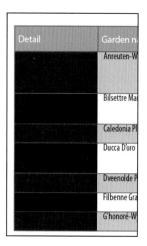

4   In the Table panel, select Exactly in the Row Height option and type **6p10.8**. Press
Enter.

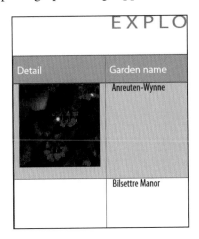

Placing graphics in table cells

To save you some time, most of the images you'll place within the table are already
placed on the pasteboard of this document. In this procedure, you'll just cut and paste
these images one by one into the cells of the first table column. To begin, you'll import
one image that is not yet part of the InDesign file.

1   Using the Type tool (T), click to place the insertion point in the first cell in the
second row (just below the "Detail" cell).

2   Choose File > Place, and locate the 09_d.tif file in your Lesson_09 folder. Double-
click to open the file. If the Import Image Options dialog box appears, click OK. The
photographic image appears in the first cell.

3 Double click on the page 3 thumbnail in the Pages panel to center page 3 in the Document window.

Make the leaves layer visible if you turned it off earlier.

4 Using the Selection tool (↖), select the top photograph on the pasteboard to the right of the spread. Then choose Edit > Cut.

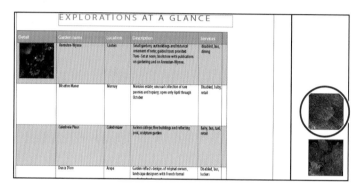

5 Double-click to place an insertion point in the third row of the first column, just below the photograph you placed in the previous step.

6 Choose Edit > Paste.

7 Continue cutting and pasting to place each of the remaining five photographs into the empty cells in column 1, proceeding from top to bottom.

💡 *You can temporarily switch between the Selection tool and the Type tool by holding the Ctrl key (Windows) or Command key (Mac OS).*

Note: You cannot simply drag items into table cells. Dragging would merely position the item above or below the table in the layout stacking order, not place the item within a cell. Tables require you to use the Type tool as you place or paste content into cells.

Placing multiple graphics in a cell

Essentially, the images you place or paste into table cells are inline graphics in text. Because of this, you can add as many images to a single cell as you need. You are limited only by the actual size of a cell.

1 Select the Zoom tool (⌕), then click and drag to isolate the upper right hand corner of page 3, along with the icons located on the pasteboard.

2 Hide the Pages panel, or any other panels if necessary, by clicking on the Pages tab, to reveal the graphics on the pasteboard of the document. Using the Selection tool (▸), select the wheelchair icon on the pasteboard.

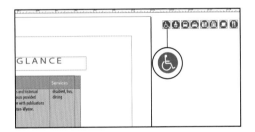

3 Choose Edit > Copy.

4 Switch to the Type tool (T), and look in column 5 for the first instance of the word disabled. Click and drag to select the entire word and the comma. It is probably easiest to also select the space between that word and the next one.

5   Choose Edit > Paste. If you selected the space after the comma, press the spacebar to add a space after the icon.

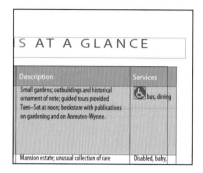

6   Find the remaining instances of the word Disabled in the remaining cells of that column, select them, and paste to replace the text with the wheelchair icon.

7   Repeat this entire process for each of the remaining words and icons: Baby, Bus, Taxi, Retail, Lockers, Coffee, and Dining.

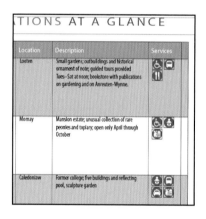

Note: If you are unsure which icon is which, select the icon with the Selection tool and then look at the Links panel to see which file is selected. The icon files have descriptive names.

Because you haven't yet adjusted the column widths, your icons may overlap each other vertically at this phase of your work. You'll fix that in the next section.

8   Click the Pages tab to reveal the Pages panel and double-click on the page 3 thumbnail to center the page.

Formatting text within a table

All that remains in your table project is to make some final adjustments so that the spacing of the text, graphics, and table are in harmony with the rest of the spread.

Editing imported paragraph styles in a table

If you are already comfortable formatting text in text frames, then formatting text in tables will be an easy and natural extension of your InDesign skills.

1 Using the Type tool (T), select the word "name" in the first row of your table. Notice in the Paragraph Styles panel that this type already carries the paragraph style "header." This style was imported along with the Microsoft Word document where it had originally been formatted. You will want to update the style to reflect new formatting.

2 In the Control panel, set following attributes:

- Font: Myriad Pro
- Style: Regular
- Size: 10 pt
- Leading: 14 pt
- Case: All Caps
- Tracking: 150
- Horizontal Scale: 125%

3 In the Swatches panel, select Black for the text.

4 In the Paragraph Styles panel, you will now see a plus sign (+) next to the header style. From the panel menu (▾☰), select Redefine Style.

If some of the text no longer fits into the cells, it will be fixed in the next step. Overset text inside of cells is represented by a red dot inside the cell.

5 In the third column, select the word "Looten." Notice in the Paragraph Styles panel that this type already carries the paragraph style "bodytable." This style was imported along with the Microsoft Word document where it had originally been formatted. You will want to update the style to reflect new formatting.

6   In the Control panel, set the following attributes:

- Font: Myriad Pro

- Style: Regular

- Size: 8 pt

- Leading: 10 pt

7   In the Paragraph Styles panel, you will now see a plus sign (+) next to the bodytable style. From the panel menu (▾≣), choose Redefine Style.

Creating a new cell style

Now you'll want to create a New Cell Style as we did in Lesson 7 that contains the paragraph style we just edited, as well as cell formatting, we want to have the text in these cells vertically aligned in the center.

1   Select the Type tool (T) and click to create an insertion point in the word "Looten."

2   Select Window > Type & Tables > Cell Styles. From the Cell Styles panel menu (▾≣), choose New Cell Style.

3   Assign a name for the style in the Style Name field. Call this style Table Body.

4   From the Paragraph Styles pop-up menu, choose the paragraph style **bodytable**. This ensures that the style is part of the cell formatting.

5   Select Text on the left side of the dialog box. In the Cell Insets section, enter **0p5** in the Top field and click Make all settings the same icon to fill in the same values for Bottom, Left and Right.

6   In the Vertical Justification section, choose Align Center from the Align pop-up menu.

Cell Options

| Text | Strokes and Fills | Rows and Columns | Diagonal Lines |

Cell Insets

Top: 0p5   Left: 0p5
Bottom: 0p5   Right: 0p5

Vertical Justification

Align: Center   Paragraph Spacing Limit: 0p0

First Baseline

Offset: Ascent   Min: 0p0

Clipping   Text Rotation
☐ Clip Contents to Cell   Rotation: 0°

☑ Preview   OK   Cancel

7 Click OK. The new Table Body cell style should appear in your Cell Styles panel.

8 With the Type tool (T), select through all rows and columns (excluding the headline row) and click Table Body to apply the new style to all the selected cells. Even though there is no type in the first column, you can still take advantage of the centering for the photos.

> *Note: If you try this and the text does not change and you still see a plus sign (+) next to the style, press the Alt (Windows) or Option (Mac OS) key as you select the style.*

9 You'll notice in the last column that the leading is too tight to accommodate the icons. You will want to adjust this.

10 With the Type tool (T), select the three icons in the top body cell of the last column.

11 In the Control panel, increase the leading to 20 pt.

12 From the panel menu (▾≡) in the Paragraph Styles panel, choose New Paragraph Style. Your new leading displays in the Style Settings box.

13 Type **Table Icons** in the Style Name field to assign a name to this new style. Click OK.

14 Choose Windows > Type & Tables > Cell Styles to access the Cell Styles panel. Since we want to use a Cell Style similar to Table Body, just with a different Paragraph Style, click the Table Body style and then, from the panel menu (▾≡), choose Duplicate Style.

15 The Duplicate Cell Style window appears, displaying all the same attributes as the original Table Body style.

16 Enter **Table Icons** in the Style Name field.

17 In the Paragraph Styles section, choose the new Table Icons paragraph style from the pop-up menu.

18 Click OK. The new Table Icons style now appears in your Cell Styles panel. With the Type tool, select all the cells with green icons (exclude the header row) and click Table Icons in the Cell Styles panel to apply the new style to these cells.

Your cell contents should now all be formatted properly, and, if necessary, you only need to adjust the column widths to accommodate the text and images.

Dragging to adjust column size

When an ordinary text frame contains text that doesn't completely fit into the assigned space, the out port for the frame displays a red plus sign, indicating that there is overset text. You can solve that either by enlarging the text frame or continuing the story in another text frame.

In tables, text or graphics that don't fit into their cells are also called overset but are indicated by a small red circle in the lower right corner of the cell. Table cells do not support linking. Overset text must be made smaller, or cells must be made larger, if contents do not fit in a cell.

For this table, you'll resize the columns so that everything fits nicely into the table.

1 Zoom into the page by pressing Ctrl+2 (Windows) or Command+2 (Mac OS) to view the page at 200%.

2 Move the Type tool (T) over the vertical line separating columns until the pointer icon becomes a double arrow (↔), and then drag the column margin to the right to resize it so that it is wider, leaving more room for the header.

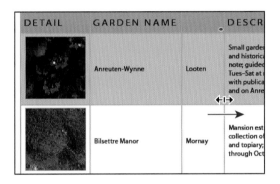

3 Moving from left to right, resize each of the columns so that the contents fit inside. Also set the right edge of the table to snap against the vertical margin guide on the right side of the page.

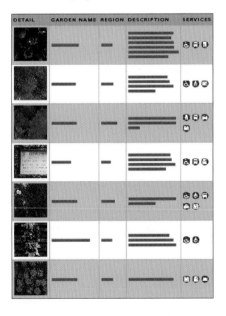

4 Deselect all, then choose View > Fit Spread in Window, and then save your work.

Finishing up

You're almost finished with your work on this lesson.

1   In the Tools panel, click the Preview Mode button.

2   Press Tab to hide all the panels and review the results of your work.

Congratulations! You have now completed this lesson.

For more information about working with tables, see "Tables" in InDesign Help.

Exploring on your own

Now that you're skilled in the basics of working with tables using InDesign, you can experiment with other techniques to expand your table-building abilities.

1   To create a new table, scroll beyond the spread to the pasteboard, and drag the Type tool (T) to create a new text frame. Then choose Table > Insert Table and enter the number of rows and columns you want in your table.

2   To enter information in your table, make sure that the blinking insertion point is in the first cell and then type. To move forward to the next cell in the row, press Tab. To move to the next cell down in the column, press the Down Arrow key.

3   To add a column by dragging, move the Type tool (T) over the right edge of one of the columns in your table, so that the pointer becomes a double-headed arrow. Hold down Alt (Windows) or Option (Mac OS) and drag a short distance to the right, perhaps half an inch or so. When you release the mouse button, a new column appears, having the same width as the distance you dragged.

4   To combine several cells into one cell, select all the cells in the new column you just created. Then choose Table > Merge Cells. To convert the table to text, choose Table > Convert Table to Text. You can have tabs separate what were previously columns and have paragraph breaks separate the columns. You can also modify these options. Similarly, you can convert tabbed text into a table by selecting the text and choosing Table > Convert Text to Table.

5   To create rotated text, click the Type tool inside the merged cell you just created. Choose Window > Table to bring the Table panel forward, and select the Rotate Text 270° option (↦). Then type the text you want in this cell.

Review

▶ **Review questions**

1   What are the advantages of using tables rather than just typing text and using tabs to separate the columns?

2   When might you get an overset cell?

3   What tool is used most frequently when you work with tables?

▶ **Review answers**

1   Tables give you much more flexibility and are far easier to format. In a table, text can wrap within a cell, so you don't have to add extra lines to accommodate cells with many words. Also, you can assign styles to individual rows, columns, and cells, including character styles and even paragraph styles, because each cell is considered a separate paragraph.

2   Overset cells occur when the dimensions of the cell are limited and the contents don't fit inside it. For this to occur, you must actively define the width and height of the cell (or its row and column). Otherwise, when you place text in the cell, the text will wrap within the cell, which then expands vertically to accommodate the text. When you place a graphic in a cell that does not have defined size limits, the cell also expands vertically but not horizontally, so that the column keeps its original width.

3   The Type tool must be selected to do any work with the table. You can use other tools to work with the graphics within table cells, but to work with the table itself, such as selecting rows or columns, inserting text or graphic content, adjusting table dimensions, and so forth, you use the Type tool.

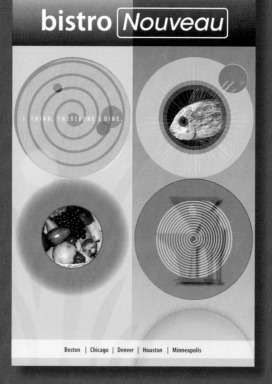

InDesign CS3 delivers an array of transparency features to feed your imagination and creativity. InDesign CS3 provides control over opacity and color blendings and you can also import files that use transparency.

10 | Working with Transparency

In this lesson you'll learn how to do the following:

- Colorize an imported black-and-white graphic.

- Change the opacity of objects drawn in InDesign.

- Adjust transparency settings for imported graphics.

- Apply transparency settings to text.

- Apply blending modes to overlapping objects.

- Apply feathering to objects.

- Apply multiple effects to an object.

- Edit and remove effects.

Getting started

The project for this lesson is a menu for a fictional restaurant, Bistro Nouveau. By applying transparency effects using a series of layers, you'll create a visually rich design.

Note: If you have not already copied the resource files for this lesson onto your hard disk from the Adobe InDesign CS3 Classroom in a Book CD, do so now. See "Copying the Classroom in a Book files" on page 4.

1   To ensure that the tools and panels function exactly as described in this lesson, delete or reset the InDesign CS3 defaults preferences following the procedure in "Saving, deleting and restoring preference files" on page 2.

2   Start Adobe InDesign CS3.

3   Choose File > Open, and open the 10_a.indd file in the Lesson_10 folder, which is located within the Lessons folder in the InDesignCIB folder on your hard disk.

4   Choose File > Save As, name the file **10_Menu.indd**, and save it in the Lesson_10 folder.

The menu appears as a long, blank page because all layers are currently hidden. You'll reveal these layers one by one as you need them, so that it will be easy to focus on the specific objects and tasks in this lesson.

5 To see what the finished project will look like, choose File > Open, and open the 10_b.indd file in the Lesson_10 folder, which is located within the InDesignCIB folder on your hard disk.

6 When you are ready to start working, you can either close the 10_b.indd file or choose Window > 10_Menu.indd to switch back to your own lesson document, leaving the sample of the finished file open for reference.

Importing and colorizing a black-and-white image

You'll begin by working with the background layer for the menu. This layer serves as a random textured background that will be visible through the objects layered above it that have transparency settings. Since there's nothing below this layer in the layer stack, you won't change this object's opacity.

1   In the Layers panel, select the Background layer, scrolling as necessary to find it at the bottom of the layer stack. Make sure that the two boxes to the left of the layer name show that the layer is visible (eye icon (👁) appears) and unlocked (layer lock icon (🔒) does not appear). The pen icon (✒) to the right of the layer name indicates that this is the layer onto which any imported objects will be placed, or where any new frames will be created.

2   Choose View > Grids/Guides > Show Guides

3   Choose File > Place, and then locate, select, and open the bg.tif file in your Lesson_10 folder.

4   Move the loaded graphics icon pointer (📄) to the upper left corner of the page where the bleed guides meet and click, so that the image fills the entire page, including any margins. After you place the graphic, it remains selected. Keep the image selected.

Note: If you don't see the bleed guides on the page, choose View > Grids & Guides > Show Guides to reveal them.

5   With the graphic still selected, choose Window > Swatches to open the Swatches panel and select the Fill box (■). Scroll down the list of swatches to find the Light Green and click to select it. Click the Tint pop-up and drag the slider to 76%. The white areas of the image are now the 76% tint of the green color, but the gray areas remain gray. Choose Edit > Deselect All to deselect the image.

6   In the Tools panel, use the Direct Selection tool ( ) to select the image again, and then select the Light Green color in the Swatches panel. The Light Green color replaces gray in the original image, leaving the Light Green 76% areas as they were.

Note: *Remember that the Direct Selection tool appears as a hand ( ) when it is over a frame, but it still selects the contents of an image frame when you click.*

7   In the Layers panel, select the empty box to the left of the Background layer name to lock the layer. Leave the Background layer visible so that you can see the results of the transparency work you will be doing above this layer.

You've learned a quick method for colorizing a grayscale image. While this method is effective for creating composites, you may find the color controls available in Adobe Photoshop CS3 more effective for creating your final work.

Applying transparency settings

InDesign CS3 provides extensive transparency controls. You can adjust the opacity of strokes and fills applied to objects, text, and even imported objects. Additional controls for blending modes, drop shadows, feathering and other effects provide creative opportunities to experiment with transparency effects.

In this project, practice using various transparency options on each of the layers of the menu.

About the Effects Panel

Use the Effects panel (Window > Effects) to specify the opacity and blending mode of objects and groups, isolate blending to a particular group, knock out objects inside a group, or apply a transparency effect.

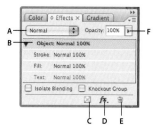

A. *Blending Modes.* **B.** *Levels.* **C.** *Clear Effects*
D. *Fx button.* **E.** *Delete.* **F.** *Change Opacity.*

Effects panel overview

Blending Mode—Specifies how colors in transparent objects interact with the objects behind them. (Search for Specify how colors blend in help.)

Opacity—Determines the opacity of an object, stroke, fill, or text. (Search for Set the opacity of an object in help.)

Level—Tells you the Object, Stroke, Fill, and Text opacity settings of the object, as well as whether transparency effects have been applied. Click the triangle to the left of the word Object (or Group or Graphic) to hide or display these level settings. The FX icon appears on a level after you apply transparency settings there, and you can double-click the FX icon to edit the settings.

Isolate Blending—Applies a blending mode to a selected group of objects. (Search for Isolate blending modes in help.)

Knockout Group—Makes the opacity and blending attributes of every object in a group knock out, or block out, underlying objects in the group. (Search for Knock out objects within a group in help.)

Clear All button—Clears effects—stroke, fill, or text— from an object, sets the blend mode to Normal, and changes the Opacity setting to 100% throughout the object.

FX button—Displays a list of transparency effects. (Search for Apply transparency effects in help.)

—From InDesign Help

Changing the opacity of solid-color objects

With the background graphic complete, you can start adding transparency features to the layers stacked above it. You'll start with a series of simple shapes that were drawn using InDesign CS3.

1   In the Layers panel, select the Art1 layer so that it becomes the active layer, and click the small box on the left of the layer name, unlocking the layer. Click in the box to the far left of the Art1 layer name, so the eye icon (👁) is displayed, indicating that the layer is visible.

2   Using the Selection tool (➤), click the circle filled with the Yellow/Green swatch on the right side of the page. This ellipse frame with a solid fill was drawn in InDesign.

Note: Choose Window > Swatches to open the Swatches panel for this exercise. The shapes mentioned will be named by the color swatch applied to the fill of the object.

3   Choose Window > Effects to open the Effects panel.

4   In the Effects panel, click the arrow to the right side of the Opacity percentage, and an Opacity slider adjustment is displayed. Drag the slider to 70%. You can also type **70%** in the Opacity option and press Enter if you do not wish to use the slider to adjust the transparency level.

After you adjust the transparency, the purple bar is now visible beneath the Yellow/Green filled ellipse.

5 Select the Light Green filled semicircle at the top, left of the page, go to the Effects panel and set the Opacity value at 50%. The semicircle now appears as just a subtle variation in color against the background.

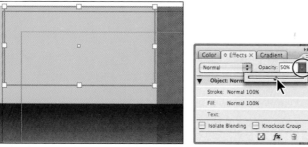

Select the image.   Change the opacity to 50%

6 Repeating the process used in step 5, change the remaining circles on the Art1 layer, using the following settings to change the opacity of each of the circles:

- Left side, middle ellipse filled with the Medium Green, swatch, Opacity = **60%**

- Left side, bottom ellipse filled with the Light Purple swatch, Opacity = **70%**

- Right side, ellipse filled with the Light Purple swatch and a black stroke, Opacity = **60%**

- Right side, bottom semicircle filled with the Light Green swatch, Opacity = **50%**

Applying a blending mode

An Opacity setting creates a color that combines the color values of the object with the objects below it. Blending modes give you another way to create color interactions between layered objects.

In this procedure, you'll first change the opacity and then apply the Multiply blending mode to the same objects.

1 Using the Selection tool (↖), select the Yellow/Green filled circle on the middle, right side of the page.

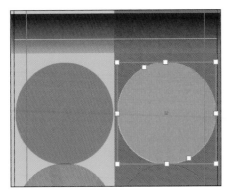

2　In the Effects panel, open the blending mode pop-up menu, which currently displays Normal as the selected blending mode, and select Overlay. Notice the change in the appearance of the colors.

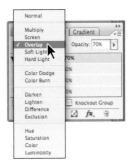

3　Select the Light Green filled half-circle at the bottom of the right side of the page, and then hold down the Shift key and select the half-circle at the top of the left side of the page, and apply the Multiply blending mode, using the same method as in step 2.

4　Choose File > Save.

For more information about the different blending modes, see "Specify how colors blend" in InDesign Help. This topic describes the results generated by each of the blending modes.

Adjusting the transparency settings for EPS images

You have applied various transparency settings to objects drawn using InDesign. You can also set the opacity values and blending mode for imported graphics in programs such as Adobe Illustrator.

1   In the Layers panel, unlock and make visible the Art2 layer.

2   In the Tools panel, make sure that the Selection tool (⬀) is selected.

3   On the left side of the page, click the black spiral image, which is on top of the Medium Green colored circle. With the black spiral still selected, press and hold the Shift key and click to select the spiral that is above the Light Purple circle on the right side of the page. Both spiral objects should now be selected.

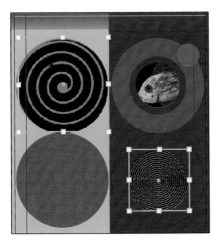

4   In the Effects panel, select Color Dodge blending mode and set the Opacity to 30%.

5   In the Layers panel, click the box to the left of the Art2 layer name to lock the Art2 layer, and then choose File > Save to save your work.

Next you will apply a blending mode to the stroke of an object.

6   With the Selection tool, click on the fish image on the right side of the page. From the Effects Panel, click on the Stroke option beneath Object. This will apply an opacity or blending mode changes you make to the stroke of the selected object.

7   Choose Hard Light from the Blending Mode options.

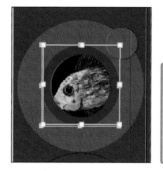

Select the image.   Select the Stroke option.   Choose Hard Light.

Adjusting transparency for Photoshop images

In this procedure, you'll apply transparency to an imported Photoshop file. Although this example uses a monochromatic image, you can also apply InDesign transparency settings to complex multicolor photographs.

1   In the Layers panel, select the Art3 layer. Click to unlock this layer and to make it visible. You can hide either the Art1 and Art2 layers to make it easier to work. Be sure to keep at least one underlying layer visible so that you can see the results of the transparency interactions.

2   Using the Selection tool (⬀), click the black starburst image on the upper right side of the page.

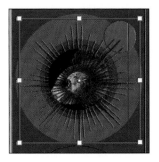

3   On the Effects panel, enter **70%** as the Opacity value.

4   Switch to the Direct Selection tool (↖), move the pointer over the starburst image so that it changes to a hand (✍), and then click once on the image.

5   In the Swatches panel, select the Red color swatch so that the red color replaces the black areas of the image. If other layers are visible below the Art3 layer, you can see the starburst as a muted orange color. If no other layers are visible, the starburst is red. Leave the starburst image selected, or reselect it with the Direct Selection tool now.

6   In the Effects panel, select Screen blending mode and leave the Opacity value at 100%. The starburst changes colors based upon the layers that are visible beneath it.

Importing and adjusting Illustrator files that use transparency

When you import Adobe Illustrator files into your InDesign layout, InDesign CS3 recognizes and preserves any transparency interactions that were applied in Illustrator. You can also apply additional transparency settings within InDesign, adjusting the opacity, blending modes, and feathering to the entire image.

1   Make sure that the Art3 layer is the active layer in the Layers panel. Choose the Selection tool (↖) from the Tools panel, and then choose Edit > Deselect All.

2   Choose View > Fit Page in Window.

3   Choose File > Place. Activate the Show Import Options feature at the bottom of the Place window.

4 Locate the 10_d.ai file in your Lesson_10 folder, and double-click to select it.

5 In the Place PDF dialog box, be sure that the Bounding Box option for Crop to: is selected, then click OK.

6 Position your cursor, which becomes a loaded graphics icon (🖉), over the purple circle in the middle of the right side of the page. Click to place the graphic image. If necessary, drag the image so that it is approximately centered over the purple circle. Be careful not to place the graphic in an existing frame.

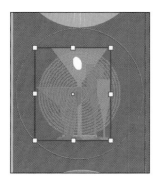

7 In the Layers panel, click to hide the Art2, Art1, and Background layers so that only the Art3 layer is visible. This allows you to see the transparency color interactions within the original image. After viewing the placed image on its own, click within the Layers panel to make the Art2, Art1, and Background layers visible. Notice that the white "olive" shape is completely opaque while the other shapes of the drinking glasses are partly transparent.

8 With the glasses graphic still selected, change the Opacity setting in the Effects panel to **80%**. You can now see the spiral behind the white olive and that the glasses are more subdued in color. Keep the image of the glasses selected.

9 In the Effects panel, select Color Burn as the blending mode. Now the colors and interactions of the image take on a completely different character.

10 Choose File > Save to save your work.

Applying transparency settings to text

Changing the opacity of text is as easy as applying transparency settings to graphic objects in your layout. Next, you'll change the color and opacity of some text that you will add to the layout.

1 In the Layers panel, click to lock the Art3 layer and then click to unlock and make visible the Type layer to the layout.

2 In the Tools panel, choose the Selection tool (▶), then click on the text frame "I THINK, THEREFORE I DINE." If necessary, zoom in so that you can read the text easily.

3   In the Effects panel, click on the Select Overlay blending mode and type **70%** as the Opacity value.

Note: You cannot specify transparency options when the Type tool is active. By switching to the Selection tool, the transparency options can be applied to the text frame and its contents.

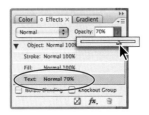

4   Choose Edit > Deselect All and then choose File > Save to save your work.

Applying transparency settings to text frame fill

Changing the opacity of text is as easy as applying transparency settings to graphic objects in your layout. Next, you'll change the color and opacity of some text that you will add to the layout.

1   In the Tools panel, choose the Selection tool (➤), then click on the text frame at the bottom of the page that contains, "Boston | Chicago | Denver | Houston | Minneapolis." If necessary, zoom in so that you can read the text easily.

2   Choose Fill from the Effect panel and change the Opacity to **70%.**

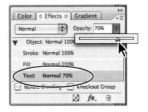

3   Choose Edit > Deselect All and then choose File > Save to save your work.

Working with effects

InDesign offers nine transparency effects. Many of the settings and options for creating these effects are similar.

Transparency effects

Drop Shadow—Adds a shadow that falls behind the object, stroke, fill, or text.

Inner Shadow—Adds a shadow that falls just inside the edges of the object, stroke, fill, or text, giving it a recessed appearance.

Outer Glow and Inner Glow—Add glows that emanate from the outside or inside edges of the object, stroke, fill, or text.

Bevel and Emboss—Adds various combinations of highlights and shadows to give text and images a three-dimensional appearance.

Satin—Adds interior shading that makes a satiny finish.

Basic Feather, Directional Feather, and Gradient Feather—Soften the edges of an object by fading them to transparent.

—From InDesign Help

Applying basic feathering to the margins of an image

Feathering is another way to apply transparency to an object. There are three types of feathering found in InDesign CS3, including: Basic Feather (softens or fades) the edges of an object over a distance that you specify), Directional Feather (softens the edges of an object by fading the edges to transparent from directions that you specify) and Gradient Feather (softens the areas of an object by fading them to transparent.). Feathering creates a more subtle transition between the object and any underlying images. In this first part, you will apply a Basic Feather, then move onto the Gradient feather.

1   With the Selection tool, unlock the Art 1 layer and then select the Light Purple filled circle on the left side of the page.

2   Choose Object > Effects > Basic Feather. The Effects dialog box opens.

3   In Feather Width, type **0.375 in**. Leave the Corners option set as Diffused. Change the Choke to **10%** and the Noise value to **10%** as well. Make sure Preview is checked and then notice how the margins of the purple circle are now blurred. Click OK to close the Effects dialog box.

4   Choose File > Save.

Applying a Gradient feather

You can use the Gradient Feather effect to soften the areas of an object by fading them to transparent. This type of effect is new to InDesign CS3 and one that we have been using a lot.

1   Unlock the Art1 layer if not already unlocked. Choose the Selection tool (⬧) and click on the Light Purple filled vertical bar on the right side of the page on the Art1 layer.

2   In the Effects panel, click on the Fx button (*fx.*) at the bottom of the panel and choose Gradient Feather from the pop-up menu.

3   The Effects dialog box should appear. From the Effects dialog box, click on the Reverse Gradient button ( ) to reverse the black and transparent colors. Click OK to close the dialog box.

Note: The Effects dialog box shows you which effects are applied to a selected object (indicated by a check mark on the left side of the dialog), and allows you to apply multiple effects to a single object.

4   The purple rectangle should fade to transparent from right to left. Now you will control the direction of the transparency. In the Tools panel, click and hold down the mouse button on the Gradient Swatch tool to reveal the Gradient Feather tool. Select the Gradient Feather tool. With the cursor, hold down Shift and drag from bottom to top across the purple rectangle to change the gradient direction. If you don't get it right the first time, try it again.

5 Choose Edit > Deselect All and File > Save to save your work.

Next you will apply multiple effects to a single object, then edit them.

Applying multiple effects to objects

There are several different types of effects that can be applied. You can create the impression that an object is embossed by using the Bevel and Emboss effect or create the illusion of an object floating above the page by adding a drop shadow. These are just two of the effects that you will use.

1 Using the Selection tool (➤), select the Light Green filled half-circle in the upper left corner of the page.

2 In the Effects panel, click on the Fx button (*fx.*) at the bottom of the panel and choose Bevel and Emboss from the pop-up menu.

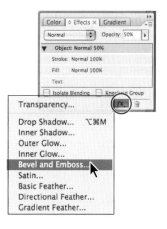

3 In the Effects dialog box, select the following settings under the Structure options. Make sure that Preview is selected to be able to see the effects on your page.

- Change the Size to **0.3125 in**.

- Change the Soften value to **0.3125 in** as well.

- Change the Depth to 30% by clicking on the arrow to the right of the Depth field and dragging the slider that appears.

4   Leave the rest of the settings alone and leave the Effects dialog box open.

For more information about the Effects settings, such as for the Bevel and Emboss, see "Bevel and Emboss" in InDesign Help. This topic describes the settings for the transparency effects.

5   With the Effects dialog box still open, click the checkbox to the left of Outer Glow on the left side of the dialog box. This will add an outer glow to the half-circle as well.

6   Click on the words Outer Glow on the left side of the Effects dialog box to edit the effect and confirm the following settings:

- Choose Multiply from the Mode settings pop-up menu.

- In Opacity, type **80%**.

- In Size, type **0.25 in**.

- In Spread, type **10%**.

7   Click OK to close the dialog box.

Next you will apply the same settings to the other half-circle on the page.

8 Double-click on the Hand tool (✋) to fit the page in the window.

9 With the green half-circle in the upper left corner still selected and the Effects panel visible, use the Selection tool to click and drag the Fx symbol (to the right of the Object option) directly on top of the green half-circle in the bottom right corner of the page.

Note: *If you miss the half-circle, you can choose Edit > Undo and try again.*

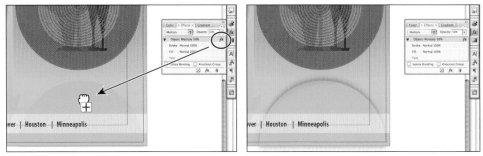

Drag the Fx icon onto the other half-circle   The result.

10 In the Layers panel, click the eye icon to turn off the visibility for the Art3 layer. Click and drag the same effect onto the gray circle above and to the right of the fish.

11 Choose File > Save to save your work.

Note: *When you export your InDesign document as an Adobe PDF, transparency is preserved when you create a file using Adobe Acrobat 5.0 or later as the compatibility setting.*

Editing and removing effects

Effects that are applied can easily be edited or removed. You can also do a quick check to see if any effects have been applied to an object.

1 In the Layers panel, make sure that the Art1 layer is unlocked and that it is visible.

2 With the Selection tool (▶), click on the black bar behind the text "bistro Nouveau."

3 With the Effects panel showing, click on the Fx button (*fx.*) at the bottom of the panel. Notice in the pop-up menu that appears, the Gradient Feather effect has a check mark next to it. Choose the Gradient Feather option in the menu.

4   The Effects dialog box will appear. Under the Gradient Stops options, click on the color stop at the right end of the gradient ramp to select it. Change the Opacity to **30%**. Change the Angle value to **90°**.

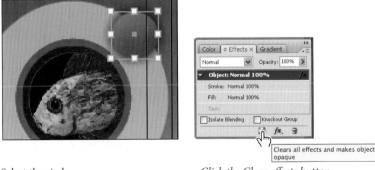

5   Click OK to close the Effects dialog box.

Now you will remove an effect from an object.

6   With the Selection tool, click on the small, gray circle to the right and above the fish image on the right side of the page.

7   At the bottom of the Effects panel, click on the Clear effects button (▨) to remove all of the effects applied to the circle.

Note: This would also remove any transparency changes such as opacity from the object.

Select the circle.   Click the Clear effects button.

💡 *If you would like to remove only any effects applied and not any opacity or blending mode changes, choose Object > Effects > Clear Effects.*

8   In the Layers panel, turn on the visibility for the Art3 layer.

9   Choose File > Save to save your work.

Congratulations! You have completed the lesson.

Exploring on your own

Try some of the following ways of working with InDesign transparency options:

1   Scroll to a blank area of the pasteboard and create some shapes (using the Drawing tools or by importing new copies of some of the image files used in this lesson) on a new layer. Position your shapes so that they overlap each other, at least partially. Then:

•   Select the topmost object in your arrangement of shapes and experiment with other blending modes, such as Luminosity, Hard Light, and Difference, by selecting them in the Effects panel. Then select a different object and select the same blending modes to compare the results. When you have a sense of what the various modes do, select all of your objects and select Normal as the blending mode.

•   In the Effects panel, change the Opacity value of some of the objects but not others. Then select different objects in your arrangement and use the Object > Arrange > Send Backward and Object > Arrange > Bring Forward commands to observe different results.

•   Experiment with combinations of different opacities and different blending modes applied to an object. Then do the same with other objects that partially overlap the first object to explore the enormous number of different effects you can create.

2   Double-click the Page 1 icon in the Pages panel to center it in the document window. Then try clicking the eye icons for the different Art layers one at a time, to see the differences this creates in the overall effect of the project.

3   Make sure all layers are unlocked in the Layers panel. Click on the graphic of the glasses to select it. Apply a drop shadow using the Effects panel.

Review

▶ **Review questions**

1 How do you change the color of the white areas of a black-and-white image? The black areas?

2 How can you change transparency effects without changing the Opacity value of an object?

3 What is the importance of the stacking order of layers and of objects within layers when you work with transparency?

4 Will the transparency effects you create in InDesign CS3 appear in a PDF that you export from InDesign?

▶ **Review answers**

1 To change the white areas, select the object with the Selection tool and then select the color in the Swatches panel. To change the black areas, select the object with the Direct Selection tool and then select the color you want to use in the Swatches panel.

2 Besides selecting the object and changing the Opacity value in the Effects panel, you can also create transparency effects by changing the blending mode, feathering an object several ways, adding drop shadows, bevel and emboss effects and more. Blending modes determine how the base color and the blend color will be combined to produce a resulting color.

3 The transparency of an object affects the view of objects below (behind) it in the stacking order. For example, objects below a semitransparent object can be seen behind it—like objects behind a colored plastic film. Opaque objects block the view of the area behind them in the stacking order, regardless of whether the objects behind them have reduced Opacity values, feathering, blending modes, or other effects.

4 Yes, if you export the PDF using compatibility settings of Acrobat 5.0 or later, the transparency is preserved in the resulting PDF file.

You can assemble your individual InDesign documents into multi-file books. Automatic page numbering from file to file is just the beginning. You can also create tables of contents and indexes for the entire book. Additionally, using the book features, multiple files can be printed or converted to PDF in one step.

11 | Working with Long Documents

In this lesson you'll learn how to do the following:

- Join multiple InDesign documents into a book.
- Control page numbering across separate documents.
- Create running headers and footers.
- Create a Table of Contents for a book.
- Assign a source document for defining styles.
- Update book files after modifying documents.
- Create text variables.
- Create index references.
- Generate an index file and sort entries.
- Edit index references.

Getting started

In this project, you'll gather together a collection of several InDesign CS3 documents, each representing one chapter of a cookbook. Using InDesign CS3, you'll assemble these chapters into a book so that you can easily create common elements, such as a table of contents, index, unified page numbering, styles, and color definitions.

Note: If you have not already copied the resource files for this lesson onto your hard disk from the Adobe InDesign CS3 Classroom in a Book *CD, do so now. See "Copying the Classroom in a Book files" on page 4.*

To ensure that the tools and panels function exactly as described in this lesson, delete or reset the InDesign CS3 defaults preferences following the procedure in "Saving, deleting and restoring preference files" on page 2.

Defining a book

Your project will pull together six existing chapters into a book. Defining a book means that you specify the relationships among multiple existing InDesign files, including which files are included in the book and in what order they appear.

The sample files you'll use for this project are from the *Powerful Food for Powerful Minds & Bodies* cookbook.

Creating a book file

The first task is to define which InDesign documents will be part of the new book.

1   Start Adobe InDesign CS3.

2   Choose File > New > Book.

3   In the New Book dialog box, type **Cookbook.indb** as the filename, and save the file in the Lesson_11 folder. The Book panel opens. The panel is empty, as you have not yet specified any InDesign files to be a part of the book.

Note: An .indb file is a book file, which opens the book panel. It contains references (links) to all the InDesign documents that are a part of the book—but it does not contain copies of the actual documents.

4   In the Book panel menu (▾☰), choose Add Document to open the Add Documents dialog box.

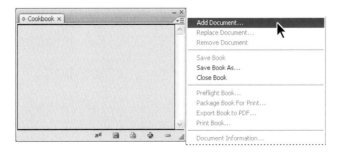

5 Open the Lesson_11 folder and select the following InDesign CS3 documents: breakfast, lunch, dinner, intro, snacks, and treats. Do not select the index and table of contents (TOC) files.

To select multiple files in one step, click one of the six documents and then Ctrl+click (Windows) or Command+click (Mac OS) each of the other five files. Or, you can add documents one at a time, repeating steps 4–5 for each one of the six files.

6 With all six files selected, click Open.

The six document names now appear in the Book panel. Notice that the page numbers for each chapter also appear in the panel.

7 Examine each of the documents listed in the Cookbook Book panel and notice the order of the files. The order in your Book panel may differ from the illustration above, depending on the order in which you selected and added the files.

Setting the order and pagination

The plan for the cookbook is to organize the chapters in the order they will appear in the book. The book will start with the introduction, and the meals will begin with breakfast, then lunch, dinner, snacks, and finally treats. Your next task is to organize the chapters in the order appropriate for the book, so that the sequence and page numbers flow appropriately.

1   In the Book panel, click and drag the intro file to the top of the list. When a black bar appears just under the tab in the panel, release the mouse. Notice that the pagination changes to reflect the new sequence of the files in the book.

2   Drag the other files into position on the list so that they appear in the following order (from top to bottom): intro, breakfast, lunch, dinner, snacks, treats.

Notice that the treats chapter starts on an even-numbered page. You want each chapter to start on an odd numbered page, keeping the start of each chapter consistent. Next you'll set the documents to always start on an odd numbered page.

3   In the Book panel menu (▼≡), choose Book Page Numbering Options.

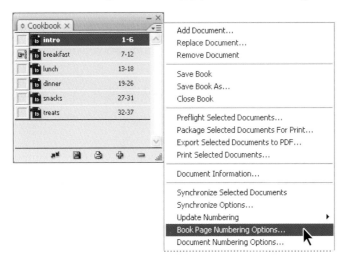

4   In the dialog box that appears, in the Page Order section, select Continue on next odd page. Also click Insert Blank Page, so InDesign will add a blank page at the end of a document to facilitate starting each new chapter on an odd page. If it isn't already selected, also click Automatically Update Page & Section Numbers to allow InDesign to keep page numbering updated. After choosing these options, click OK. All chapters will now begin on an odd-numbered page.

Now you'll change the starting page number of the current book.

5   In the Book panel, click once to select the intro file and then choose Document Numbering Options from the Book panel menu.

Note: Selecting the Document Numbering Options command in the Book panel menu will also automatically open the file.

6   Select the Start Page Numbering at option and type **3** so that the first page of the document appears on page 3. Then click OK.

7   Choose File > Save and then choose File > Close to close the intro document, but do not close the Book panel.

Working with a table of contents

A table of contents (TOC) for a book can be a separate InDesign document, or it can be placed in an existing document that is part of the book. You can also create a table of contents inside a single document, even if you have not created a book file. Here you will create a TOC for the section titles and recipe names in the cookbook.

Adding the table of contents file

If you create a new file to be used for the book TOC, be certain to carefully select the same document-setup specifications used in the other chapters of the book, such as the page size and paper orientation. For this lesson, the TOC file has already been created for you, but it is empty and you will add the actual content.

1   In the Book panel menu (▾≡), choose Add Document, and then locate and double-click the TOC.indd file in your Lesson_11 folder.

2   Drag the TOC document to the top of the Book panel list, so it is the first file listed in the Book panel.

3   In the Book panel, double-click the TOC file name to open it in the document window. You will now set the page numbering of the TOC to use Roman numerals.

4   From the Book panel menu, choose Document Numbering Options.

Note: You can also double-click the page numbers of a file in the Book panel list to open the Document Numbering Options for a specific file.

5   Select the Start Page Numbering at option and type **1**.

6   Under Style in the Document Page Numbering Options dialog box, select the lowercase Roman numerals option, i, ii, iii, iv..., and then click OK.

7   Choose File > Save to save the document, and then in the Book panel, choose Save Book from the Book panel menu (▾≡) to save the book file. Keep the TOC file open.

Generating a table of contents for the book

You will now have InDesign create the TOC listings for you. The TOC listings can be generated from any text where paragraph styles have been applied. You simply choose which paragraph styles you want to use. In this section, you will use text styled with the section_start, headline_intro and recipes paragraph styles.

1   In the TOC file, choose Layout > Table of Contents.

2   At the top of the dialog box, choose TOC Cookbook from the TOC Style menu. The Title changes to "Powerful Food" as the Title and other attributes of the TOC have been partially prepared for you. The Style, located to the right of the Title, changes to TOC Title. The words "Powerful Food" will appear at the top of the Table of Contents page, formatted in the TOC Title paragraph style.

The section_start and headline_intro styles have already been added to the Include Paragraph Styles list. You need to add the recipes style.

3 Under the Other Styles list on the right side of the dialog box, select recipes, and then click the Add button. This places the recipes style in the Include Paragraph Styles list along the left side of the dialog box.

4 Select recipes in the Include Paragraph Styles list. Under Style: recipes, select TOC cookbook body text for the Entry Style. This applies the selected paragraph style to the listings which will be created in the Table of Contents.

Because Include Book Documents is selected, all text in any of the book documents that is styled with the recipe Paragraph Style will be listed in the TOC.

5 Select Create PDF Bookmarks. This automatically creates PDF bookmarks using the TOC entries. The PDF bookmarks enhance navigation of the document if you convert the book files to PDF.

6 Click OK to generate the table of contents. The generated TOC appears as a loaded text icon.

7 Position the loaded-text icon (⊟) over the center of the page, and click to place the generated TOC text. The TOC flows onto the page, showing the separate chapter names, headlines, and recipes.

8 Choose File > Save.

Note: In this file, custom paragraph styles for the table of contents were created for you. When working with your own documents, you can adjust and format the text and style definitions of the TOC entries as you would any other text frame.

⋃ *If the text in the book has changed and the TOC needs revisions, open the file containing the TOC, insert the cursor in the TOC text and choose Layout > Update Table of Contents.*

Maintaining consistency across book files

You can ensure that paragraph-style specifications and color definitions are consistent throughout the book, creating a unified look for your long publication. To make this easier to manage, InDesign designates one of the files as the style source document. The style and color definitions in this source document are then used in all the other documents. By default, the first file that you place in the book becomes the style source. This is not necessarily the file at the top of the list in the Book panel.

You can tell which file is the style source by looking in the Book panel. A style source icon (⊟) appears in the box to the left of the designated source file. This box is empty for all other book files.

Reassigning the style source

Designating a file as the style source is an easy, one-click process. Here you'll make the dinner file the style source file with just one click.

- In the Book panel, click the empty box to the left of the dinner file.

The style source indicator now appears in the box next to the dinner file.

Synchronizing book documents

When you synchronize documents, InDesign automatically searches all the style and swatch definitions in the selected files and compares them to the definitions in the designated style source file. When the set of definitions in a file does not match the set in the style source file, InDesign adds, removes, and edits the definitions in the selected file so that they match those in the style source file. After synchronizing, all documents in the book have identical sets of styles, ensuring consistency throughout the book.

Currently, the paragraph definitions for several of the paragraph styles are defined differently in the various chapters of the book. You'll update the style and color definitions of each file using one simple process.

1   Make sure that the style source icon (🔲) appears next to the dinner file in the Book panel, indicating that it is the designated style source file.

2   Holding down Control (Windows) or Command (Mac OS) and clicking, select these five files in the Book panel: breakfast, lunch, dinner, snacks, and treats. It is not necessary to select the TOC or intro files.

3 In the Book panel menu (▾☰), select Synchronize Selected Documents.

Note: If all documents are selected, the option will be to Synchronize Book as opposed to Synchronize Selected Documents.

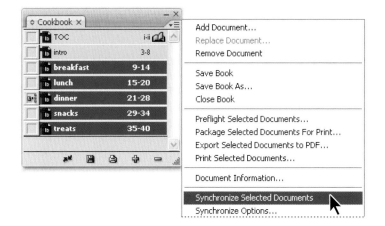

4 After a short delay, a message appears, telling you that synchronization was successful and that some documents may have changed. Click OK.

Indexing the book

Creating a good index is an art, as every reader who has tried to find a reference to a specific topic appreciates. Indexing is also a work that traditionally requires extraordinary attention to detail, with precise checking and rechecking of the entries. InDesign CS3 makes the job easier by facilitating the mechanical aspects of the process.

To create an index using InDesign CS3, you embed index references in the text. When you add or delete text, and the pagination changes, the embedded index references flow with the text. This ensures that an updated index always shows the correct page. These embedded index entries can display markers to show their location, or you can disable their visibility as you work. The index markers themselves never appear in the printed document.

You can create indexes for individual chapters, but you'll usually want to publish just one index at the end of this book, covering the entire contents of all chapters.

Creating index references

Some indexing has already been embedded in the project documents for this lesson. You'll add some index markers so you'll know how to do this yourself.

1   In the Book panel, double-click to open the breakfast document.

2   Navigate to page 10 to view the "Eggs & Fruit breakfast" recipe.

3   Choose Window > Type & Tables > Index to open the Index panel.

4   Select the Type tool (T) in the Tools panel, and select the words Eggs & Fruit breakfast in the recipe title.

5   Press Ctrl+U (Windows) or Command+U (Mac OS) then click OK in the New Page Reference dialog box that appears. The entry Eggs & Fruit breakfast is added to the Index panel. If necessary, scroll down the list to the letter E and click the arrow to see the new page reference.

6   With the Eggs & Fruit breakfast recipe title still selected on the page, choose New Page Reference on the Index panel menu. This adds another index reference to the same page.

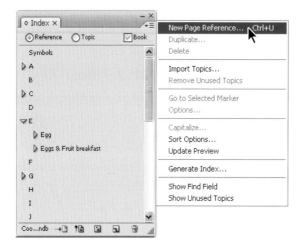

7   In the dialog box that opens, under Topic Levels, click the downward facing arrow, moving the Eggs & Fruit breakfast to Topic Level 2. Type **Breakfasts** in the box labeled 1. This creates an entry for "Breakfasts" and the specific breakfast will be listed under this heading as well in the final index. Click OK.

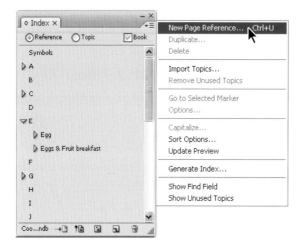

8   In the Index panel, scroll to review your new page references in the index list. If necessary, click the arrows adjacent to the letters to expand and collapse items in the index list.

Creating index cross-references

Many indexes include cross-references to other listings within the index. In this procedure, you'll add a cross-reference directing readers who are looking in the index for entries under "melon" to look under "cantaloupe" instead.

1   In the breakfast.indd file, choose Edit > Deselect All.

2   In the Index panel menu (▾≡), choose New Cross-reference.

3   In Topic Level 1, type **melon**.

4   In the Type pop-up menu, select See.

5   In the Referenced text field, type **cantaloupe**.

6   Click Add, then click Done.

7   Scroll down the list in the Index panel to see the new cross-reference. Choose File > Save to save your work.

Generating the index

As with the table of contents, you can place the index in a separate InDesign document or add it to a file in your book that already contains other content. In this project, you'll put the index in a separate file.

1   In the Book panel, choose Add Document from the panel menu (▾≡).

2 Locate the index.indd file in your Lesson_11 folder and double-click to add the file to the book. If the index file is not at the bottom of the list in the Book panel, drag it to that position now, so it becomes the bottom document listed in the Book panel.

3 In the Book panel, double-click the index file name to open the index document.

4 If the Index panel is not already open, choose Windows > Type & Tables > Index, and then select Generate Index from the Index panel menu (▾≡).

5 In the Generate Index dialog box, if necessary, select Include Book Documents and deselect Replace Existing Index, then click OK.

Note: *InDesign may require you to save the files before the index is generated.*

Generate Index		
Title: Index		OK
Title Style: Index Title		Cancel
☐ Replace Existing Index		More Options
☑ Include Book Documents	Book Name: Cookbook.indb	
☐ Include Entries on Hidden Layers		

6 After a short pause, the pointer appears as a loaded text icon (▤). Move the cursor to the center of the document page. Click with the loaded cursor, and the text flows onto the page, filling all three columns.

7 Choose File > Save.

The index combines all index references embedded in the book files into one unified index.

💡 *Always use the Index panel to enter and edit index entries. Although you can edit the index directly, like any other text frame, those changes will be lost when you regenerate the index.*

Congratulations! You have completed this lesson.

For more information about creating, refining, and formatting table of contents and index files, see "Tables of Contents" and "Indexes" in the InDesign Help.

Exploring on your own

1   Open the snacks file and delete several pages. Save the file. Then update your book numbering by doing the following:

• In the Book panel menu, choose Repaginate > Update Number > Update all Numbers..

• In the index file, using the Index panel menu, choose Generate Index. Make sure that the Replace Existing Index and the Include Book Documents check boxes are selected, and click OK.

• In the TOC file, select the table-of-contents text frame and choose Layout > Update Table of Contents.

In each case, notice the changes in the page numbering on the Book panel, index references, and table-of-contents references, respectively.

2   Examine the available options when you select all the files in the Book panel and then choose the following commands (one at a time) on the Book panel menu:

• Preflight Book.

• Package Book for Print.

• Export Book to PDF.

• Print Book.

3   Create an index reference for a range of pages. For example, in the breakfast file, select the word "Fruit" on page 10 and choose New Page Reference on the Index panel menu. Then, under Type, select the To End of Section option to create an index reference from pages 10 to 14.

Review

▶ Review questions

1   What are the advantages of the book feature in InDesign CS3?

2   Describe the process and the results of moving a chapter file in a book.

3   What is the best way to edit an index? Why?

▶ Review answers

1   The book feature makes it easy to coordinate related elements in a long document that consists of multiple files. By defining documents as a book, you can automate what would otherwise be time-consuming work, including the following:

- Maintaining the proper sequence of documents.

- Updating the pagination of the entire book after adding or removing pages.

- Generating a book-wide index and table of contents with accurate page references.

- Specifying options for preflight, packaging, exporting, and printing the entire book.

2   To move a file within a book, first select the file in the Book panel, then drag it to the desired location in the list of book files. After repositioning a book file, the index and table of contents entries for the book may become inaccurate. If automatic repagination has been disabled for the book, you will want to choose the repaginate command from the book panel. When you repaginate the book, update the index, and update the table of contents; all page references that involve pages that were below the moved file now change. Although the file is moved in the book, the file is not changed on your hard disk.

3   Always update index page references in the Index panel. To do this, double-click the index reference you want to edit in the Index panel (or select it and choose Topic Options on the Index panel menu), and then make your changes in the dialog box and click OK. When you finish making changes to index references, open the Index file. Then, on the Index panel menu, choose Generate Index and replace the existing index for all book documents.

It is important to do your editing in the Index panel instead of simply editing the index text directly. The reason is that any edits you make directly in the index text will be lost when you regenerate the index. If you then make changes in the book pagination, you risk having many incorrect index page references. If you edit in the Index panel, all those references are automatically updated when you generate a new index to update the existing one.

REFINE DESIGN '07
www.refinedesignconference.com

WHEN
June 19-20, 9:00am – 5:00pm
(registration begins at 8:30am)

WHERE
Seattle Central Library
(1000 Fourth Ave., 4th Floor)

Keynote Speaker:
Coming Soon!

Session Speakers:
Brian Wood,
VP/Director of Training, eVolve
evolveseattle.com
Gary Affonso, greywether.com
Liz Atteberry, Expedition Tea
and more to come...

Refine Design

Hone your skills and learn new time-saving tricks in
Adobe's new **Lightroom**, **Creative Suite 3**, and others.
Whether you're looking to learn **CSS**, delve deeper into
Flash or sharpen your **InDesign** and **Photoshop** skills,
this is one event you won't want to miss!

Sessions include:
» **Dreamweaver**: Tables to XHTML + CSS
» **InDesign** High Voltage: Work smarter not harder
» **Photoshop** & **Flash** Integration: Optimizing Pixels
  and Workflow
» Interactive Portfolio: **PDF** like you've never seen
» A new era in Digital Asset Management: **Adobe
  Lightroom**
» Adobe **Illustrator** CS3: Taming complex illustrations
» Rescuing, Retouching and Restoring with **Photoshop**
» **Flash ActionScript** workshop **and much more...**

Sign up before May 15th for the early bird rate!

www.refinedesignconference.com/

Hosted by:

eVolve
Computer Graphics Training Inc.

You can use Adobe InDesign
CS3's advanced printing and print
preparation controls to manage your
print settings, regardless of your
output device. With Adobe InDesign
CS3, you can easily print to a laser
printer, inkjet printer, high resolution
film, or computer-to-plate imaging
device.

12 | Output and PDF Exporting

In this lesson you will learn how to do the following:

- Confirm that an InDesign file and all of its elements are ready for printing.

- Generate a PDF file for proofing.

- Assemble all necessary files for printing or delivery to a service provider or printer.

- Print documents containing spot colors.

- Select appropriate print settings for fonts and graphics.

- Create a Print preset to automate the printing process.

Getting started

In this lesson, you'll work on a single page product marketing sheet that contains full-color images and also uses a spot color. The document will be printed on a color inkjet or laser printer for proofing and also on a high-resolution imaging device, such as a computer-to-plate or film imagesetter. Prior to printing, the file will be sent for review as an Adobe PDF file, which you will export from Adobe InDesign CS3.

Note: Even if you don't have a printer or you only have access to a black-and-white printer for proofing, you can still follow the steps for this lesson. You will use some default print settings that help you better understand the controls and capabilities that InDesign CS3 offers for printing and imaging.

Note: If you have not already copied the resource files for this lesson onto your hard disk from the Adobe InDesign CS3 Classroom in a Book *CD, do so now. See "Copying the Classroom in a Book files" on page 4.*

1   To ensure that the tools and panels function exactly as described in this lesson, delete or reset the InDesign CS3 defaults preferences following the procedure in "Saving, deleting and restoring preference files" on page 2.

2   Start Adobe InDesign CS3.

3   Choose File > Open and open the 12_a.indd file in the Lesson_12 folder, located inside the Lessons folder within the InDesignCIB folder on your hard disk.

4   An alert message informs you that the document contains missing or modified links. Click Don't Fix, as you will correct this problem later in this lesson.

When you print or generate an Adobe PDF file, InDesign CS3 must access the original artwork that was placed into the layout. If the original artwork is moved, its name has changed, or the location where the files are stored is no longer available, InDesign CS3 alerts you that the original artwork cannot be located. This alert occurs when a document is first opened, when a document is printed or exported, and when a document is checked for printing using the Preflight command. Additionally in the Links panel, InDesign CS3 shows the status of all files necessary for printing.

5   Choose File > Save As, rename the file **12_brochure.indd** and save it in the Lesson_12 folder.

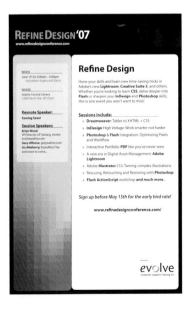

Using Preflight

Adobe InDesign CS3 provides integrated controls for checking the availability of all files necessary for imaging a document. You can use these controls to preflight a file, confirming that all graphics and fonts used in the file are available for printing. You can also check the colors used in the document, including fonts and colors used in placed graphics.

1   Choose File > Preflight. The Preflight dialog box opens.

2   In the Preflight dialog box, review the summary panel that appears. InDesign alerts you to several potential concerns, noted by the yellow triangle adjacent to the information. These include:

- One image is missing.

- One image uses RGB colors.

- Duplicate spot-colors may exist.

The summary section of the Preflight dialog box provides a fast overview of possible concerns in a document. For more detailed information you can click each of the six options along the left side of the dialog box.

3   Click the Fonts option to see a detailed list of fonts used in the document. You can learn about the fonts used in this job and whether they are OpenType, PostScript, or TrueType. You can also obtain additional information about fonts used in this job, including:

- Whether a font is available for printing, and whether it is missing, or incomplete.

- If a font is protected from embedding in a PDF by the font manufacturer.

- The first page on which the font is used.

- The location of the font file being used.

4   While continuing to examine the Fonts, click to select the Show Problems Only checkbox at the bottom of the Preflight dialog box. Notice how no fonts are listed, as all fonts are available for printing and there are no problems with them.

5   Click the Links and Images option along the left side of the Preflight dialog box.

Notice that information regarding all images used in the file is displayed. We want only to view possible problems.

6   Click to select Show Problems Only. Notice that two images are displayed as possible problems. One file, top_banner.psd, uses RGB colors. Because the document will be printed using CMYK colors, this could be a problem. The other image, rdlogo_red.ai is missing and needs to be located before the document can be printed.

You will replace the RD logo with a revised version that includes a color change. You will also address the RGB image in the printing process.

7   Click the Repair All button. Browse to the Links folder inside the Lesson_12 folder. This folder is located inside the Lessons folder within the InDesignCIB folder on your hard disk. Double-click the rdlogo_red_new.ai. The new file is now linked, in place of the original file.

8   Click to select the rdlogo_red_new.ai then click Update.

Because the file name is different, InDesign did not automatically update the image. If the selected file had not been modified since it was originally placed, InDesign would not have required you to update the link.

Note: The Repair All allows you to repair missing or modified links. It does not allow you to change the color space defined in a placed graphic. You can do this by opening the linked image in Photoshop and changing its color space or you can have InDesign convert the colors for printing.

9   Click the Colors and Inks option.

Notice that the four subtractive primary colors are listed: Cyan, Magenta, Yellow, and Black along with three variations of Pantone 1817. The C is for coated, M is for matte, and U is for uncoated. Because we will not want all three of these colors to print independently, we will want to correct this at the time we print this document.

10   Click the Cancel button.

Note: *You could directly package the file as the next step in preparing your file for delivery. For this lesson we have decided to create the package as a separate step.*

Using Package

You can use the package command to gather a copy of your InDesign document, all linked items, including graphics. InDesign also copies all fonts needed for printing.

1   Choose File > Package.

2   Click Continue in the dialog box that warns of possible problems discovered during Preflight.

Whenever you Package a file, InDesign CS3 automatically uses the Preflight command to confirm that all elements are available and that there are no possible problems. Because you still have not corrected the RGB image, InDesign CS3 alerts you to its presence. You will convert this image to CMYK for printing using InDesign CS3 later in this lesson.

3   In the Printing Instructions window, enter the file name for the instructions file that will accompany the InDesign document and also enter your contact information, then click Continue.

Note: The instructions file name cannot be the same as the document file name.

Adobe InDesign CS3 uses this information to create an instructions text file that accompanies the InDesign file, links, and fonts. This can be used by the recipient of the file to better understand work you want done on the file, or how to contact you if they have questions.

4   In the Create Package Folder dialog box, browse to locate the Lesson_12 folder and confirm that the folder being created for the package is named 12_brochure Folder. InDesign automatically names the folder based upon the document name, which you created in the Getting Started section of this lesson.

5   Confirm that the following are selected:

- Copy Fonts (Except CJK).
- Copy Linked Graphics.
- Update Graphic Links In Package.

6   Click the Package (Windows) or Save (Mac) button.

7   Read the Font Alert message that informs you about the various licensing restrictions that may affect your ability to copy fonts, then click OK.

8   Switch to your operating system and navigate to the 12_brochure Folder in the Lesson_12 folder (located inside the Lessons folder within the InDesignCIB folder on your hard disk).

Notice that Adobe InDesign CS3 created a duplicate version of your document and also copied all fonts, graphics, and other linked files necessary for high resolution printing. Because you selected the Update Graphics Links In Package, the duplicate InDesign file now links to the copied graphic files located in the package folder instead of the original linked files. This makes the document easier for a printer or service provider to manage, and also makes the package file ideal for archiving.

Close the 12_brochure Folder when finished viewing its contents.

Creating an Adobe PDF proof

If your documents need to be reviewed by others, you can create Adobe PDF files easily and efficiently to share them. Adobe InDesign CS3 exports directly to the Adobe PDF file format.

1   Choose File > Export.

Choose Adobe PDF from the Save as type (Windows) or Format (Mac OS) pop-up menu, and for Save as (file name) enter **proof**. If necessary, navigate to the Lesson_12 folder, then click Save. The Export Adobe PDF window opens.

2   From the Adobe PDF Preset pop-up menu, choose [High Quality Print]. This setting creates PDF files suitable for output on an office laser printer.

3   From the Compatibility pop-up menu, choose Acrobat 6 (PDF 1.5). This allows you to use more advanced features in the PDF file, including layers.

4   In the Options section of the window, click to enable the following two options:

• View PDF after Exporting.

• Create Acrobat Layers.

Automatically viewing the PDF after exporting is an efficient way of checking the results of the file export process. The Create Acrobat Layers option coverts the layers from the InDesign CS3 layout into layers that can be viewed in the resulting Adobe PDF file.

5   Choose Visible Layers from the Export Layers pop-up menu.

New in InDesign CS3 is the ability to choose InDesign layers to be exported when creating the PDF. Click on the pop-up menu next to Export Layers and you will see All Layers, Visible Layers, Visible & Printable Layers.

6   Click the Export button.

A warning window may be displayed, informing you that some objects in the layout are on hidden layers. Click OK to close this window if it does appear. An Adobe PDF file is generated and displays on your monitor.

7   Review the Adobe PDF file, then return to Adobe InDesign CS3.

Viewing a Layered Adobe PDF file using Adobe Acrobat 8

Use the following steps to view a layered PDF file created from Adobe InDesign CS3.

1 Click the Layers icon along the left side of the document window, or choose View > Navigation Panels > Layers, to display the Layers panel.

2 Click the plus sign (+) located to the left of the document name in the Layers panel.

The layers in the document are displayed.

3 Click the eye icon (👁*) to the left of the Text layer. As the icon is hidden, so are all objects on this layer.*

4 Click the empty box to the left of the Text layer to turn the visibility back on for the text.

5 Choose File > Close to close the document. Return to Adobe InDesign CS3.

Separation preview

If your documents need to be color separated for commercial printing, you can use the Separations Preview panel to gain a better understanding of how each portion of the document will print.

1   Choose Window > Output > Separations Preview.

2   Click to select Separations from the View pop-up menu in the Separations Preview panel.

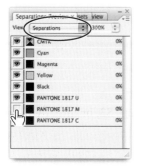

3   Click the eye icon (👁) adjacent to each of the Pantone 2582 colors to disable each color.

Notice how certain objects, images and text disappear as you click to disable viewing each color separation. Each of these objects has a different variation of the Pantone color associated with it. You will correct this later using the Ink Manager feature.

4   Choose Off from the View pop-up menu in the Separations Preview panel to enable viewing of all colors.

Transparency flattener preview

The images in this brochure have been adjusted using the transparency feature. You use the Transparency Flattener to determine how the transparency will impact the final printed version.

1   Choose Window > Output > Flattener Preview.

2   Choose Affected Graphics from the Highlight pop-up menu in the Flattener Preview panel.

3   If not already selected, choose High Resolution from the Preset pop-up menu. This is the setting you will use later in this lesson when imaging this file.

Notice how a red highlight appears over some of the objects on the page. These are the objects that will be impacted by the transparency that has been used in this document. You can use this highlight to help identify areas of your page that may be unintentionally affected by transparency and can adjust your transparency settings accordingly.

Transparency can be applied in Photoshop CS3, Illustrator CS3, or directly in the InDesign CS3 layout. The Flattener Preview can identify transparent objects, regardless of whether the transparency was created using InDesign or imported from another program.

4   Choose None from the highlight menu in the Flattener Preview panel.

About flattening transparent artwork

If your document or artwork contains transparency, to be output it usually needs to undergo a process called flattening. Flattening divides transparent artwork into vector-based areas and rasterized areas. As artwork becomes more complex (mixing images, vectors, type, spot colors, overprinting, and so on), so does the flattening and its results.

Flattening may be necessary when you print or when you save or export to other formats that don't support transparency. To retain transparency without flattening when you create PDF files, save your file as Adobe PDF 1.4 (Acrobat 5.0) or later.

You can choose a flattener preset in the Advanced panel of the Print dialog box or of the format-specific dialog box that appears after the initial Export or Save As dialog box. You can create your own flattener presets or choose from the default options provided with the software. The settings of each of these defaults are designed to match the quality and speed of the flattening with an appropriate resolution for rasterized transparent areas, depending on the document's intended use:

[High Resolution] is for final press output and for high-quality proofs, such as separations-based color proofs.

[Medium Resolution] is for desktop proofs and print-on-demand documents that will be printed on PostScript color printers.

[Low Resolution] is for quick proofs that will be printed on black-and-white desktop printers and for documents that will be published on the web or exported to SVG.

—From InDesign Help

Previewing the page

1   Double-click the Hand tool (✋) to fit the document to the available window size.

2   Choose Edit > Deselect All.

3   In the bottom of the Tools panel, click and hold down on the Preview Mode button. Choose Preview from the menu that shows. Any guides, frame edges, or other non-printing items are hidden.

4   Click and hold the Preview Mode button and choose Bleed Mode. Additional space outside the perimeter of the final document size is displayed. This confirms that the color background will print outside the edge of the document. After the job is printed, this excess area will be trimmed, or cut off, to produce the final document size.

5   Click and hold the Bleed Mode button in the bottom right corner of the Tools panel, then choose Slug Mode. The page now displays additional space beyond the edge of the bleed area. This additional area is often used to print production information about the job. You can see this information below the bottom of the document in the center of the screen. The Slug area is setup by choosing File > Document Properties and clicking on the More Options button to reveal the Slug options.

After confirming that the file looks acceptable, you are ready to print it.

Printing a laser or inkjet proof

InDesign makes it easy to print documents to a variety of output devices.

1   Choose File > Print.

2   From the Printer pop-up menu, choose your inkjet or laser printer.

Notice how Adobe InDesign CS3 automatically selects the PPD (printer description) that was associated with this printer at the time you installed the printer.

Note: If you do not have a printer connected to your computer or computer network, choose PostScript File from the Printer list and choose Device Independent from the PPD list. This allows you to follow the steps in this lesson without being connected to a printer.

3   In the General options on the left side of the Print window, choose Visible Layers from the Print Layer pop-up menu.

New in InDesign CS3 is the ability to choose All Layers, Visible Layers or Visible & Printable Layers.

4   Click the Setup option on the left side of the Print window and choose the following options:

- Paper Size: Letter.

- Orientation: Portrait.

- Scale to Fit.

Note: If you selected PostScript File along with the Device Independent PPD, as opposed to an actual printer, you will not be able to apply scaling or adjust the positioning of where the file will image.

5 Click the Marks and Bleeds option on the left side of the Print window and click to enable the following options:

- Crop Marks.

- Page Information.

- Use Document Bleed Settings.

- Include Slug Area.

Enter a Marks offset value of **.125 in**. This value determines the distance from the page where the specified marks and page information will image.

The crop marks print outside of the page area and provide guides showing where the final document will be trimmed (cut) after printing. The page information automatically adds the document name along with the date and time it was printed, to the bottom of the document.

Using the document bleed and slug settings causes InDesign to print objects that extend outside the edge of the page area. These check boxes eliminate the need for entering the amount of extra area that should be imaged.

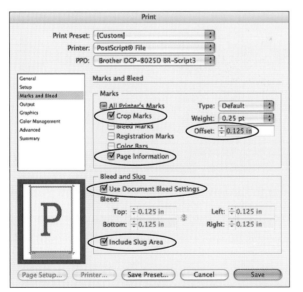

In the Preview area, lower left in the Print dialog box (the big letter P on the page), you can see the blue shaded box below the page area. This is the bleed area.

6   Click the Output option on the left side of the Print window. Confirm that Color is set to Composite CMYK in the Color pop-up menu.

This setting causes any RGB objects, including images, to be converted to CMYK at the time of printing. This setting does not change the original, placed graphic. This option is not available if you are printing to a PostScript file.

Note: You can have InDesign maintain the existing colors used in a job by choosing Composite Leave Unchanged in the Color pop-up menu. Additionally, if you are a printer or service provider and need to print color separations from Adobe InDesign CS3, choose Separations or In-RIP separations based upon the workflow that you use. Also, certain printers, such as an RGB proofer, may not let you choose Composite CMYK.

7   Click the Ink Manager button in the lower right corner of the Print Window.

You can use the Ink Manager to convert spot colors, such as Pantone colors, to process (CMYK) colors, and to manage duplicate spot colors. You will address both of these issues.

8   In the Ink Manager window, click the spot icon (◉) to the left of the Pantone 398 C color swatch. It changes to a CMYK icon (⊠). This color will now print as a combination of CMYK colors as opposed to printing on its own, separate color plate. Keep the Ink Manager window open.

9 In the Ink Manager window, click the Pantone 1817 M color swatch and then select Pantone 1817 U from the Ink Alias pop-up menu. The Ink Alias tells Adobe InDesign CS3 to treat these two colors as if they are identical, so they will print as one color separation rather than as multiple separations.

Applying an Ink Alias means that all objects with this color will now print on the same separation as its Alias color. Rather than getting two separate color separations, you will get one. Repeat this process to select Pantone 1817 C and choose Pantone 1817 U from the Ink Alias pop-up menu. Now all three duplicate Pantone colors will print on the same separation. Click OK.

10 Click the Graphics option on the left side of the Print window. Confirm that Optimized Subsampling is selected from the Send Data pop-up menu.

When Optimized Subsampling is selected, InDesign sends only the image data necessary for the printer you have selected in the Print window. To have the entire high-resolution image information sent to the printer, which may take longer to image, select All from the Send Data pop-up menu.

Note: This option cannot be changed if you selected the Device Independent PPD.

Note: When printing to a PostScript file, this option is not available.

11 If necessary, select Complete under the Font Download pop-up menu.

This causes all fonts used in the job to be sent to the output device.

Options for printing graphics

When you are exporting or printing documents that contain complex graphics (for example, high-resolution images, EPS graphics, PDF pages, or transparent effects), it will often be necessary to change resolution and rasterization settings in order to obtain the best output results.

Send Data—Controls how much image data in placed bitmap images to send to the printer or file.

All—Sends full-resolution data, which is appropriate for any high-resolution printing, or for printing grayscale or color images with high contrast, as in black-and-white text with one spot color. This option requires the most disk space.

Optimized Subsampling—Sends just enough image data to print the graphic at the best possible resolution for the output device. (A high-resolution printer will use more data than a low-resolution desktop model.) Select this option when you're working with high-resolution images but printing proofs to a desktop printer.

Note: InDesign does not subsample EPS or PDF graphics, even when Optimized Subsampling is selected.

Proxy—Sends screen-resolution versions (72 dpi) of placed bitmap images, thereby reducing printing time.

None—Temporarily removes all graphics when you print and replaces them with graphics frames with crossbars, thereby reducing printing time. The graphics frames are the same dimensions as the imported graphics and clipping paths are maintained, so you can still check sizes and positioning. Suppressing the printing of imported graphics is useful when you want to distribute text proofs to editors or proofreaders. Printing without graphics is also helpful when you're trying to isolate the cause of a printing problem.

—From InDesign Help

Options for downloading fonts to a printer

Printer-resident fonts are stored in a printer's memory or on a hard drive connected to the printer. Type 1 and TrueType fonts can be stored either on the printer or on your computer; bitmap fonts are stored only on your computer. InDesign downloads fonts as needed, provided they are installed on your computer's hard disk.

Choose from the following options in the Graphics area of the Print dialog box to control how fonts are downloaded to the printer.

None—Includes a reference to the font in the PostScript file, which tells the RIP or a post-processor where the font should be included. This option is appropriate if the fonts reside in the printer. TrueType fonts are named according to the PostScript name in the font; however, not all applications can interpret these names. To ensure that TrueType fonts are interpreted correctly, use one of the other font downloading options.

Complete—Downloads all fonts required for the document at the beginning of the print job. All glyphs and characters in the font are included even if they're not used in the document. InDesign automatically subsets fonts that contain more than the maximum number of glyphs (characters) specified in the Preferences dialog box.

Subset—Downloads only the characters (glyphs) used in the document. Glyphs are downloaded once per page. This option typically results in faster and smaller PostScript files when used with single-page documents, or short documents without much text.

Download PPD Fonts—Downloads all fonts used in the document, even if those fonts reside in the printer. Use this option to ensure that InDesign uses the font outlines on your computer for printing common fonts, such as Helvetica and Times. Using this option can resolve problems with font versions, such as mismatched character sets between your computer and printer or outline variances in trapping. Unless you commonly use extended character sets, you don't need to use this option for desktop draft printing.

—From InDesign Help

12 Click the Advanced Tab and set the Transparency Flattener Preset to High Resolution from the Preset pop-up menu.

You can choose the appropriate transparency flattener preset for your needs. The preset determines the quality of placed artwork or images that include transparency. The preset also impacts the quality of objects with transparency applied to them using InDesign's transparency feature, including objects with drop shadows or feathering.

13 Click the Save Preset button and name the preset **Proof** and click OK.

Creating a Print preset saves these settings so you do not need to individually set every option each time you print to the same device. You can create multiple presets to meet various quality needs of individual printers you may use. When you want to use these settings in the future, you can choose them from the Print Preset pop-up menu at the top of the Print dialog box.

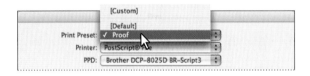

14 Click the Print button.

If you are creating a PostScript file, click Save and browse to the Lesson_12 folder, located inside the Lessons folder within the InDesignCIB folder on your hard disk. The PostScript file could be provided to your service provider, commercial printer or converted to an Adobe PDF using Adobe Acrobat Distiller. If you do not have Adobe Acrobat Distiller, you can delete the PostScript file after you have completed this lesson.

💡 *You can use absolute page numbering when working with documents that are broken into sections. For example, to print the third page of a document you can input +3 in the Page Range section of the print dialog box. You can also use section names. For more information see "Specifying pages to print" in the InDesign Help.*

Exploring on your own

1   Create a new Print preset by choosing File > Print presets > Define. Use the resulting dialog boxes to create presets to use for oversize printing or for printing to various color or black-and-white printers you may use.

2   Open the 12_brochure.indd file and explore how each color separation can be enabled or disabled using the Color Separation Preview. Switch to viewing the Ink Limit preview using the same panel. See how the total ink settings used in creating CMYK colors affects how various images will print.

3   Using the 12_brochure.indd file, Choose File > Print. Then click the Output option on the left side of the Print window and examine the different choices for printing color documents.

4   Choose Ink Manager from the Swatches panel menu and experiment with using add ink alias for spot colors and with converting spot colors to process.

Review

▶ **Review questions**

1   What elements does InDesign gather when it packages a file?

2   What problems does InDesign look for when using the preflight command?

3   If you want to print the highest quality version of a scanned image on a lower resolution laser printer or proofer, what options can you select?

▶ **Review answers**

1   Adobe InDesign CS3 gathers a copy of the InDesign document along with copies of all fonts used in the document and copies of all graphics used in the original document. The original items remain undisturbed.

2   You can confirm that all items necessary for high-resolution printing are available by choosing File > Preflight. This command looks to confirm that all fonts used in the document or inside-placed graphics are available. InDesign also looks for linked graphic files and even linked text files to confirm that they have not been modified since they were initially imported.

3   InDesign sends only the image data necessary to an output device as its default setting. If you want to send the entire set of image data, even if it may take longer to print, you can choose All from the Send Data pop-up menu in the Graphics options of the Print window.

Snow & Ski Report

Family Fun

Super Skiing

Facilisismodo consed magna conum volorercilla feugiat inciduis aliquate tie doluptat, quamet, velisicidunt nostrud tat nim dolobore tio exer suatis nibh eum irit at nim vel dionae min hendre magnit wis nim quis adit, vullum qui blaore vel duiscipit am vel et am augait velendit duisl iriustio dolore do do dolut pratisismod modolob orperisrem inim nonse consenisi bla feuguerci tat, quis eu facin hendipit init ut veliquisit. Volorem nons elit elit iriat hut vulla facil ip eugue conse consequis nis nullam illaoreet vulputat, velisitisit accum duis num at. Ut la aliquatummy nim vel ex ectem iure er summodolore min ullan henit loborem aliquisit irit consequate venim nibh elisisl. To coreе sim vel utet vent wiscin

Great Year to Ski

Elenit lan utem do od magna feum irit lore dolum aliquat, vullaor per-aessi.

Senim alit loreet vulput autpat. Er suscili quisci et et, quamcorme feuisi ectem nissi etum ad esto odolorp erosto cons dolobortio ea feugait praese quipis erci tat.

Ectem er, si. In exer irit wis el inisi. Quat. La faccumm olorper aessi. On ectetum sandre mod modio cortial do od mincincilit wisi tat.

Tat la faccummy nostismodio dolesequat.

Doluptat. Ommy nibh el ilissequam, sim dit nim doluptatue delendreet, vel ilis nostie modipsustrud te feu faciliquisit iustrud tetuer ilisi.

Isl deleniscip ex ex exero delesto odipsum dolummy nos alit aut lup-

tat. Secte magna alissequis aliquam nullutat lumsandion utem adignit atueros nullan benim nons acing eu feugait ipisi.

Nim ilit ut prat ulputpat am, commodolorem autarinibh exercin

iamet, veliquis dolore et deliquat illutpatem nos dit exerosto ex et eugait amet, quam, sum delendit alit vullut wiscipsum enim quisim ver

sed miocing eugiam, commodiatuer susto dolum ea aut augait praessim quat lorer sed modignim eugiamet il ea amet vulputatum iure feugait euis et, sequam do del in et, commy nulputpat amconsequat. Tis nim vendrem el ea feu facilit prat vent nummoloreet ut iusto cortin ulla feuipsustie dolore dunt la augue eu feugiamcon heniam del duissi.

Good Snow

Tio el eu feugiat, commod modigna commolorting exerosto odolore doloreet velessim volore ming eugiam ercincil del dunt nonsequis alis nullam dolorerilla conulla aliquis acidunt auguerit, sum quis eu faccum exerci eugait wissi.

Urerosto dolobore modiam dunt ad dolore venit vulput ea cortie ming euguerc iliquis autat. Ciliquat, si bla alisis elit amet, velesequisit utat, minit nit ullandio odip elit dolorpetilit nos niat.

Use the powerful XML capabilities of InDesign CS3 to build and share documents for multiple destinations. InDesign CS3 supports tagging of content, including text, tables, and graphics. Tagged objects can be organized in the Structure pane and then exported as XML. InDesign CS3 lets you import XML and place it into a structure layout either automatically or manually.

13 | Using XML

In this lesson, you'll learn how to do the following:

- Import XML tags.

- Apply XML tags.

- Map styles and tags.

- Use the Structure pane.

- Import XML.

- Export XML.

Getting started

In this lesson, you'll take a completed InDesign layout and apply XML tags to the document. You'll then confirm the structure of the document, export the contents as XML, and then import the XML into another InDesign layout. Before you begin, you'll need to restore the default preferences for Adobe InDesign CS3.

Note: If you have not already copied the resource files for this lesson onto your hard disk from the Adobe InDesign CS3 Classroom in a Book *CD, do so now. See "Copying the Classroom in a Book files" on page 4.*

1   To ensure that the tools and panels function exactly as described in this lesson, delete or reset the InDesign CS3 defaults preferences following the procedure in "Saving, deleting and restoring preference files" on page 2.

2   Start Adobe InDesign CS3.

To begin working, you'll open an existing InDesign document.

3   Choose File > Open, and open the 13_a.indd file in the Lesson_13 folder, on your hard disk.

4   Choose File > Save As, rename the file **ski_brochure.indd**, and save it in the Lesson_13 folder.

About XML

eXtensible Markup Language (XML) is used to distribute content, including text and images, to multiple destinations. XML separates content from its appearance on a page or in a layout. XML files use tags that identify the content in the file. Because the content of an XML file is identified with tags, it can be repurposed for distribution in print, on-line, or in some other format, such as PDF.

XML files are not dependent upon a specific layout, and can be formatted to match the needs of the viewer or viewing device. For example, an XML version of a typical brochure might be formatted to display as a traditional vertical layout when printed. The same information can be converted to a horizontal layout for on-screen viewing as a PDF. The same content can also be converted to HTML and placed onto a web page.

While XML allows for data to be presented in a variety of formats, it also has advantages for revising and customizing print layouts. When InDesign documents are converted to XML, you can easily extract some or all of the data to re-use in other InDesign layouts. For example, a single XML file can be the source for a sales brochure, a price list, and a catalog.

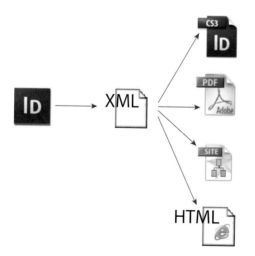

If you design web sites using Adobe Dreamweaver or other programs, you may be familiar with Hyper Text Markup Language (HTML). While XML and HTML have similar names, and both markup languages include tags, they are actually quite different. HTML tags describe the appearance of the content in an HTML file, and how it should be formatted. Conversely, XML tags describe the content itself and do not describe formatting. With XML, formatting decisions occur when the XML is placed into a specific layout.

To use the XML features of InDesign CS3, you do not need extensive XML knowledge. To learn more about the XML capabilities of InDesign CS3, choose Help > InDesign Help. Then select XML in the InDesign Help Contents.

Viewing XML tags

InDesign CS3 uses XML tags to identify the type of content that is, or will be, placed on a page. These tags are used when XML is either imported or exported from an InDesign layout. Frames can be tagged, or specified, to contain certain types of text, such as stories or headlines. Frames can also be tagged to contain graphics. The same tags may be used multiple times within a document. For example, a document may contain multiple headlines, and each headline may contain the same tag name identifying it as a headline.

If you regularly work with XML, you may be more familiar with XML elements. Tags applied using InDesign CS3 identify the specific occurrence of an XML element.

In this exercise you'll examine some existing XML tags that have been applied to an InDesign CS3 layout.

1 Choose Window > Tags to open the Tags panel. The Tags panel opens, displaying a list of XML tags that have previously been created with this document.

2   Choose the Selection tool (➤) and click the text frame containing the text "Snow and Ski Report" along the top of the document. Notice that the Title tag in the tags panel becomes highlighted as this frame is selected. The highlighting indicates that the Title tag is applied to this text frame.

3   Choose Edit > Deselect all.

4   Choose the Type tool (T) and click in the headline text "Great Year to Ski." In the tags panel, the tag Head2 becomes highlighted, indicating that this text also has an XML tag applied to it.

5   Choose View > Structure > Show Tagged Frames. The two text frames we've examined display a colored border and background.

The border and background color corresponds to the color of the XML tags that are applied to the frames. Notice that the Title tag is Magenta and this is the color that is displayed around the title of the publication.

6   Choose the Zoom tool (🔍) and click and drag a box around the text "Great Year to Ski" along with several lines of type beneath this text. The magnification of this area of the page increases.

7   Choose View > Structure > Hide Tag Markers. The XML tag markers at the start and end of the Great Year to Ski headline disappear. Choose View > Structure > Show Tag Markers. Markers are displayed to the left of the word Great and the right of the word Ski. The markers are purple, which corresponds to the color of the Head2 tag in the Tags panel.

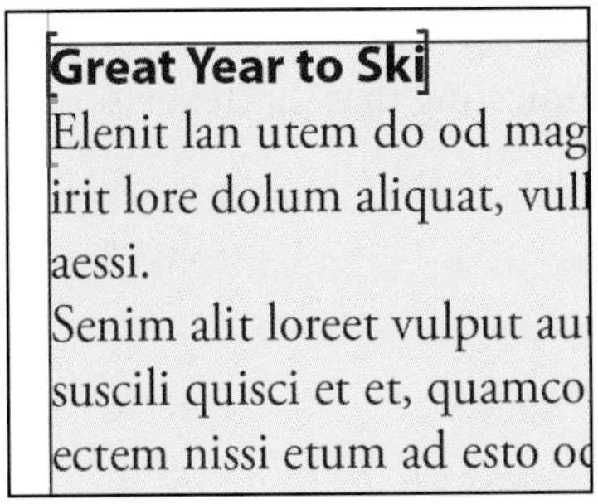

Great Year to Ski
Elenit lan utem do od mag
irit lore dolum aliquat, vull
aessi.
Senim alit loreet vulput au
suscili quisci et et, quamco
ectem nissi etum ad esto o

💡 *Tag markers are also visible in the Story Editor.*

8   Double-click the Hand tool (✋) to view the entire page.

Note: The tag indicators help identify which objects have been tagged, and these markers display only on screen, not when a document is printed.

Importing and applying XML tags

You can create XML tags within your InDesign CS3 layout, or you can import them from another InDesign CS3 document or a Document Type Definition (DTD). In this exercise, you will import several new tags, and then apply the tags to objects in the layout.

1   Select the Type tool (T) and click anywhere in the text of the sidebar titled "Super Skiing" along the right side of the document. No tags in the Tags panel are highlighted, as tags have not been applied to this text.

When the cursor is placed within tagged text, or when a tagged object is selected, the tag applied to the text or object is highlighted in the Tags panel. Because this text is not yet tagged, no tag name is highlighted. You will import several new tags, and then apply them.

2   Choose Edit > Deselect All.

3   In the Tags panel, choose Load Tags from the panel menu. Navigate to the Lesson_13 folder and choose the tags.xml file, then click Open. InDesign adds two new tags into the Tags panel: Head1 and Image. You will apply these tags to objects and text in your layout.

Note: The names of the tags must exactly match those used in your XML workflow. XML is very precise, causing head1 and Head1 to be considered different tags.

4   In the tools panel, choose the Selection tool (*), click the text frame containing the headline text "Family Fun," and click the Head1 tag in the Tags panel. The Head1 tag is now applied to this text frame and all its contents. The frame containing the Family Fun text becomes blue, reflecting the tag that has been applied to it.

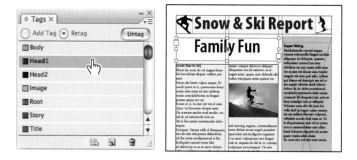

5   In the Tools panel, select the Type tool (T). Click and drag to select the headline "Good Snow" in the second column. This text sits within a frame that has been tagged as Story. Click the Head2 tag in the Tags panel to change this text. The tag is applied to the selected text. Brackets appear at the start and end of the selected text, identifying that the text is tagged. The color of the brackets corresponds to the color of the tag. If necessary, choose View > Structure > Show Tag Markers to display the text tags.

Note: You may need to deselect the text to clearly see the tag markers that are applied to it. Choose Edit > Deselect All to deselect the text.

6   Click and drag to select the body text that follows the "Good Snow" headline. Be sure to select the text in the final two paragraphs of this story, at the bottom of the second column. While the text is selected, click the Body tag in the Tags panel.

7 If necessary, scroll to view the sidebar in the far right column of the page. Continuing to work with the Type tool, click and drag to select the "Super Skiing" headline, and then click the Head2 tag to apply the tag to this text.

As the Head2 tag is applied, tag markers are displayed at the start and end of the tagged text. The frame also changes colors, as a tag was applied to it at the same time you applied a tag to the headline. This is because a frame must have a tag if any of the contents are also tagged. The tag applied to the frame may be different from the tag applied to the text.

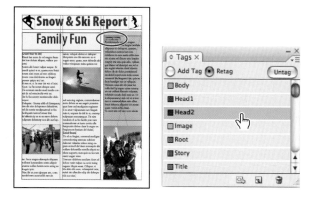

8 Continuing to work in the sidebar, click and drag to select the remaining text in the third column. Be sure to select all the text that follows the "Super Skiing" headline, without selecting the headline itself. With the text selected, click the Body tag in the Tags panel.

You have completed tagging all the text in the layout.

9 Choose Edit > Deselect All.

10 Choose File > Save.

Tagging images

1   In the Tools panel, choose the Selection tool (➤).

2   Click the image of the snow volleyball players in the far left column to select it. In the Tags panel, click the Image tag so that it is applied to this graphic.

3   Click the image of the downhill skier in the second column to select it. Right-click (Windows) or Ctrl+click (Mac OS) and choose Tag Frame > Image from the contextual menu that is displayed. (You may need to scroll down to see the Tag Frame option.)

You can use the contextual menus to apply tags to frames as well as text.

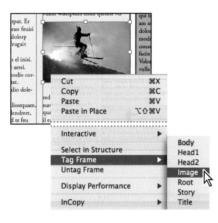

4   Repeating the process from the previous step, click to select the image of the two skiers in the third column, and then right-click (Windows) or Ctrl+click (Mac OS) and choose Tag Frame > Image from the contextual menu.

You have completed the process of tagging all the frames for content that will be exported as XML.

Viewing and organizing structure

Before exporting the document as XML, you want to confirm that the structure of the XML matches the hierarchy of your layout.

1 Choose View > Structure > Show Structure. The Structure pane is displayed.

The Structure pane displays the tags that have been applied to objects in the layout, in the sequence in which they were applied.

Note: You may need to move your Tools panel to view all the contents of the Structure pane.

2 In the Structure pane, click the triangle (▷) to the left of the Root tag. The Root tag is the highest-level tag; all other tagged objects appear beneath the Root tag. All documents must have at least one Root tag.

The Root tag can be renamed if your workflow uses a different name for its top-level tag.

3 Click the triangle to the left of the top Story tag. All the structured elements under this tag are displayed, including both Head2 tags and both Body tags.

You can see the tags that you applied, as well as tags that had been previously applied to the document. The Head2 and Body tags are children of the Story tag, which was previously applied for you. The tags are listed in the order they were applied to objects on the page, and should match the relationship of objects in the layout. For example, all related text is typically placed under the same parent tag. In this case, the Head2 and Body tags are related, so they are placed together under the Story tag. Each Head2 tag is placed before each Body tag, just as the headlines are before the body text in the layout.

4   In the Structure pane, click the menu in the upper right corner and choose Show Text Snippets. The Structure pane now shows the first portion of the text to which each tag is related.

5   In the Structure pane, click the Head1 Tag, which displays the text snippet "Family Fun." In the layout this is the highest-level headline, placed immediately beneath the title. In the Structure pane, this tag is positioned between two Story tags. As a primary headline, it should be one of the top-most items in the structure. Because InDesign adds items to the Structure pane in the order in which they are tagged, it is incorrectly positioned. Click and drag the Head1 tag up so that it is positioned under the Title tag. Release the Head1 tag when a black line appears under the Title tag. The position of the tag in the Structure pane now reflects the position of this headline in the layout.

Note: InDesign CS3 also supports using DTDs to validate the structure. For more information about using DTDs to validate structure see InDesign Help.

6   Choose File > Save.

Viewing and applying attributes

Tagged objects may also include additional information about the objects. This information which describes the tagged object is known as an attribute.

1   In the Structure pane, click the triangle to the left of the top Image tag. InDesign displays the attribute icon (●) followed by the location of the image file.

2   Continuing to work in the Structure pane, click to select the Title tag with the text snippet "Ski & Snow Report." Right-click (Windows) or Ctrl+click (Mac OS) the Title tag and choose New Attribute. The New Attribute window opens.

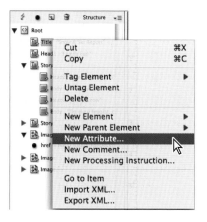

3   In the New Attribute window, for Name enter **Issue_Number**. Press the Tab key, and for Value enter **12**. Click OK and the attribute is added to the Title tag.

Attributes can be used to provide additional descriptive information such as the publication date or copyright status.

4   Choose File > Save to save the document.

Exporting XML

After applying XML tags to the text and graphics in the InDesign layout, you can create an XML file.

1   Choose File > Export. The Export window opens.

2   If necessary, in the Export window, navigate to the Lesson_13 folder, then choose XML from the Save as type pop-up menu (Windows) or Format pop-up menu (Mac OS). Enter the file name **snow.xml**. Click the Save button and the Export XML window opens.

3 In the Export XML window, click the Images tab. Confirm that all the options are unchecked.

When exporting XML from InDesign CS3, you can have images from the layout copied or moved into the same folder as the XML file by selecting the options under the Copy to Images Sub-folder section of this window. This allows for images that have been tagged to be re-used in other print or web layouts. Because you will be working with the XML file using the same computer that extracted the XML, none of these options is necessary.

4 Click the Export button. The XML file is generated. Keep this document open, as you will return to work in it later in this lesson.

Importing XML

Next you will open an existing InDesign layout that already includes XML tags, and you will import XML that was created in the previous exercise.

1   Choose File > Open, and open the 13_b.indd file in the Lesson_13 folder, on your hard disk.

2   Choose File > Save As, rename the file **online_brochure.indd**, and save it in the Lesson_13 folder.

3   Choose View > Structure > Show structure. The Structure pane is displayed.

4   In the Structure pane, click the triangle to the left of the Root tag. All the tags that have been applied to objects in this document are displayed.

Note: The top-level structure of the online brochure matches the structure used in the original print layout.

5   Choose File > Import XML. The Import XML window opens.

In the Import XML window, make sure that Show XML Import Options and Merge Content radio button are selected. Click to select the snow.xml file, then click the Open button. The XML Import Options window opens.

6   In the XML Import Options window, confirm the Mode pop-up menu is set to Merge content and deselect all the check boxes so that all the options are unchecked, and click OK. The XML is imported into the horizontal layout designed for on-screen viewing.

All the text and graphics which were tagged in the original document are flowed into their new layout. The text will be formatted in the next section of this lesson.

Appending versus merging XML

When importing XML, you can either append or merge the XML content into your document. Appending adds the new XML content to your document, leaving the existing structure and content unchanged. Merging replaces existing content and, depending on the options you select, adds new content where it finds no equivalent elements. You merge XML into a document in the following situations:

- The document contains placeholder frames that you want to fill with the incoming XML file.

- The document contains XML that you want to replace with the incoming XML file.

- The document doesn't contain any XML structure, and you want InDesign to replace the default root with the root of the incoming XML file.

XML import options

When importing XML files using the Merge Content option, the XML Import Options dialog box has the following options:

Create Link—Links to the XML file so that if the XML file is updated, you can update its XML data in your InDesign document.

Apply XSLT—Applies a stylesheet to define the transformation of the imported XML. Select Browse (Windows®) or Choose (Mac OS®) to select an XSLT file (.xsl or .xslt) from the file system. Use Stylesheet From XML, the default option, causes InDesign to use an XSLT processing instruction, if one is present in the XML file, to transform the XML data.

Clone Repeating Text Elements—Replicates the formatting applied to tagged placeholder text for repeating content. Create one formatting instance (for example, an address), and then reuse its layout to create other instances automatically. (See Working with repeating data.)

Only Import Elements That Match Existing Structure—Filters the imported XML content so that only elements from the imported XML file with matching elements in the document are imported.

Import Text Elements Into Tables If Tags Match—Imports elements into a table if the tags match the tags applied to the placeholder table and its cells. For example, use this option to place database records into a table when generating price lists or inventory sheets.

Do Not Import Contents Of Whitespace-only Elements—Leaves any existing content in place if the matching XML content contains only whitespace (such as a return or tab character). Use this if you've included text between elements in your placeholder frames and want to preserve this text. For example, when laying out recipes generated from a database, you might add labels such as "Ingredients." As long as the parent element that wraps each recipe contains only whitespace, InDesign leaves the label in place.

Delete Elements, Frames, and Content That Do Not Match Imported XML—Removes elements from the Structure pane and the layout of the document if they don't match any elements in the imported XML file. Use this option to filter data from the document. For example, when importing names and addresses, you might have placeholder text for an element containing the company name. If one of the names doesn't include the company element, InDesign deletes the element containing the placeholder text.

Import CALS Tables As InDesign Tables—Imports any CALS tables in the XML file as InDesign tables.

Mapping tags to style

Now that you have imported XML into the document, you will format and style the text. Because the document is structured with tags, you will automate the process of formatting by establishing a relationship between the tags and styles.

1   In the Structure pane, click the menu option in the upper right corner and choose Map Tags to Styles. The Map Tags to Styles window opens.

2   In the Map Tags to Styles window, click the Map By Name button. Because this document already includes paragraph styles with names that are identical to the XML tags, InDesign CS3 can apply styles to this text. Keep the Map Tags to Styles window open.

3   Click the Preview checkbox. The tagged text becomes formatted as the Paragraph styles are applied to it. Click OK.

4   Choose File > Save.

Using XML snippets

A snippet is an XML file that is a full representation of InDesign content, including page items and any XML structure applied to those page items. A snippet lets you reuse the content, formatting, tags, and structure of a document. You can store snippets in an Object library, and place them in other documents. Use snippets to easily reuse objects—even those with complex formatting.

1   Choose Window > ski_brochure.indd to switch to the original document you worked on earlier in this lesson.

2   Choose the Selection tool (↖), and click anywhere on the document.

3   Choose View > Fit Page in Window.

4   Arrange your application window (Windows) or document window (Mac OS) so that you can see both your desktop and the InDesign layout.

5   Click to select the outline image of the snowboarder to the left of the headline. The outline of the skier and the arc across the top of the page all become selected, as they are part of a group.

6   Click and drag the two images and arc to the desktop of your computer. An icon appears on the desktop with a name that begins as Snippet, followed by a series of numbers and letters. You can rename this file if you like. This XML snippet file includes all the information necessary to reproduce these images in another InDesign layout.

7   Choose Window > online_brochure.indd. If necessary, arrange your InDesign windows so that you can see both the snippet file you dragged to your desktop as well as the InDesign layout.

8 Click and drag the snippet file from your desktop onto your layout. The images and the arc are imported into the document.

Snippets retain the x and y coordinates of the original objects, making them perfect for objects that need to be reused in multiple versions of an identical document. In this case, we are using a different sized layout, so we'll move the images.

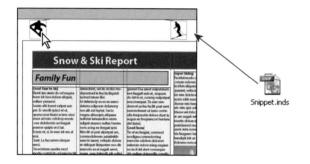

9 Click and drag the outline image of the snowboarder and position it to the left of and above the Snow & Ski Report headline text.

10 Choose File > Save.

Congratulations. You have completed this lesson.

Exploring on your own

1 Explore the Structure pane by right-clicking (Windows) or Ctrl+clicking (Mac OS) the various tags. Examine the options available in the Structure pane menu.

2 Apply XML tags to your own document and export the XML. Practice importing the XML into another InDesign layout.

3 Import XML into an InDesign layout and map the tags to InDesign styles used in the document, formatting the XML text.

Review

▶ **Review questions**

1 How and why are XML tags used in InDesign CS3?

2 What steps are necessary before an InDesign CS3 layout can be exported as XML?

3 What is the Structure pane, and what role does it play in exporting or importing XML?

▶ **Review answers**

1 XML tags are applied to content in an InDesign CS3 layout, including text, graphics and frames. Tags describe the content, allowing for it to be exported as XML. Additionally, tagged frames can have XML imported into them.

2 Prior to exporting an InDesign CS3 layout as XML, all objects that will be a part of the XML must be tagged. Additionally, the sequence of the XML tags must be verified in the Structure pane, and any attributes necessary must be added in the Structure pane.

3 The Structure pane provides a listing of all tagged objects used in an InDesign CS3 layout. It is used to import, manage and export XML. It is used to organize the hierarchy of tagged objects, apply attributes, and establish the relationship between tags and styles.

Index

A

adding
  colors to the swatches panel
    218
  column break 165
  graphics 210
  page continuation note 177
  rule below a paragraph 127
  words to a dictionary 17
adding sections 189
adjusting gradient direction
    242
adjusting text inset 305
adjusting vertical spacing 6
adjusting view quality 108
Adobe ACE engine 145
Adobe Acrobat 407, 418
Adobe Bridge 255
Adobe certification 167
Adobe Illustrator 167
  color management 197
  embedding a profile 163

B

background
  removing 307
baseline grid 191
  for aligning text 54
bitmap graphics 299
bleeds 117, 413
blending mode 363
blending modes 357, 360,
    361, 364, 367, 378,
    379
book
  creating 383
  order 383

pagination 389
bringing objects forward. *See
    also* arranging objects
Bringing objects forward.
    See layers; *See also* ar-
    ranging objects

C

CALS Tables 437
cell
  heading formatting 339
  options 286
  strokes 286, 348
  styles 33, 90
cell styles
  creating 95, 73
center point 35
Character Formatting Con-
    trols button 197
Character panel 179
characters
  special 273
character styles
  applying 274
  creating 44
  nested 255
check spelling 250
  dynamically 306
clipping paths
  working with 240
color management
  Adobe Illustrator 214
  Adobe Photoshop CS3 238
  assigning a profile 246
  engines 241
  full-resolution display 165
  needs assessment 52, 238,
    239

overview 229
  profiles. *See* ICC Profiles
  rendering intent 219
  setting up in InDesign 231
Color profiles 229
colors
  about spot and process 234
  adding to the swatches
    panel 238
  applying to objects 238
  applying to text 170
  creating a spot 140
  creating a tint 61
  multiple color gradients
    166
color space 82
  device-independent 82
column break
  adding 350
  creating text 393

D

dashed strokes
  creating 222
decorative font character 2
defaults, restoring 216, 265,
    297, 331, 357, 382,
    400, 423
default working spaces
  setting up 244
deleting columns 341
Deselect All command 178,
    338, 359, 367, 370,
    374, 393, 410, 428,
    429
device-independent color
    space 239
dictionary

adding words 99
document-specific 181
documents
  switching between 179
Document Window
  About 202
drag and drop editing 199
drop caps 284
drop shadow 360, 371

E

effects
  blending mode 363
  changing opacity 362
  drop shadow 371
  editing 376
  feathering 371
  overview 361
  removing 376
  transparency 360
  transparency for EPS images 364
  transparency for Photoshop images 366
  transparency for text 369, 370
  transparency for text frame fill 370
embedding a profile 7
Enhanced workspace 112
export
  Adobe PDF 406
exporting
  XML 434

F

facing pages 85
feathering
  gradient 372
  image margins 371
find and change
  text formatting 2
Find Font command 159
Fit Page in Window command 163

Fit Spread in Window command 173
flowing text 168
  automatically 199
  into an existing frame 87
  semi-automatic 38
Flush Space command 195
fonts
  changing 23
  decorative 154
  finding and changing missing 155
  installing 101
  managing 23
footers 381

G

gamut. See color space
globally updating styles 291
gradient feather 372
gradients
  adjusting direction 226
  applying to an object 235
  applying to multiple objects 235
  creating multiple colors 234
  working with 130, 100
gradient swatches
  applying 224
  creating 224
graphics
  black and white
    colorizing 359
  frames 301
  identifying 299
  importing 318
  inline 300
  managing links 136
  placing 316
  placing native files 303
  updating links 299
  vector 299
  vector vs. bitmap 342
  within tables 130
  wrapping text around 130

graphics frames
  changing the shape 132
  creating 147
  editing 189
  replacing content 147
  resizing 147
grids
  baseline 100

H

Hand tool 70
hanging indent 205
  creating 208
Help 75
High Quality Display 247
HTML 424, 425

I

ICC profiles 215, 216, 239, 240, 249, 260, 262, 263, 312
images
  moving within a frame 75
  resizing 108
importing
  Adobe Illustrator files 299
  graphics 318
  inline graphics 316
  native files 293
  styles 334
  text 436
  XML 318
InDesign Help 318
index
  generating 390
indexing 391
  creating references 393

J

jump lines. See continuation note
justification
  vertical 348, 339

K

kerning
  adjusting 202

L

layer
  locking 43
layers
  working with 56, 59, 60, 121,
     120, 119, 120, 121, 122, 130,
     132, 135
leading 189
letter spacing 204
library 323
  creating 325
links
  adjusting view quality 305
  identifying 301
  importing graphics 43, 299
  managing 300
  relinking 252
  updating 303
  viewing information 302
loading styles 100

M

magnet icon (tabs) 206
magnification
  changing 8
Managing fonts 83
managing links 300
mapping tags 438
margins 170, 93
Margins and Columns command 9
master pages
  adding additional 86
  adding guides 93
  applying 85
  creating 93
  multiple 86
  overriding items 92

  renaming 85
  working with 83
measurements 108, 162
Menu Customization 331
Microsoft Excel 155, 86
Microsoft Word 81

N

navigating 66
  Navigator panel 71
Navigator panel 71
nested character styles 274
  creating 274
New Color Swatch 218
new document
  creating 224, 107
New Gradient Swatch command
  107, 166
new pages
  adding 228

O

objects
  aligning 145
  applying colors 219
  deselecting 111
  grouped 147
  library 323
  rotating 144
  scaling grouped 147
  selecting 74
  wrapping text around 98
object styles
  applying 285
  creating 281
overset text
  in tables 347, 350

P

Package 404
page numbering

changing 47, 54, 66
pages
  arranging 166
  continuation note 83
  facing 66
  targeting 82
panels
  docking 30
  viewing and arranging 221
paper color 192
paragraph
  change spacing above and below
    197
paragraph alignment
  changing 204
paragraph composer
  applying 94
paragraph rules 108
paragraph styles
  applying 266
  creating 274
  nested character styles 142
PDF
  creating 406
  layered 407
  proof 406
placeholder frame 343
placing text 217
Portable Document Format.
  See PDF
preference files
  deleting 249, 251, 254, 256, 400,
    423
  restoring 400, 423
  saving 245, 400, 423
Preflight 401
Preview Mode 410
printing 399, 400, 401, 402, 403,
    404, 405, 407, 410, 413,
    414, 415, 416, 417, 419,
    420, 398
  downloading fonts to a printer
    417
  graphics 416

laser or inkjet proof 410
Package 404
Preflight 401

R

Rectangle Frame tool 97
Rectangle tool 97
Redefine Style command 194, 293, 347, 348
reference color space 239
rendering intent
    specifying 246, 247
resizing a graphics frame 144
rows
    dimensions 342

S

saturation 240
scaling
    grouped objects 147, 70
scroll bars 70
scrolling 70
    hand tool 70
    scroll bars 38
sections 105, 74, 418
    adding 74
selecting
    objects behind other objects 74
    table 338
    tables 336
    tools 67
Separation preview 407
shapes
    converting 176
single-line composer 179
    applying 192
snippets
    XML 439
source profiles
    assigning 202
spacing
    change above and below para-

graph 197
kerning 176
letter 182
tracking 161
vertical 171
special characters 229
spell checking 229
spread
    targeting 222
Story Editor 286
strokes
    creating dashed 291
styles
    applying paragraph 274
    cell 281
    character 266
    globally updating 286
    loading from another document 224

T

table of contents
    adding 385
    generating 386
tables
    alternating row colors 336
    borders 348
    cell styles 342
    column and row dimensions 341
    deleting columns 338
    editing cell strokes 347
    editing imported paragraph styles 334
    formatting 336
    formatting borders 347
    formatting text 342
    graphics within 339
    heading cells 334
    importing 290
table styles
    applying 208
    creating 205, 164
tabs

hanging indent 205
leaders 156
markers 202
    working with 202
text
    adjusting kerning 231
    adjusting tracking 192
    aligning with baseline grid 156
    applying color 174
    change spacing above and below
        paragraph 159
    creating 163
    entering 159
    find and change formatting 168
    flowing 167
    flowing automatically 108
    flowing manually 128
    flowing semi-automatically 347
    formatting within a table 167
    horizontal text alignment 98
    placing 85
    vertically aligning 127
    vertical text alignment 122
    wrapping 49
text frames
    adjusting text inset 125
    creating 122
    creating columns 59
    editing 227
    reshaping 202
    resizing 195
tracking
    adjusting 360
transparency
    Adobe Illustrator files 364
    applying 366
    changing opacity 369
    EPS images 370
    flattener preview 408
    flattening 409

U

ungroup 219

updating
  links 303
  revised graphics 303

V

vector graphics 299
vertically aligning text 128
view quality
  adjusting 305

W

work area 46, 47, 48, 61, 77, 55
working with pathfinders 139
workspace
  customizing 98
wrapping text around a graphic 137

X

XHTML 1, 12
XML 1, 13
  about 424
  applying attributes 433
  applying tags 427
  exporting 434
  importing 436
  importing tags 427
  import options 437
  mapping tags 438
  organizing structure 431
  snippets 439
  tagging images 430
  viewing attributes 433
  viewing tags 425
XSLT 437

Z

Zoom In 64
Zoom Out 64
Zoom tool
  using 64

Production Notes

The *Adobe InDesign CS3 Classroom in a Book* was created electronically using Adobe InDesign. Additional art was produced using Adobe Illustrator and Adobe Photoshop.

A special thank you to Dr. Rene Thomas for the use of her recipes from her *Natures Mighty Bites Cookbook* for use in Lesson 11. Also, thanks to istockphoto.com for supplying photographic images in many of the lessons. Other references to company names in the lessons are for demonstration purposes only.

Team credits

The following individuals contributed to the development of new and updated lessons for this edition of the *Adobe InDesign CS3 Classroom in a Book*:

Project coordinator: Wyndham Wood

Technical writing: Brian Wood and T. Elizabeth Atteberry

Production: eVolve Computer Graphics Training, Inc., Brian Wood and T. Elizabeth Atteberry

Proofreading and beta testing: Wyndham Wood, Jeffrey Hannibal and Marni Nemer

Technical editing: Jeffrey Hannibal

Typefaces used

Set in the Adobe Minion Pro and Adobe Myriad Pro OpenType families of typefaces. These along with Adobe Caslon, Adobe Chaparral Pro and Adobe Garamond Pro are used throughout the lessons. More information about OpenType and Adobe fonts visit www.adobe.com/type/opentype/.

Images

Photographic images and illustrations are intended for use with the tutorials only.

Images provided by Claudia Murray Photography: Lesson 11 (cookbook). Illustrations for Lesson 11 provided by Jennifer M. Smith.

Images provided by iStockphoto.com for Lesson 5: Norman Reid, Jeffrey Waibel, Janusz Doboszynski

Images provided by Expedition Tea Company for Lessons 4 and 7: T. Elizabeth Atteberry.